MEDIEVAL INDIA

Other Works by the Author:

Parties and Politics at the Mughal Court 1707-1740: Aligarh 1959, 1972, 1979, 2002.

Letters of a Kingmaker of the Eighteenth Century – Balmukundnama, 1972.

Uttar Mughal Kalin Bharat, 1975, 1980, 1993.

(eds.) *Marwar under Jaswant Singh (1658-1678): Jodhpur Hukumat ri Bahi,* 1976.

Medieval India: A text-book for Class XI, 1978, 1990, in Japanese, 1999.

Medieval India: Society, the Jagirdari Crisis and the Village, 1982.

Congress and the Concept of Secularism, 1985.

The Eighteenth Century in India: Its Economy and the Role of the Marathas, the Jats, the Sikhs and the Afghans, 1986, 1991.

(ed.) *The Indian Ocean – Explorations in History, Commerce and Politics,* 1987.

(eds.) *Essays in Medieval Indian Economic History,* 1987.

(eds.) *The Indian Ocean and Its Islands: Strategic, Scientific and Historical Perspectives,* 1993.

Mughal Religious Policies, the Rajputs and the Deccan, 1993, 1994.

Historiography, Religion and State in Medieval India, 1996, 1997.

Medieval India: From Sultanat to the Mughals: Part II — Mughal Empire (1526-1748), 1999

Essays on Medieval Indian History, 2003.

History of Medieval India (800-1700) (2003)

Social Change and Development in Medieval Indian History, 2008

State, Pluralism and the Indian Historical Tradition, 2008

MEDIEVAL INDIA

FROM SULTANAT TO THE MUGHALS

PART ONE
DELHI SULTANAT:
(1206-1526)

(REVISED EDITION)

SATISH CHANDRA

HAR-ANAND
PUBLICATIONS PVT LTD

HAR–ANAND PUBLICATIONS PVT LTD
E-49/3, Okhla Industrial Area, Phase-II, New Delhi-110020
Tel.: 41603490 Fax: 011-41708607
E-mail: info@haranandpublications.com
Website: www.haranandpublications.com

Published by Ashok Gosain and Ashish Gosain for
Har-Anand Publications Pvt Ltd

Printed in India at Vinayak Offset

Preface to the Fourth Edition

In this new edition, I have tried to bring together recent thinking on the downfall of the Mughal Empire, using modern data on prices, population and growth of cropped area in order to present a more realistic picture of the economic developments, and the challenges facing the Empire.

SATISH CHANDRA

Preface to the Third Edition

The pattern of Asian trade before the arrival of the Portuguese has been revised, and a note added on the problem of conversions. Inadvertent mistakes have also been corrected.

SATISH CHANDRA

Preface to the Second Edition

I am happy that this work which has been reprinted twice since its first publication in 1997, is now in its second edition.

A few textual corrections have been carried out in the new edition, and a few modifications made where considered necessary.

SATISH CHANDRA

PREFACE

This work has been in the offing for a long time. During the past several years, friends, both within the country and outside, have been asking me to write a book on Medieval India which would bring together recent thinking and research on the subject, and could be of use both to the general readers and to the students. However, I could not get down to the work in real earnest till I had finished my third trilogy, *Historiography, Religion and State in Medieval India* (1996); the two earlier ones being *Medieval India: Society, Jagirdari Crisis and the Village* (1982), and *Mughal Religious Policies, the Rajputs and the Deccan* (1993).

The present work covers only the Sultanat period from 1206 to 1526. I have adopted the traditional division, but have tried to bring out the continuities so that the self-imposed demarcation of periods does not affect an understanding of the broader movement of history.

The present book would hardly have been possible without the friendly, prompting and personal interest of Shri Narendra Kumar, Chairman, Har-Anand Publications Pvt Ltd.

I am grateful to Shri B. Sahay, Librarian, Indian Council of Historical Research; the Librarian, Nehru Memorial Museum and Library, and Dr. A.P. Srivastava, the then Director of Libraries, Delhi University, for their constant help in providing books and reference materials.

I am also grateful to Shri J.K. Gosain of the Society for Indian Ocean Studies, assisted by Ms. Monika Moorjani, who have gone through the difficult task of reducing the pages of my manuscript to fine type-written pages, and carrying out the corrections.

Lastly, I am grateful to my wife, Mrs. Savitri Chandra, for her constant help and support, and bearing with me at all times while I was busy with my writing.

SATISH CHANDRA

CONTENTS

1. **West and Central Asia Between the 10th**   13
   and 12th Centuries, and Turkish Advance
   towards India

   i.   Developments in West and Central Asia   14
   ii. The Turkish Advance towards India: 16
        the Hindushahis
   iii. Rajput Kingdoms in North India (10th-   19
        12th centuries), and the Ghaznavids
   iv. The Rise of the Ghurids and their   22
        Advance into India: the Battles of
        Tarain—Turkish Expansion into the
        Upper Ganga Valley—Comparison of Muizzuddin
        Muhammad Ghuri and Mahmud Ghazni
   v.   Causes of the Defeat of the Rajputs   29
   Map: Delhi Sultanat (13th Century)   35

2. **Establishment and Territorial Consolidation**   36
   of the Delhi Sultanat (1206-1236)

   i.   Qutbuddin Aibak and Iltutmish: 38
        Establishment of the Delhi Sultanat:
        (a) Punjab and Sindh (b) Turkish
        Conquest of Bihar and Lakhnauti
   ii. Internal Rebellions, Conquest of   44
        Ranthambhor and Gwaliyar, and Raids
        into Bundelkhand and Malwa
   iii. Estimate of Iltutmish as a Ruler   45

3. **Struggle for the Establishment of a**   47
   Centralized Monarchy (1236-1290)

   i.   Razia and the Period of Instability   47
        (1236-46)

ii.	The Age of Balban (1246-87)	51
	(a) Balban as *naib*—struggle with the Chihalgani	
	(b) Balban as a ruler	
iii.	Struggle for the Territorial Integrity of the Sultanat	58
iv.	Assessment of Balban	62

4. The Mongol Threat to India during the 13th-14th Centuries — 64

i.	The Mongol Incursions (upto 1292)	64
ii.	The Mongol Threat to Delhi (1292-1328)	68
	Map: India (Century 1200)	74

5. Internal Restructuring of the Delhi Sultanat, and its Territorial Expansion (1290-1320) — 75

i.	Jalaluddin and Alauddin Khalji's Approaches to the State	75
ii.	Agrarian and Market Reforms of Alauddin	78
iii.	The Territorial Expansion of the Delhi Sultanat (upto 1328): (a) Gujarat— (b) Rajasthan—(c) Malwa—(d) Maharashtra and South India (a) First Phase: Conquest (b) Second Phase: Annexation	86

6. Problems of a Centralised All-India-State— Ghiyasuddin and Muhammad bin Tughlaq (1320-1351) — 96

i.	Problems and Approaches	97
ii.	Experiments and Reforms	99
	(a) Administrative and Political Measures: Exodus to Deogiri—The Khurasan and Karachil Expeditions	
	(b) Economic and Agrarian Reforms: Token Currency—Agrarian Reforms	
iii.	Rebellions and Changes in the Ruling Class	108

7. Reassertion of a State Based on Benevolence— Disintegration of the Delhi Sultanat — 113

i.	Firuz's Concept of Benevolence and Peoples' Welfare	113

ii. Military Expeditions of Firuz and the Impact   116
     of their Limited Success: The Bengal
     Campaigns—Jajnagar (Orissa) and
     Nagarkot—The Thatta Campaign (1365-67)
iii. Reorganisation of the Nobility and the   119
     Administration
iv. Developmental Activities—Agrarian   122
     and Urban
v.   Disintegration of the Delhi Sultanat and its   126
     Causes

8.   **Government and Administration under**   **129**
     the Delhi Sultanat (13th-14th Centuries)

     i.   The Sultan—the Ministries: The Wazir,   129
          Diwan-i-Arz, Diwan-i-Insha, Diwan-i-
          Risalat, Other Ministries
     ii. Court and the Royal Household   139
     iii. Provincial and Local Governments   140

9.   **Economic and Social Life in North India**   **144**
     Under the Delhi Sultanat

a. *Economic Life*
     i.   Agricultural Production, Village   145
          Society and the Revenue System
     ii. Non-agricultural Production: 151
          Textiles, Metallurgy, Building Industry,
          Other Crafts including Paper-making
     iii. Trade: (a) Domestic Trade (b) Foreign   154
          Trade
b. *Social Life*
     i.   The Ruling Classes: (a) The Nobility   158
          (b) The Chiefs—Emergence of Zamindars
     ii. Adjuncts to the Ruling Class: Judicial   164
          and Junior Administrative Officers, and
          the Ulema
     iii. The Trading and Financial Classes   166
     iv. Standard of Living   167
     v.   Towns and Town Life—Artisans and   169
          Slaves
     vi. Women, Caste, Social Manners and   172
          Customs

10. **Politics, State, Society and the Economy in South**   175
    India under Vijayanagar and Bahmanid Rule
    (c. 1350-1565)

     i.   The Vijayanagar Empire—its Nature and   175
             Conflict with the Bahmani Kingdom
     ii.   The Bahmani Kingdom—its growth and   183
             disintegration—Age of Mahmud Gawan
             (1463-82)
     iii.   Climax of the Vijayanagar Empire and   188
             its Disintegration

11. **Establishment of Portuguese Control**   192
    in the Indian Seas and its Economic
    and Political Impact

     i.   The Asian Oceanic Trade Network before   194
             the Coming of the Portuguese
     ii.   The Portuguese *Estado da India*   199
     iii.   The Portuguese Impact on the Indian   202
             Ocean Trade Network

12. **Rise of Regional Kingdoms in North India**   **210**
    and a System of Balance of Power

     i.   Eastern India: Bengal, Assam and   **211**
             Orissa
     ii.   Western India: Gujarat, Malwa and   **217**
             Rajasthan
     iii.   North-West and North India: the Sharqis,   **224**
             the Lodi Sultans and Kashmir

13. **Religious and Cultural Life Under the**   **230**
    Delhi Sultanat

     i.   Architecture   232
     ii.   Religious Ideas and Beliefs: 236
             (a) The Sufi Movement: Early Origins—
             The Chishti and The Suhrawardi
             Silsilahs
             (b) The Bhakti Movement: Early Origins—
             The Popular Bhakti in North India—
             The Vaishnavite Movement
     iii.   Literature and Fine Arts: Sanskrit, Arabic   259
             and Persian, and Regional Languages; Music

14. The State in India under the Sultanat 265

    i.   Legal, Political and Social Character of   266
        the State
    ii.   Relations with the *ulema*   271
    iii. Position of the Hindus   273
    iv. Despotism, benevolence and   277
        development

  Glossary   281

  Index   285

MAPS

1. India c.1200   35

2. Delhi Sultanat 13t h Century   74

1

WEST AND CENTRAL ASIA BETWEEN THE 10TH AND 12TH CENTURIES, AND TURKISH ADVANCE TOWARDS INDIA

West and Central Asia are connected to India geographically across mountain barriers which demarcate India from Central and West Asia but do not pose an insurmountable barrier, like the Himalayas to the north. In consequence, nomadic and semi-nomadic hordes have constantly tried to enter India through these mountain passes, attracted by India's well watered plains with fertile soil, extending from the Punjab to the eastern borders of Bengal, its rich and flourishing cities and ports, and its fabulous wealth generated by the hard working peasants and skillful artisans, and experienced traders and financers.

The rise of Islam, its conquest of West Asia and Iran, and its slow expansion into Khurasan, and Central Asia, particularly the fertile tract called Mawara-un-Nahar or Transoxiana, i.e. the areas between the rivers **Amu'** (Oxus) and Syr, led to a gradual contraction of India's cultural and political influence in the area, which was largely Buddhist. It also adversely effected India's over-land trade with China and West Asia. Trade from the sea-ports of Western India was also effected for some time. However, this trend was soon countered by the rise of Arab sea traders who revived and strengthened India's sea trade, both with West Asia and with the countries of south-east Asia and China. There is no reason to believe that the Indian traders were displaced from this sea trade, or kept themselves away on account of the growth of the sentiment in some quarters that travel across the salt-seas or beyond the areas where the *munj* grass grew would lead to the loss of one's caste. Thus, there is evidence of Indian traders living in the areas around the Persian Gulf and beyond, and of Indian *Vaids* and craftsmen being welcomed at the court of the Abbasid Caliph at Baghdad. There is also evidence of Arab traders settling down in Malabar. The powerful Rashtrakuta rulers who dominated western India, Malwa and parts of south India upto the 10th century, also welcomed the Arab traders, and even permitted them to build mosques for worship.

i. Developments in West and Central Asia

The Abbasid empire, which reached its zenith in the 9th century, comprised at its height the areas from the environs of Constantinople and Egypt to Central Asia and the Arabian peninsula. It was thus the most powerful empire which arose in the area since the days of Dairius the Great of Iran (5th century A.D.). However, its energies were spent more in fighting the heathen Turks of Central Asia, and expanding the empire towards the west, rather than making a serious bid for the conquest of India. The situation began to change from the end of the 9th century when the Abbasid empire disintegrated, and a series of aggressive, expansionist states arose. These states were independent in all but name, but they accepted the nominal suzreignty of the Caliph who legitimised their position by granting them a formal letter or *manshur*. In course of time, the rulers of these states began to be called Sultans. Most of these sultans were Turks. The Turks who were nomads and lived in areas now known as Mongolistan and Sinkiang had, since the 8th century, been infiltrating into the region called Mawara-un-Nahar (Transoxiana), which was the "transitional zone" between Central Asia and the lands of ancient civilisations in East Asia. The Iranian rulers of the area, and the Abbasid Caliphs, brought in the Turks as mercenaries and slaves, and recruited them as palace guards, after converting them to Islam. The Turkish military commanders quickly assimilated the Iranian language and culture which was dominant in the region. Even earlier, both Arabic and Persian had been the languages of the ruling classes, and Persian culture and administrative practices had influenced the Abbasids.

Thus, the Turkish immigrants became Islamized and Persianised. It was they who set the political agenda of the future, fighting both the Turkish tribes which had not converted, and expanding into India.

The most powerful dynasty which arose in the region after the fall of the Abbasids was the Samanid dynasty (874-999) established by a converted Iranian noble from Balkh who was governor of Samarqand, Herat, etc. This was followed after sometime by the Ghaznavids (962-1186). Its founder, Alap-tigin, was a Turkish slave officer of the Samanids. The Ghaznavids were displaced by the Seljukids, and then by the Khwarizmi empire with its capital at Merv. The Khwarizmi empire was destroyed by the Mongol, Chengiz Khan, in the 13th century. These empires fought each other, as also smaller potentates in the region whom they tried to subordinate. In this they were not very different from the various Rajput rajas who dominated different areas in India, and continually fought each other. However, in the fierce battle for survival in West and Central Asia, military efficiency was considered the most valuable asset. This led to the growth of a militarism which spelt immediate danger to India and its outlying areas—Zabulistan and Afghanistan which till, then, had not been converted to Islam.

The aggressiveness of the newly Islamized Turks was added to by a number of factors. They had at their disposal the finest horses in the world. These horses which roamed the steppes of Central Asia in wild herds, were bred by the Turks who were considered hardy warriors and skillful horsemen. These horses were imported into Arabia and India from time immemorial. Horses bred in India could not match the Central Asia horses in swiftness, nor could the Indians match the Turkish horsemen in their skill and speed of manoeuver. Perhaps, developments in West and Central Asia limited the import of these horses into India. The mountains around Ghur were also rich in metals, particularly iron, and there was a tradition of production of war materials there, as also in many cities of the region. Thus, the Turks had a plentiful supply of horses and war materials, both of which were important for warfare in those times.

Secondly, there was a growth of what is called the *'ghazi'* spirit in West Asia at that time. Iranian rule in Transoxiana and its neighbouring areas was being gradually replaced by Turks, including the nomadic Turks who were called Turkmen or Turkomans. Iranian and Turkish Muslim rulers of the area had to face the continuous pressure of the nomadic, non-Muslim Turkmens, such as the Guzz or Oguzz and other tribes living in Kara-Khitai, or the steppes of Central Asia. While defending themselves, the Turkish rulers were themselves making continuous raids into the Turkmen held Central Asian steppes for capturing slaves who were in high demand in the slave-markets of Samarqand and Bokhara. The responsibility of this defensive-offensive warfare devolved in part on the volunteers who were fired by the spirit of defending and spreading Islam. These volunteers were not paid regularly, and made up for their pay by plunder. These were the *'ghazis.'*

The *ghazi* spirit which was first used for fighting against the non-Islamic Turks was later used against the "unbelievers" in India. Amongst the figures most closely associated with this movement, the first was Mahmud of Ghazna whose "exploits" in India are well-known. The second was Sanjar, the Seljukid ruler, who suffered a sharp defeat in 1142-43 at the hands of the non-Muslim hordes of Gur Khan of Khitai (Central Asia). We are not concerned with Sanjar's life—he was defeated and imprisoned by the Oguzz or Ghuzz in 1152, escaped, but died soon after. It shows, however, the vulnerability of the Muslim Turks, and of the Muslim rulers in general. During the period, even some of the most powerful Muslim states could not contend successfully against the non-Muslim Turks from Central Asia. Later, they succumbed to the Mongols.

On the positive side, some institutional factors helped in the growth of Turkish military power in Khurasan and Iran. The most important of these was the *"iqta"* system. The *iqta* was a territorial assignment which gave to the holder the right to collect from the peasants the land revenue and other taxes due to the state. It did not, however, imply the holder interfering with the existing land rights, or granting them any rights over the person, wealth, wives and children of the cultivators. In return, the holder was under the obligation of maintaining a fixed number of troops, and to furnish them to the sultan at his call.

This institution suited the Turkish sultans because it implied that the existing rights of the Iranian land holders, called the *dehkans*, would not be interfered with. Nor would the Turkish military leaders develop any hereditary rights in land, but would be completely dependent on the sultan who could deploy them as and where he chose. It was this highly mobile military force, dependent for its sustenance upon the backing and support of the ruler, which became the main instrument for further expansion of Muslim power under the aegis of the Turkish sultans.

ii. *The Turkish advance towards India: The Hindushahis*

It was only a question of time before these hardy, highly mobile, centralized predatory forces turned their attention towards India, the traditional land of gold.

We are told that it was only in 870 A.D. that Zabulistan was finally conquered by one Yakub who was the virtual ruler of the neighbouring Iranian province of Seistan. The king was killed, and his subjects were made Muslims. In 963 Alp-tigin, who had been the commander of the Samanid rulers in Khurasan, marched to Ghazni in south Zabulistan, and set himself up as an independent ruler. The Hindu ruler *(Shahi)* of Afghanistan, who are called Hindu-Shahis, tried to meet this emerging threat on their border by allying themselves with the former Samanid Governor of Ghazni, with the Bhatti rulers who dominated the area near Multan, as also with the Muslim amir of Multan across the Bolan pass. These rulers were willing to join Jayapal, the Hindu Shahi ruler, because they had been harassed by slave raids into their territories by the rulers of Ghazni. However, Jayapal's invasion of Ghazni failed, and the coalition built by him soon collapsed. Sabuk-tigin who succeeded Alp-tigin (977), carried the fight into the Hindu Shahi territories, and laid waste the frontier tract of Lamghan, i.e. Kabul and Jalalabad. In about 990-91, the Hindu-Shahi ruler suffered a decisive defeat. The 17th century historian, Ferishta, tells us that Jayapal was assisted in this battle by the Rajput rulers of Delhi, Ajmer, Kalinjar, and Kannauj. However, modern historians are doubtful of the veracity of this statement because it is not mentioned by any contemporary historian. Nor was Delhi an important state at that time. Ajmer had not been founded, and the rulers of Kannauj were in decline. Thus, Ferishta's account seems to be based on a desire to exaggerate the scale of the Ghazanavid victory. Following the battle, the provinces of Kabul and Jalalabad were annexed to Ghazni. The contemporary historian Utbi says, "from this time the Hindus drew in their tails and sought no more to invade the land (of Ghazni)."

The point to note is that by the end of the 10th century, the outer bastions of India, Zabulistan and Afghanistan, had been lost. An invasion of proper India was, therefore, the next likely step. In preparation for such an invasion the Yamini rulers of Ghazni had improved the road communications from Ghazni to Kabul and Jalalabad. Meanwhile, the Hindu Shahi ruler, Jayapala, had tried to make up for the loss of territory in the west by extending his kingdom towards the east. Thus, he overran Lohvara (Lahore) in 991. The local ruler was allowed to rule for sometime as a feudatory, but in 999, Lahore was annexed to the Shahi kingdom which now extended from Peshawar to the river Beas.

In 999, Mahmud ascended the throne at Ghazni, and vowed to conduct operations in India every year. After making initial raids

against frontier outposts, in 1001 he marched against the Shahis.
In a furious battle which was fought near Peshawar, Mahmud's forces
consisted of 15,000 picked cavalry, a large corps of *'ghazis'*, and
Afghans. Jayapal's army is estimated at 12,000 cavalry, 30,000 foot,
and 300 elephants. It appears to have bean a battle of cavalry, combined with skillful tactical movements. Jayapala was defeated and
Mahmud advanced to the Shahi capital Waihind (Udbhanda or
Peshawar) which was thoroughly ravaged. According to some accounts, Jayapala was captured and taken to Ghazni, but released
after some time on payment of a large ransom. But this story appears to be a concoted one because we are told that following his
victory, Mahmud made peace with the Shahi ruler, annexing only
the territory west of the Indus. This would hardly have been likely if the Shahi ruler had suffered a complete defeat and been made
a prisoner. However, Jayapala felt his defeat to be a great humiliation, and entered the funeral pyre a few years later. He was succeeded by his son, Anandpala.

Despite this set back, the Shahis were strong enough to pose a
serious obstacle to Mahmud's further advance into India. The
Ghaznavids had to fight two serious battles near the Indus before
they could penetrate into the Punjab proper. In a hard fought battle in 1006 near the Indus, Mahmud conquered the upper Indus
region. This gave him access to the Punjab. But Punjab proper remained outside his control till 1009 when in a decisive battle fought
on the eastern side of the Indus in the plains of Chhachh, Mahmud
triumphed over Anandapal, and followed his victory by over-running Nandana in the Salt Ranges to which the Shahis had shifted
their capital from Waihind (Peshawar), after their earlier defeat.
Mahmud also captured the fort called Bhimnagar or Nagarkot (to
be distinguished from Nagarkot in Kangra). For some time,
Anandapal was allowed to rule over the Punjab as a feudatory.
But in 1015, Mahmud advanced upto Lahore and plundered it. Soon
the Ghaznavid empire extended upto the river Jhelum. Meanwhile,
Multan which was ruled over by a Muslim ruler who had allied
himself with Anandapal against Mahmud, was also overrun. However, an attempt to conquer Kashmir in 1015 failed, due largely to
inclement weather. This was the first defeat of Mahmud's armies
in India.

Thus, the period from 990-91 to 1015 was a period of protracted struggle during which Afghanistan, and then Punjab and Multan
were lost to the Ghaznavids. The way was now open for Turkish
advance into the Gangetic plains.

iii. Rajput Kingdoms in North India (10th—12th centuries) and the Ghaznavids

The middle of the 10th century saw the decay of two of the most powerful Rajput states which had dominated north and central India during the two preceding centuries. These were the Gurjar-Pratihar empire with its capital at Kannauj, and the Rashtrakuta empire with its capital at Manyakhet. The Gujarat-Pratihar empire extended from the foothills of the Himalayas to Ujjain in the south, and from Gujarat in the west to Mongyr in the east. It contended with the Rashtrakutas for the mastery of Gujarat and Malwa, and with the Pala rulers of Bengal for the mastery of Bihar and modern east U.P. In the north-west, its rule extended to Thaneshwar. It declined rapidly during the second half of the 10th century, remaining confined largely to modern U.P. In the meantime, a number of kingdoms rose up, the most prominent among them being the Chandels of Kalinjar and Mahoba, the Chauhans of Sakambhar in Rajasthan, the Paramars of Malwa, and the Chaulukyas of Gujarat These, in turn, had many feudatories which some times helped their overlords, but more often conspired to become independent. Kashmir was under the powerful queen, Didda, who reigned for twenty six years, and even murdered her grandsons to retain power. She had an old standing rivalry with the Shahis and hence forbore to give them any help in their struggle with Mahmud. Nor did any of the other Rajput rajas help Anandpal in his struggle against Mahmud, despite Ferishta's statement to the contrary.

After over-running the Punjab, Mahmud undertook three expeditions into the Ganga Valley. The purpose of these raids was to acquire wealth for his Central Asian campaigns, as also to destabilize the states in the area so that no coalition of powers against him could emerge.

Towards the end of 1015, Mahmud left Ghazni, marching rapidly along the foot hills of the Himalayas. Aided by feudatory rulers, he crossed the Yamuna and defeated a local Rajput ruler at Baran (Bulandshahr) in modern western U.P. Moving towards the pilgrim centre, Mathura, he was opposed by the Kalachuri ruler Kokkala II, one of major Rajput kings of the area. The battle was hotly contested, the Rajput ruler deploying a large number of elephants. His defeat was again the defeat of slow moving forces by rapidly moving cavalry forces. After plundering Mathura and Vrindavan, Mahmud moved toward Kannauj, the capital of the Pratihar ruler. The Pratihar ruler who was in a greatly weakened condition, sought safety by flight across the Ganga. After thoroughly sacking Kannauj, Mahmud returned to Ghazni, defeating several minor opponents on the way. This was the most spectacular and profitable forage into the Ganga valley made by Mahmud. He had by now also triumphed over his Turkish enemies in Central Asia, and extended his control over Iran. The Khalifa at Baghdal received his envoy, bearing tidings of his Indian victories, with marks of special honour.

The next two invasions of the Ganga valley by Mahmud, in 1019 and 1021, did not lead to any special gains. The first one of these expeditions was meant to break up an incipient Rajput coalition against Mahmud. At the instance of the powerful Chandel ruler of Bundelkhand, the Pratihar ruler of Kannauj had been displaced for his disgraceful failure to resist Mahmud. The Rajput ruler of Gwaliyar had joined, and help been provided to Trilochanpala, the displaced Shahi ruler of Punjab. Moving rapidly, Mahmud defeated the Shahi ruler Trilochandpal, and the Chandel protege at Kannauj, also named Trilochandpal. He then turned against the Chandel ruler, Vidyadhara, who is said to have fielded an army of 145,000 foot soldiers, 36,000 horse and no less than 640 elephants. Despite skirmishes, no decisive engagement took place, neither side wanting to risk a show down. In 1021, Mahmud again over-run Gwaliyar, but an engagement with the Chandel ruler near Kalinjar was avoided. The latter, on his part, promised a nominal tribute.

These expeditions did not lead to the expansion of Mahmud Ghazni's territories beyond the Punjab, but they did succeed in making the upper part of the Ganga duab as a kind of a neutral territory in which no powerful king could establish himself. Negatively, it kept the Chandels from expanding their control over the area. The expeditions also ended, once for all, the attempt of the Shahis to recover their lost dominions.

The story of Mahmud's last plundering raid in 1025 across Rajasthan to Somnath is too well-known to be repeated here in detail. This expedition once again demonstrated the capacity of the Turks of swift movement over unknown and hostile territory, and a spirit of daring and enterprise rare even among the Turkish nomadic tribes of the times. To this was added the lure of gold, and the *ghazi* spirit of waging an all-out war against the enemies of Islam.

The military capabilities of Mahmud of Ghazna can hardly be disputed. He was a bold warrior, and leader of men who almost singly carved out one of the biggest empires in West and Central Asia. With the riches plundered from India he adorned his capital, Ghazni, with magnificent buildings. He also gave patronage to literary men

and poets, such as Firdausi, and carried forward the Persian renaissance which had begun with the Samanids. But he built no lasting
institutions which could outlive him. Moreover, his rule outside
Ghazni was tyranical. Thus, the Ghaznavid historian, Utbi, says with
reference to Khurasan, the eastern part of Iran and the cradle of
Persian renaissance:

"Affairs were characterised there by nothing but tax levies, sucking
which sucked dry, and attempt to extract fresh sources of revenue,
without any constructive measure." Hence, after a few years there
was nothing more to be got in Khurasan, "since water had been
thrown on her udder, not a trickle of milk could be got nor any
trace of fat."

Thus, despite his political achievements and military exploits,
Mahmud is remembered in India as a plunderer, and did not earn
a good name for himself even outside India among his contemporaries. Painting him and Sanjar as the heroes of Islam was the work
of later historians.

The period of 150 years between the death of Mahmud of Ghazna
in 1030 to the beginning of Ghurid invasion towards the end of the
12th century was a period of great flux and confusion in north
India. There was constant internecine warfare between the various
Rajput principalities of the region, without any one of them emerging
as a dominant power. Following the raids of Mahmud on Kannauj,
the Pratihar power had collapsed, with the rise of small feudatories.
It was only towards the end of the 11th century that a new dynasty,
the Gahadvars, rose to power in the doab. The Gahadvars whose
seat of power was the Varanasi area, constantly fought with the
Palas of Bengal, and the Tomars of Delhi. Another dynasty, the
Chahman or Chauhan arose in Rajasthan whose later representative
was the famous Prithviraj Chauhan. The Chauhans constantly
fought with the Chaulukyas of Gujarat, and with the Paramaras of
Malwa. Another powerful dynasty was the Chandelas of Khajuraho
whose rivals were both the Paramaras of Malwa and Gahadvalas
of Kashi. Although the Gahadvalas over-ran Kannauj and also
established their over-lordship over Delhi, the Rajput states,
individually or as a group, were unable or unwilling to join hands
to expel the Ghaznavids from the Punjab, despite the rapid decline
of Ghaznavid power in West and Central Asia following the death
of Mahmud. On the other hand, the successors of Mahmud were
able to continue making debilitating raids into the doab as far as
Varanasi. In consequence, as a modern writer C.E. Bosworth says,
the "temple treasures of India continued to be brought back to

Ghazni.. the flow of bullion continued to keep the economy of the Ghaznavid empire buoyant and the currency of high quality.."

Despite these plundering raids, the Ghaznavids were in no position to expand their territories in India. This process began with another turn in West and Central Asia politics, and the rise of the Ghurids.

iv. The Rise of Ghurids and their advance into India

The rise to power of the Ghurids at Ghur, a small isolated area located in the mountain fastness between the Ghaznavid empire and the Seljukids, was an unusual and unexpected development. The area was so remote that till the 11th century, it had remained a pagan enclave surrounded by Muslim principalities. It was converted to Islam in the early part of the 12th century after Mahmud raided it, and left teachers to instruct the Ghurids in the precepts of Islam. Even then it is believed that paganism, i.e. a variety of Mahayana Buddhism persisted in the area till the end of the century.

The Shansbanis, who were originally a family of petty chiefs among many in Ghur, played a principal part in firmly planting Islam in the area, and by a policy of ruthlessness made themselves supreme there. By the middle of the 12th century they felt strong enough to intervene in Herat when its Governor rebelled against Sanjar, the Seljukid ruler. The Ghaznavids felt threatened and Bahram Shah captured the brother of the Ghurid ruler, Alauddin Husain Shah, and had him poisoned. In retaliation, Alauddin defeated Bahram Shah and captured Ghazni. For seven days, the city was turned over to plundering and destruction, with some of the finest buildings being razed to the ground. This earned for Alauddin Husain Shah the title of *jahan soz* or "world burner", and marked the final decline of the Ghaznavids and the emergence of Ghur as the strongest power on the fringe of the Islamic world. The Ghurids were no longer content to be tributaries of the Seljukids, but assumed like them the title of *al-sultan al-muazzam.*

Like their predecessors, the Ghurids constantly fought with the Seljukids for control of the prosperous areas of Khurasan and Merv. Like Ghaznavids, the Ghurids too were unpopular in Khurasan on account of their financial levies, and found it difficult to maintain their authority there. This, and the perpetual conflict with the Seljukids and the Turkish tribes across the Oxus were factors which impelled the Ghurids towards India.

In 1163, Ghiyasuddin Muhammad assumed the throne of Ghur. Recalling a Turkish tribal tradition, he appointed his younger brother, Muizzuddin Muhammad, ruler at Ghazna. This unique partnership enabled one brother, Muizzuddin, to engage all his energies for the conquest of India, and the elder brother, Ghiyasuddin, to concentrate on Central and West Asian problems.

Meanwhile, in north India, the Chahmans or Chauhans were trying to expand towards Gujarat and also towards Delhi and Mathura. As such, they had to bear the brunt of the plundering raids of Mahmud Ghazni's successors. The greatest of the Chauhan rulers was, perhaps, Vigraharaj who captured Chittor. It seems that he captured Delhi from the Tomar rulers in 1151, and extended his sway upto the Siwalik, i.e. the range of hills upto Delhi and Hansi which had been a bone of contention between the Tomars and the Ghaznavids. However, the Tomars were allowed to continue to rule as feudatories. Vigrahraja was a patron of poets and scholars, and himself wrote a Sanskrit drama. He also built many magnificent temples, including a Sanskrit College at Ajmer, and the Anasagar lake there.

The most famous among the Chauhan rulers was Prithviraj III who ascended the throne at Ajmer at the young age of eleven, in or about 1177. It is assumed that he took the reigns of administration in his hands at the age of 16, and immediately commenced a vigorous policy of expansionism at the cost of smaller states in Rajasthan. The most famous expedition, however, was the one against the Chandelas of Khajuraho and Mahoba. As we have seen, the Chandelas constituted the most powerful state in the region, and which had a history of resistance against the Ghaznavids. The fight in which the famous warriors, Alha and Udal, died fighting to save Mahoba has been immortalised in the Hindi epics, *Prithviraj-raso* and *Alha-Khanda*. Since these were written later, the historical veracity of the account is doubted by historians. However, we can conclude that Prithviraj gained a significant victory against the Chandelas. Though he did not acquire additional territories, he came home after acquiring considerable booty.

Between 1182 and 1187, Prithviraj turned his attention towards his ancient rivals, the Chaulukyas of Gujarat. The struggle was long drawn out and it seems that the Gujarat ruler, Bhima II, who had earlier beaten off an invasion by the Ghurid ruler, Muizzuddin, defeated Prithviraj also. This forced Prithviraj to turn his attention towards the Ganga Valley and the Punjab. According to tradition, there was a long drawn-out tussle between him and the Gahadvalas of Kannauj, who had the most extensive kingdom in the area. The cause of this conflict is supposed to be Prithviraj's abduction of Sanyogita, the beautiful daughter of the ruler, Jai Chand, at her *svayamvara*, and Jai Chand's subsequent defeat in battle. While historians are doubtful of the veracity of this story in the absence of any contemporary corroboration, the rivalry between the Chauhans and the Gahadvalas for control over Delhi and the upper Ganga doab was well-known, and may account for the subsequent attitude of the Gahadvalas.

The point to note is that by leading expeditions against all his neighbours, Prithviraj had isolated himself politically. This cost him dear when he had to face the Turkish armies of Muizzuddin Muhammad a few years later.

We have already referred to Muizzuddin's ascending the throne at Ghazna in 1173. His first expedition against India was launched in 1175 when he attacked and captured Multan which was under the Carmathians or Karamatis who were spread on the borders of India and Iran, and whose religious ideas formed a half-way house between Islam and Buddhism. The following year Muizzuddin captured Uchch. In 1178-79, he marched through Multan and Uchch to Neharwala in Gujarat. However, the Gujarat ruler inflicted a crushing defeat on Muizzuddin near Mt. Abu. We are told that the Chaulukyas had requested Prithviraj for help. However, his ministers declined to help, considering both the Ghurids and the Chaulukyas to be enemies of the Chauhans. Since Prithviraj was barely twelve at the time, he can hardly be blamed for the decision.

After the failure of his Gujarat expedition, Muizzuddin changed his whole plan of operations. Conquering Peshawar from the Ghaznavids in 1179-80, he marched on Lahore in 1181. The Ghaznavid ruler, Khusrau Malik, surrendered. He was allowed to rule at Lahore while Muizzuddin continuously expanded his control over the Punjab, including Sialkot, and also consolidated his control over Sindh upto the coast. Finally, in 1186, Muizzuddin removed the Ghaznavid ruler who was sent to prison in a fort and was put to death a couple of years later. The stage was now set for the conflict between the Gurids and the Rajput rulers of north India.

The Battles of Tarain

After consolidating his position in Sindh and Punjab, in 1191

Muizzuddin attacked and captured the fortress of Tabarhinda which was strategically important for the defence of Delhi. Realising its importance, and without giving the Turks time to consolidate, Prithviraj immediately marched towards Tabarhinda. In the battle, Prithviraj attained a complete victory, Muizzuddin being saved, according to a contemporary account, by a Khalji horseman who carried the wounded Sultan to safety. After his victory, Prithviraj did not try to pursue the dispirited Ghurid army, either because he did not want to venture into hostile territory far away from his base, or because he thought that, like the Ghazanavids, the Ghurids, too, would be satisfied to rule over the Punjab. Thus, he treated the siege of Tabarhinda only as a frontier fight and was satisfied with capturing it after a siege of a few months.

That Prithviraj treated the struggle with Muizzuddin as only a frontier fight is strengthened by the fact that after his victory he made little preparations for a future contest with the Ghurid chief. The *Prithviraj Raso* accuses Prithviraj of neglecting the affairs of the state, and of being busy merry-making. This may not be true, but there is little doubt that he seriously underestimated the danger from the side of the Ghurids.

The second battle of Tarain in 1192 is regarded rightly as one of the turning points in Indian history. Muizzuddin had made careful preparations for the contest, disgracing many amirs who had not stood firm in the field of battle earlier. It is difficult to form a precise estimate of the forces on the two sides. According to the information of the contemporary chronicler, Minhaj Siraj, the army of Muizzuddin had 120,000 men fully equipped with steel coats and armour. The seventeenth century historian, Ferishta, places Prithviraj's forces at 3,000 elephants, 300,000 horsemen, and considerable infantry. These figures appear to be grossly exaggerated, perhaps to emphasise the challenge faced by Muizzuddin and the scale of his victory. However, we may conclude that the forces fielded by Prithviraj were larger than those brought to the field by his opponent. Ferishta also states that on an appeal from Prithviraj, all the leading 'Rais of Hind' joined his banners. That, too, appears doubtful. As we have seen, Prithviraj had alienated all his powerful neighbours by his militaristic policies. Nor does Ferishta name any of the prominent Rais. Perhaps, Prithviraj's forces included many of his feudatories including Govindraj, the ruler of Delhi. This was a source of weakness rather than strength because these feudal levies lacked any central direction or leadership, unlike the armies of Muizzuddin.

The battle of Tarain was more a war of movement than of position. The lightly armed mounted archers of Muizzuddin kept harassing the slow moving forces of Prithviraj, and attacked from all sides when they had created confusion in his ranks. Prithviraj suffered a complete defeat and fled, but he was pursued and caught near Sarsuti or modern Sirsa in Hissar district. The historian Minhaj Siraj says that he was executed immediately. But according to another contemporary writer, Hasan Nizami, he was taken to Ajmer and allowed to rule. This is supported by numismatic evidence, showing coins of Prithviraj, with the words 'Sri Muhammad Sam' on the reverse. He rebelled after sometime, and was executed to on a charge of treason. His son succeeded him, and continued to rule for sometime as a feudatory. Hence, there is no truth in the story that Prithviraj was taken to Ghazni and that blind-folded, he killed the Ghurid sultan with an arrow, and that he was then killed by his bard, Chand.

Prithviraj is remembered as a great fighter and as a patron of poets and pandits. As a general, he had many victories to his credit. But as a modern historian, Dashrath Sharma, observes "his conduct on the battle field in the second battle of Tarain is a blot on his generalship as well as statesmanship."

Turkish Expansion into the Upper Ganga Valley

After the victory at Tarain the entire Chauhan dominion lay at the feet of the Ghurids. However, Muizzuddin adopted a cautious policy. He annexed the whole Siwalik territory, i.e. the area upto Ajmer, and Hissar and Sirsa in modern Haryana. He placed Hissar and Sirsa under his trusted slave, Qutubuddin Aibak. Govindraj, the Tomar chief of Delhi, had died in the battle at Tarain. His son was, however, installed at Delhi as a vassal. Prithviraj was reinstated at Ajmer, as mentioned earlier. Muizzuddin then returned to Ghazni.

This arrangement was bound to be tentative. It was tenable if the Ghurids were to confine themselves to Punjab and its immediate neighbourhood. If, however, the Turks were to expand into the upper Ganga valley, Delhi was too strategic to be left in alien hands.

Rebellions both at Ajmer and Delhi decided the issue. To quell the rebellions in Ajmer against the son of Prithviraj who had accepted Turkish vassalage, Aibak pressed on to Delhi in 1192, and occupied it. Delhi now became the main base of Turkish operations in India. The Tomara chief was retained for some more time but removed from the throne in 1193 when he was found to be involved in some treasonable activities. Ajmer was also occupied after defeating Hari Raj, the brother of Prithviraj, who had been leading the Rajput resistance. Hari Raj entered the funeral pyre to atone for his defeat. A Turkish governor was now placed in charge of Ajmer. Govind, the son of Prithviraj, was displaced and forced to move to Ranthambhor.

Having consolidated their position in the Delhi region, the Turks were now poised for attack on the Gahadvalas of Kannauj, reputed to be the most powerful kingdom in the country. In 1194, Muizzuddin returned to India. The areas of Meerut, Baran (modern Buland-shahr) and Koil (modern Aligarh) in the upper doab which had been under the control of the Dor Rajputs, had been occupied by the Turks shortly after the battle of Tarain. Although the Dors had offered stiff resistance, and the area had great strategic value, Jai Chand, the Gahadvala ruler, had not come to their help. Earlier, in a false sense of security, he had rejoiced at the defeat of Prithviraj at the hands of Muizzuddin, and the event was celebrated at his court.

In 1194, Muizzuddin advanced towards Kannauj and Banaras with 50,000 horsemen. The battle was fought at Chandawar in the modern Etawah district. As usual, contemporary literary works indulge in gross exaggerations. They place Jai Chand's army at 80,000 men in armour, 30,000 horses, 300,000 infantry, 200,000 bowmen and a host of elephants. Jai Chand, who is not known to have been a great warrior, suffered a disastrous defeat. After great slaughter and plunder, the fort of Asni (Fathehpur district) which contained the Gahadavala treasure-house was plundered. Varanasi, which was the early capital of the Gahadavalas, was also plundered, and large number of temples destroyed. Kannauj was finally captured in 1198.

The battles of Tarain and Chandawar laid the foundations of Turkish rule in the Ganga valley. Apart from sporadic uprisings, there was no large scale resistance in the area to Turkish rule. However, it took the Turks another fifty years to stamp out all opposition, and to consolidate their hold over the area. To protect their southern and western flanks, as also to provide future bases of operations, the Turks tried to conquer the strategic forts between Delhi and Malwa. Thus, in 1195-96, Muizzuddin occupied Bayana fort. Gwaliyar, which was a most powerful fort, was besieged, but it took a siege of a year and a half before the ruler could be persuaded to hand over the fort. A little later, Kalinjar, Mahoba and Khajuraho were wrested from the Chandel rulers of Bundelkhand who were the most powerful rulers of the area after the Gahadvalas.

Efforts at expansion beyond the upper Ganga valley and eastern Rajasthan were made in two directions—Gujarat in the west,
and Bihar and Bengal in the east. In the west, Muizzuddin's slave
invaded Anhilwara in Gujarat, largely in retaliation of the Rai having
aided earlier a Rajput rebellion which had forced Aibek to take refuge
at Ajmer till he was rescued by an army sent from Ghazni. The
Rai was defeated and Anhilwara occupied, but the Turks could not
hold it for long. This showed the limits of Turkish power in India—they were still not strong enough to keep hold of places far
away from their base of operations, Delhi. The conquest of Bihar
and Bengal by Muhammad-bin-Bakhtiyar Khalji was a special case
which we shall deal with separately.

Muizzuddin suffered a sharp reversal in 1204 when he was defeated at a great battle at Andkhui near the river Oxus by the pagan Kara Khanid Turks of Samarqand. In consequence, he lost control
of Merv and most of Khurasan. Rumours of Muizzuddin's death
led to a rebellion by the Khokhars in the Punjab. Muizzuddin
marched to India to suppress it.

We are told that Muizzuddin wanted to renew the conflict with
the Kara Khanids of Samarqand, and that a boat bridge had been
built across the river Oxus for the purpose. However, on his way
from the Punjab, Muizzuddin was killed on the banks of the river
Indus (1206) by a band of Karamatias which, as we have seen, were
a fanatical sect which had absorbed many features of Hindu/Bud-
dhist beliefs and which Muizzuddin had persecuted in his life time.

Muizzuddin Muhammad and Mahmud of Ghazna

There has been a tendency to compare Muizzuddin Muhammad
bin Sam with Mahmud of Ghazna. It has been argued that Mahmud
of Ghazna was a better general than Muizzuddin because, unlike
the latter, he never suffered a military defeat. However, the fact that
Muizzuddin could recover and take lessons from his defeats, and
change his entire approach showed both a dogged tenacity of
purpose and a grim sense of political realism. Thus, after his defeat
at Anhilwara in Gujarat, he changed his entire approach towards
India, shifting the axis of attack from Rajasthan to the Punjab. The
speed and skill with which he recovered from his defeat at the
hands of Prithviraj in the first battle of Tarain showed his mettle.

Both Mahmud of Ghazna and Muizzuddin used religion for their
essentially secular purposes, when it suited them to do so. For both,
the wealth gathered from India was important for furthering their

Central and West Asian ambitions. However, it would be wrong to consider Mahmud as a mere robber and plunderer in India. It was he who breached the outer defences of India by ousting the Hindu Shahis from Afghanistan, and by conquering the Punjab, he provided a secure base for future Turkish expansion into India. Thus, Mahmud laid the foundations on which Muizzuddin built. However, both worked in completely different circumstances.

Both enriched their capitals with fine buildings, and patronised poets and learned men. However, we know little about their administrative achievements. As we have shown, both were unpopular in Khurasan for their financial rapacity and exactions. Little is known about the nature of Ghaznavid administration in the Punjab. Muizzuddin had no time to form any new administrative system in India. Perhaps, he made little change in the existing administrative system, leaving his commanders to levy tribute or taxes through the existing channels as best as they could.

v. Causes of the defeat of the Rajputs

The causes of the defeat of the Rajputs and the success of the Turks should not be seen merely in the context of the events following the succession of Muizzuddin bin Sam at Ghazni in 1173, or his first entry into the north western parts of India (Peshawar) in 1181. As a modern writer, A.B.M. Habibullah, rightly observes, the success of Muizzuddin was "the consumation of a process which extended over the whole of the 12th century". In fact, the reconnoitering activities to obtain a foot-hold in Hindustan outside Sindh had begun at least a century earlier, with the rise of Mahmud Ghazni.

The conquest of Afghanistan and the Punjab by Mahmud Ghazni breached the outer defences of India. It enabled hostile forces to stage their forces in the area, and to make forays into the vital areas of India at will. Thus, India was tactically put on the defensive. It is to be noted that during this entire period, the Rajput states of the area showed a singular lack of understanding or strategic insight. Thus, no effort was made by them to join together to oust the Ghaznavids from the Punjab even after the death of Mahmud, when the outbreak of internal struggles among his successors led to the loss of their control over most of West and Central Asian territories. On the other hand, even in their weakened conditions, the successors of Mahmud remained tactically on the offensive, raiding Indian territories in Rajasthan upto Ajmer and beyond, and the Gangetic areas upto Kannauj and Varanasi. All the credit that the Rajput rajas of the period could take was their success in repelling the raids of *hammira* who had become "the cause of anxiety to the world."

This lack of strategic consciousness may be explained by lack of political unity, or by the absence of a dominant power in north-west India. This should not, however, be confused with size or resources. In terms of size and resources, many of the Rajput principalities of the time were superior, both in terms of population and revenue resources, to almost any of the successor states which arose in West and Central Asia after the downfall of the Abbasid empire. Except a few fertile regions such as Khurasan, Transoxiana, Khwarizm, much of the terrain in the region was mountainous or arid and inhospitable. Moreover, it had been thoroughly plundered for long by the Ghuzz tribes across the Oxus. On the other hand, the tracts under the control of the Rajputs, outside Rajasthan and Bundelkhand, were very fertile and productive. In terms of human resources or population, too, the Rajput-held areas were in an advantageous position. These were the reasons why in any battle, the number of human beings and other trappings of war on the side of the Rajput rajas were far larger than those at the disposal of the Turks. Thus, it would be misleading to think that on account of the working of the iniquitous caste system, the Rajput rajas were not able to find sufficient soldiers to man their armies. In fact, it is erroneous to think that the Rajput armies consisted only of Rajputs. Warrior groups such as the Jats, Meenas or groups called "*kuvarna*" (lower castes) in later sources, were not excluded from the armed forces of the Rajputs.

Nor was the defeat of the Rajputs due to their lack of a martial spirit, courage or bravery as compared to the Turks. War was a sport for the Rajputs, and their prolonged resistance to Turkish inroads, as compared to the easy defeat of another ancient civilisation, the Iranian, and their success in a number of battles against the Turks, does not betoken any absence of a martial spirit.

Nor is there any reason to think that the Turks had weapons which were superior to those of the Rajputs. It has been argued that the Turks used iron-stirrups which enabled them to use spears without the rider being thrown off the horse as a result of the impact. However, the use of the iron-stirrup which is supposed to have come for China or Korea, was spreading in India from the 8th century, though we have no means of knowing how widely it was used. The Central Asian horses were superior to those born or bred in India. In recognition of this, since ancient times, there had been a lively trade in horses, both by sea and land, between

India and the countries of West and Central Asia. The trade in horses had not stopped with the rise of Islam. In fact, colonies of Muslim horse-traders had existed in distinct places in north India during the 12th century. That is why, we are told, Muhammad bin Bakhtiyar Khalji was able to proceed all the way upto Purnea, pretending to be a horse-trader, before he attacked the Sena ruler, Lakshman Sena.

The question arises, what then were the factors responsible for the defeat of the Rajputs and the victory of the Turks? First and foremost, although the Rajput forces were not inferior in numbers, or in the quality of their mounts and weapons, they were definitely inferior in terms of organisation and leadership. The large Rajput armies which faced the Turks did not have a unified command, being brought to the field and led by their own feudatory rulers. It was difficult to manoeuvre such hetrogenous forces. Moreover, the Rajputs gave greater weight to men than to mobility. The Turkish warriors were used to quick movements, of rapid advance and retreat, and of shooting arrows while mounted. The Rajput forces tended to be a heavy, slow moving mass, centred on their elephants. They were beaten by swift cavalry forces which attacked their flanks and rear. While elephants themselves were not a source of weakness, what mattered was how they were used. They provided stability, and were most effective when combined with skilled and highly mobile cavalry. The Turks were reputed to be the most skillful horsemen in the world. Also, they were used to manoeuvre together because the Turkish sultans were accustomed to maintaining large standing armies. The troops were either paid in cash, or by means of the *iqta* system to which we have referred to earlier. Many of the Turkish commanders were slaves who had been brought up by the sultans and trained for warfare. This was specially so among the Muizzi sultans of Ghur. While as an institution slavery is hardly to be commended, in the immediate context, it provided the Turkish sultans with a body of commanders who were totally loyal and devoted.

We have little knowledge about the internal organisation of the Rajput armies at this time. It has, however, been assumed that there was a sharp decline in the number of soldiers in the standing armies maintained by individual Rajput rulers. This, in turn, has been linked to the growth of "feudalism", or a process by which administrative authority, including the collection of land-revenue and maintenance of the army, was delegated more and more to a body of hereditary land-holders, called *samanta*. These *samantas* were difficult to control, and were always eager to set themselves up as in-

dependent rulers whenever a suitable opportunity arose. The social structure of the Turks was different. However, among the Turks
tribal loyalties were an ever present source of danger, and there
were constant attempts on the part of local commanders setting themselves up as independent rulers. That is how both the Ghaznavid
and the Ghurid, and others, such as the Seljukid and Khwarizmi
empires arose. But as long as any of these empires existed, they
were more highly centralised than any of the Rajput states. This,
again, was on account of the working of the *iqta* system, each commander or amir being not hereditary but dependent on the will of
the sultan for his position.

We should be careful not to allow our criticism of the Rajput
social system to cloud our historical judgement. It has been sug-.
gested by an eminent modern historian that on account of the caste
system, and the working of the feudal system which was hierarchical in nature, the Indian people watched with "sullen indiffer-
ence" the fate of the Indian governing classes, and that in consequence, the towns fell like ripe fruits, that only the forts put up
some resistance, but they felt helpless when the enemy controlled
the countryside. This is based on a misunderstanding of the nature of medieval polity in India and elsewhere. According to K. S.
Lambden, among the states in West and Central Asia at the time,
"patriotism was an unknown virtue. All the sultan expected of his
subjects was that they should pay their taxes and pray for his welfare,
while they expected from him security and justice. The state did
not demand, or receive, the loyalty of the common man." The situation in India was little different. Loyalty was accorded to caste,
clan, village or city, and to the defence of hearth and home. The
question of religion we shall discuss separately. As far as forts or
fortified towns were concerned, their defence, again, had to be combined with a mobile cavalry force. This was a deficiency with the
Rajputs, as we have already noted.

To what extent religion was able to provide a bond of union
between peoples divided on the basis of tribe, clan, caste, ethnicity
etc. and between them and the ruling groups is a matter of debate. There is little doubt that Islam did provide a strong bond of
unity between different groups and sections, and imbued them with
a strong sense of a mission and fighting spirit. In their operations
in India, this was combined with an equally strong spirit of gain
through plunder. The Islamic spirit of equality and brotherhood was
certainly a positive point, but it did not extend to the social sphere.
Both the Turkish and Rajput societies were hierarchical, one based

on racial and family superiority, and the other on clan. Among both of them, power and office were the monopoly of narrow sections. However, on balance, there was greater social mobility among the Turks than among the Rajputs. Thus, an ironsmith established the Saffarid dynasty which ruled in West Asia for some time before the rise of the Ghazanavids. The Hindu concept of *chhut* (untouchability), and banning a section of the people from entiring temples were negative phenomena and a source of weakness. It is true that Hindu society had developed other methods of bringing the "outscaste" sections into the stream of Hindu religions consciousness, viz. through wandering sadhus, and brahmans who presided over their religious rituals. However, these could not bridge the gap between the Rajput ruling classes and the masses.

Finally, the lack of a strategic perspective on the part of the Rajputs which put them tactically on the defensive, to which we have referred earlier, and which led to long term disadvantages has to be seen in the perspective of the prevailing Indian cultural ethos. Al-Biruni, the noted scientist and scholar, who spent ten years in India and interacted with the brahmans and studied Sanskrit, noted the deep insulary of the Indians, remarking "The Hindus believe that there is no country but theirs, no nation but theirs, no kings like theirs, no science like theirs. They are haughty, foolishly vain, self-conceited and stolid. Their haughtiness is such that if you tell them of any science or scholar in Khurasan or Persia, they think you both an ignoramus and a liar."

It was this sense of insularity which restricted the Indians from going to West and Central Asia, and bring back knowledge of its sciences, its peoples and governments. We do not find an Al-Biruni among Indians to study foreign lands. The *kali varjya*, or ban on the Hindus travelling in countries where the *munja* grass did not grow or crossing the salt seas, though disregarded in practice, was an index of this attitude of growing insularity. After the break-up of the Kushan empire, and the gradual decline of Buddhism in West and Central Asia, India became more and more inward looking. This neglect and ignorance of the outside world, and loss of a strategic perspective, led to long term repercussions of which the Turkish conquest was, perhaps, the first, but not the last consequence.

Thus, the defeat of the Rajputs by the Turks have to be seen in a long-term perspective. It was the result not only of weakness in their military organisation and leadership, and of a defective understanding of military tactics. It was rooted also in the defective social organisation which led to the growth of states which were structurally weak as compared to the Turkish states. Finally, the Rajput sense of insularity which was rooted in the Indian cultural ethos, did not enable them to develop a strategic perspective whereby, through military and diplomatic means, potential invaders could be kept away from the natural defence parameter of India.

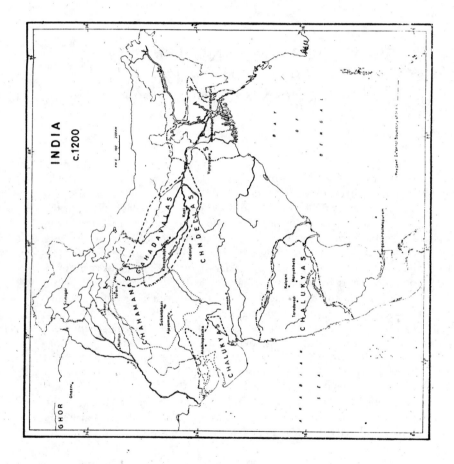

INDIA
c.1200

2

ESTABLISHMENT AND TERRITORIAL CONSOLIDATION OF THE DELHI SULTANAT (1206-1236)

By the time of Muizzuddin Muhammad's death in 1206, the Turks had by individual efforts been able to extend their sway upto Lakhnauti in Bengal, Ajmer and Ranthambor in Rajasthan, upto the boundaries of Ujjain in the south, and Multan and Uchch in Sindh. However, they had many internal difficulties to face, and their empire remained more or less stationary for almost a hundred years. The internal and external difficulties faced by the Turks were numerous. First and foremost they had to deal with the efforts of some of the ousted rulers, particularly the Rajput rulers of Rajasthan and Bundelkhand, and neighbouring areas, such as Bayana and Gwaliyar to regain their former possessions. While the struggle with them had many ups and downs, depending on the strength and cohesion of the two sides, the Rajputs never came together to try and collectively oust the Turks from India. Nor were there any serious uprisings against the Turks in the Ganga Valley or the Punjab (with the sole exception of the Khokhars during the reign of Muizzuddin). Hence, it would hardly be correct to term these isolated battles by individual Rajput rulers to regain their possessions as "Hindu reaction" to the Turks.

Secondly, the Turks had to spend a lot of time and energy in dealing with factionalism in the Turkish nobility which led to recurrent spells of political instability at the centre. Some of the Turkish rulers tried to carve out their own independent spheres of authority. Thus, Muhammad bin Bakhtiyar Khalji and his successors tried to keep Lakhnauti and Bihar free from the control of Delhi. There were strong separatist tendencies in Multan and Sindh also. For some time, there was a struggle for domination between the nobles at Lahore and Delhi. On and off, some of the powerful governors (*iqtadars*) also tried to defy.Delhi. Thus, regional factors asserted themselves.

Finally, during this period, there were important changes in Central Asian politics which affected India. Immediately following the death of Muizzuddin, the Ghurid empire broke up. Muizzuddin's favourite slave, Yalduz, succeeded him at Ghazni, while another slave, Qubacha seized control of Multan and Uchch. Qutbuddin Aibak, who had been deputizing for Muizzuddin at Delhi, was invited by the Turkish amirs at Lahore. Aibak marched to Lahore and ascended the throne there. Although both Qubacha and Aibak had married two daughters of Yalduz, they struggled against each other, particularly for the possession of the Punjab. But Aibak succeeded in keeping his control over Lahore which he made his capital. After some time, Khwarizm Shah, the ruler of Merv, which was the most powerful state in Central Asia over-ran Ghur and Ghazni. But before the Khwarizm Shah could consolidate his position in Ghur and Ghazni, and think of moving towards India, he had to face an even bigger danger, the Mongols.

As is well known, the Mongol ruler, Chingez Khan, erupted into Transoxiana and Khurasan in 1218 and, in course of time, the Mongol empire extended from China to Saxony in Central Europe. The Mongols devastated the towns and cities of Central and West Asia which offered resistance to them levelling some of them to the ground after slaughtering almost all the men there, except artisans who, along with women and children, were enslaved. But the Mongol conquest did not have negative aspects only. The unification of Central and West Asia under Mongol aegis enabled trade and merchandise to move freely, and gradually towns and town-life began to revive. However, we are concerned here only with the impact of the rise of the Mongols on the Delhi sultanat.

In 1218, after conquering North China, Chingez turned against the Khwarizm Shah who had offended him by putting to death some Muslim merchants who had received a safe conduct from Chingez for carrying on trade. The Khwarizm Shah suffered a set back in a brush with Chingez's advance guard. Afraid of a defeat when faced with the main armies of Chingez, he evacuated Transoxiana, and then retreated to the West. Samarqand and Bukhara fell to the Mongols after resistance, and suffered the fate reserved by the Mongols to those towns which resisted. However, Prince Jalaluddin Mangbarani, the son of the Khwarizm Shah, continued

to resist in Ghur and Ghazni. Chingez pursued the prince, and inflicted a sharp defeat on him on the bank of the river Indus in
1221. The prince escaped across the river with a handful of followers. Chingez loitered around in the neighbourhood for three
months, then decided to complete the conquest of Khurasan. He
then returned to Mongolia and died in 1227. This was followed by
internal troubles among the Mongols, giving the Turkish rulers in
India time to consolidate the Sultanat.

The rise of the Mongols, and the deprivation of the support and
backing of the well trained Ghurid army were important factors
which prevented the early Turkish rulers of Delhi from trying to
further expand their territories. On the other hand, the end of the
link with Ghur and Ghazni after the death of Muizzuddin (1206),
saved them from involvement in Central Asian affairs, and enabled
them to develop in India on the basis of their own resources and
inclinations. The Turkish rulers were thus forced to develop an independent state in India, with forms and institutions suited to their
own requirements and the specific conditions obtaining in the country. In consequence, gradually a new socio-cultural order evolved
in North India. We shall pay attention to these aspects while tracing the broad political developments in the country.

i. Qutbuddin Aibak and Iltutmish—Establishment of the Delhi Sultanat

As we have noted, **Qutbuddin Aibak** (1206-1210), a favourite
slave of Muizzuddin, who had played an important role in the battle
of Tarain and in the subsequent Turkish conquests in North India
had been enthroned at Lahore in 1206 on the basis of the support
of the local notables and amirs. Although prominent in India, it is
doubtful whether he had ever been nominated as his *wali-ahd* (successor or viceroy) by Muizzuddin. Thus, he rose to the throne by
personal merit. Somewhat later, he received from Sultan Mahmud
who had succeeded his father, Ghiyasuddin, at Ghur, a deed of
manumission (freeing him from his slave status, legally, a slave could
not be a sovereign), and a *chatr*, recognizing his position as a sovereign. This finally ended the legal claim of Ghazni over the Turkish conquests in Hindustan. The early break with Ghazni and Central
Asian affairs had long term consequences, as we have noted.

Aibak hardly had time to add to the Turkish conquests in India, and died in 1210, on account of a fall from his horse while
playing *chaugan* (medieval polo). But his brief reign is considered

significant because it marked the rise of the first independent Turkish ruler in India. Contemporaries praise him for his liberality, beneficence and gallantry. Thus, he is supposed to have given away lakhs but also slaughtered lakhs. This combination of liberality, emphasis on justice, and brutality in war were typical of many of the early Turkish rulers in India.

Shamsuddin Iltutmish (1210-36) who was a slave of Aibak, succeeded him at Delhi in 1210. He ruled till 1236, and was responsible not only for keeping the Delhi Sultanat together, but made it a well-knit and compact State. He may thus be called the real establisher of what came to be called the Delhi Sultanat.

Iltutmish had many difficulties to contend with. First, he faced the challenge of Aram Shah who had been put up by the Turkish amirs at Lahore. Aram Shah apparently was not the son of Aibak, because we are told that Aibak had no son and only three daughters, two of whom were married successively to Qubacha, and one to Iltutmish after he ascended the throne. Aram Shah marched on Delhi but was defeated easily by Iltutmish at a battle at Tarain. But Iltutmish's position was not secure even then. Some of the Turkish nobles were not prepared to accept Iltutmish's authority. They went outside Delhi and prepared for rebellion. Iltutmish marched from Delhi, defeated the rebels and executed most of the leaders. Nor was this the first opposition of Turkish nobles that Iltutmish had to face. According to the contemporary author, Minhaj Siraj, "On several other occasions in different parts of Hindustan, hostilities arose between him and the armies and the Turks." Iltutmish triumphed over all of them—on account of "Divine help" according to Minhaj, or according to his own careful management of affairs.

Having brought under his control Delhi and its dependencies including Banaras, Awadh, Badaun and the Siwaliks, Iltutmish found himself faced with a piquant situation. The Turkish rule in Hindustan was by this time divided into four portions: Multan and Uchch and Siwistan upto the sea in Sindh which was under the control of Qubacha, Lakhnauti under the control of the Khalji maliks, Delhi under the control of Iltutmish, and Lahore which was coveted by Yalduz, Qubacha and Iltutmish and passed under the control of one or the other according to circumstances.

(a) Punjab and Sindh

In his struggle for the control of the Punjab and Sindh, Iltutmish displayed great tact, patience and diplomatic skill. He did not get too closely involved in the struggle for the Punjab till circumstances favoured him. At first he befriended Yalduz at Ghazni, and accepted the letter of manumission and *durbash* (two-headed baton which was a symbol of royalty) sent by Yalduz, even though it implied according a superior status to Yalduz. Meanwhile, there was a complex struggle for the control of Punjab between Yalduz and Qubacha which need not concern us here. In 1215, after being ousted from Ghazni by the Khwarizm Shah, Yalduz occupied Lahore and the whole of the Punjab, expelling Qubacha. It seems that as the successor of Muizzuddin at Ghazni, Yalduz claimed not only to be the ruler of the Punjab, but also claimed a vague control over all the conquests of Muizzuddins in Hindustan. This situation was unacceptable to Iltutmish, and led to hostilities between the two in which Yalduz was defeated, imprisoned and later killed. However, the problem of the Punjab remained. At first, Iltutmish was prepared to leave Lahore to Qubacha, but there was a disagreement between the two upon its boundaries. Qubacha wanted to extend his control upto Tabarhinda and 'Kuhram which Iltutmish felt, would have threaten his position at Delhi. In the hostilities between the two which followed, Qubacha was defeated and Iltutmish occupied Lahore.

Before Iltutmish could consolidate his position in Punjab, Jalaluddin Mangabarani, the Khwarizmian prince, being pursued by Chingez, crossed the Indus in 1221 and, in alliance with the war-like Khokhars, conquered the Punjab upto Thanesar. He then sent a message to Iltutmish seeking an alliance against the Mongols so that he could recover his lost dominions. Iltutmish politely turned down the overture, refusing to be drawn into a fight with the Mongols. He also marched against him with a large army. Unable to withstand his forces, Jalaluddin quit Lahore, and moved towards Qubacha in Sindh. He inflicted a sharp defeat upon Qubacha and occupied Uchch. Meanwhile, the Mongols too invested Multan.

Thus, the effect of Jalaluddin's incursion into India was the weakening of Qubacha's position in Sindh. Jalaluddin quit India in 1224, but for fear of Chingez, Iltutmish kept a low posture in the northwest. It was only in 1228, after the death of Chingez that he decided to conquer Sindh from Qubacha, and invested Uchch. It was captured after a siege of three months. Qubacha fled to Bakkhar. Shortly afterwards when Iltutmish advanced on Bakhhar, Qubacha drowned himself in the river Indus.

Thus, by 1228, not only did Iltutmish's control extend upto the Indus, but the whole of Multan and Sindh upto the sea came under his control. This marked the first phase of Iltutmish's consolidation of the Delhi Sultanat.

(b) Turkish Conquest of Bihar and Lakhnauti

As has been mentioned earlier, during the reign of Muizzuddin, Bihar and Lakhauti had been captured by a Khalji malik, Muhammad bin Bakhtiyar Khalji. The contemporary historian, Minhaj Siraj, praises him as a man of "impetus, enterprising, intrepid, bold, sagacious and expert in warfare." The Khaljis were a Turkish tribe from southwest Ghur. However, Bakhtiyar was ungainly in appearance, and was offered only low employment when he appeared for service before Muizzuddin at Ghazni. Rejecting this as beneath him, he repaired to India, and presented himself again at Delhi. But he was rejected once more. Thereupon, he took service under the *iqtadar* (governor) of Badaun who had an extensive charge in modern west U.P. Soon after, he repaired to the service of the Commander of Awadh who assigned him two villages on the boundary of Bihar. This gave him the opportunity of making plundering raids into Bihar and Maner which, following the downfall of the Gahadavala empire, had become a kind of a no-man's land dominated by petty Gahadavala chiefs. Rai Lakshman Sena, the ruler of Bengal, who had been a rival of the Gahadavads, preferred to confine himself to Bengal, either because he was too old and feeble, or because he was under the illusion that the Turks would be satisfied with Bihar if he did not come into conflict with them.

Bakhtiyar Khalji's reputation as an enterprising warrior spread far and wide, and many Khaljis from different parts of Hindustan joined him. Even Muizzuddin sent him a special robe of distinction (*khilat*) and honoured him, though he was neither his slave nor his employee. Emboldened, Bakhtiyar Khalji now attacked a fort in Bihar with 200 horsemen which he later found was a Buddhist monastery (*vihar*). This apparently was the famous university of Nalanda. He then captured Vikramsila, another university town, and wrought much havoc there. He also captured the capital, Uddandapur, and built a fort there. This is placed in 1202.

After this victory, Bakhtiyar Khalji returned with great booty and presented himself before Qutbuddin Aibak and received from him great honour and distinction, including a robe of honour from his special wardrobe and many presents. Bakhtiyar Khalji distributed the presents to his people and returned to Bihar. This shows the nature of relationship between prominent chiefs and the Sultan at that time. The chiefs were expected to fend for themselves, and their victories were the victories of the Sultan. The chiefs on their part, acknowledged a Sultan if it suited them, or made a bid for independence. Thus, the structure of the Sultanat was rather brittle. Returning to Bihar, Bakhtiyar Khalji gathered information about Lakshman Sena. He was said to be eighty years old, and had been a famous warrior. According to Minhaj Siraj, he had never committed any oppression on his people, and was very generous in giving gifts. Apprehensive that after the conquest of Bihar, the turn of Bengal would come next, and because fear of Bakhtiyar's military prowess had spread far and wide, and on the advice of brahmans and astrologers, many brahmans and traders had left the Sena capital for a safer place of refuge in the east. But we are told that Lakshman Sena had decided to stick on.

For Muhammad bin Bakhtiyar Khalji's conquest of Lakhauti, we are dependent on one contemporary source, Minhaj Siraj, whose account has been followed by all later writers. Minhaj's account is well-known; that Bakhtiyar prepared a force and pressed on the Sena capital, Nadia, so rapidly that only 18 horsemen were able to keep up with him, that he proceeded in such a manner in which people of the place imagined that may be his party were merchants and had brought horses for sale, that reaching the palace Bakhtiyar suddenly attacked, and the Rai, taken unawares, fled by a posterior gate, and that Bakhtiyar captured the whole of his treasures, his wives, and other females and attendants etc., and that the main army arrived soon and took possession of the city and its round abouts.

There are several difficulties in accepting Minhaj's story as it stands. Minhaj states that Nadia was the capital of Lakshman Sena. From archaeological evidence, we know that the capital of the Senas was first Bikrampur (near modern Dacca), and then Lakshmanavati or Lakhnauti. Nadia was a very small town—perhaps a pilgrim centre or a centre of brahmanical learning. It is possible that, as in the case of Bihar where Bakhtiyar confused a university with a fort, he mistook a pilgrim centre, Nadia, for the Sena capital. This appears even more likely because there is no mention of any resistance by the Sena forces, although Lakshman Sena had been a noted warrior, and had been forewarned of the danger of Turkish attack.[1]

---

1. It is possible that Minhaj confused Nadia with Lakhnauti, the Sena capital which Bakhtiyar captured later. Again, there is no mention of a fight. May be the Senas had abandoned the city in anticipation of a Turkish attack. The Senas continued to rule south Bengal for another fifty years from their capital at Sonargaon, near ancient Gaur.

We have no independent corroboration of Lakshman Sena being at Nadia at the time. May be he had gone here on pilgrimage with a small military escort.

Following Nadia, Bakhtiyar captured Lakhnauti. He had the *khutba* read, and issued coins in the name of Muizzuddin, although he was independent in all but name.

Bakhtiyar Khalji's conquest of Bihar and North Bengal stands as an example of intrepid daring. It added greatly to the reputation of Turkish arms in India. But Bakhtiyar Khalji did not live long after his success. In the following year, he prepared an army of 10,000 horses for the occupation of Tibet and Turkistan. The Turks had very vague ideas of the geography of the region. Bakhtiyar apparently believed that Tibet and Turkistan were just across the mountain, and that if he could gain direct access to Turkistan, he could get military supplies from it, and set himself up as an independent ruler. The campaign was thus, destined to fail from the beginning. It seems that Bakhtiyar never went beyond Assam. The Magh rulers allowed him to come as far as he could, crossing the river Bagmati across a stone bridge. Finding that he could go no further, Bakhtiyar retreated, to find that the bridge had been destroyed. Caught between a large opposing force and the river, Bakhtiyar made a dash for the river. But the river was too deep to be forded. Most of the soldiers drowned, Bakhtiyar himself escaping with about 100 soldiers.

This was the worst disaster of Turkish arms. Bakhtiyar was deeply depressed, and took to bed where he was stabbed to death by one of his nobles, Ali Mardan Khan. This was in 1205.

Relations of Bengal with Delhi

Ali Mardan was ousted by nobles loyal to Muhammad Bakhtiyar and imprisoned. But he escaped, and after many adventures, came to the court of Qutbuddin Aibak who honoured him, and assigned him the territory of Lakhnauti. The prestige of Muizzuddin and his successors was high, and the Khalji amirs at Lakhnauti submitted to Ali Mardan who brought the whole of North Bengal under his control.

When Aibak died, and ambitious nobles such as Qubacha in Sindh, assumed airs of independence, Ali Mardan assumed the canopy of state (*chatra*) and read the *khutbah* in his name. However, he proved to be a tyrant, and was soon displaced by a Khalji amir, Iwaz, who assumed the throne under the title Sultan Ghiyasuddin. Minhaj calls

Ghiyasuddin Khalji a monarch worthy, just and beneficent. The region prospered under his rule and he undertook a number of public works which benefited the people. Taking advantage of Iltutmish's preoccupation with the north-west, he extended his authority over Bihar, and exacted tribute from many of the neighbouring rulers.

It seems that there were many clashes between Iltutmish's Maliks and Iwaz for control over Bihar. This was a repetition of an old geostrategic struggle between the masters of Kashi and Magadh. After the situation in the north-west had settled somewhat, in 1225 Iltutmish marched against Iwaz. A kind of a treaty was patched up between the two whereby Iwaz agreed to Iltutmish's suzreignty and also paid a heavy indemnity. Iltutmish awarded Bihar to his own officers. But as soon as Iltutmish's back was turned, Iwaz repudiated his suzreignty, and ousted his officials from Bihar. Iltutmish asked his son, Nasiruddin Mahmud, then Governor of Awadh, to watch the situation. Two years later, when Iwaz was campaigning in Kamrup (Assam) and Bang (East Bihar), and Lakhnauti was undefended, Nasiruddin Mahmud made a sudden move and occupied Lakhnauti. Iwaz came back, and fought a battle but was defeated, imprisoned and executed. Nasiruddin remained in charge of Lakhnauti. But he died shortly afterwards and the Khaljis again threw off the yoke of Delhi.

It was not till 1230 when Iltutmish led a second campaign that Lakhnauti was brought under his control. But Bengal always remained a difficult charge, and threw off its allegiance to Delhi at the first sign of weakness at the centre.

ii. Internal Rebellions, Conquest of Ranthambhor and Gwaliyar, and Raids into Bundelkhand and Malwa

During his long reign, Iltutmish had to face a number of internal rebellions. The ousted Gahadvaras of Kannauj had recovered Badaun and Kannauj, and there was a rebellion even at Banaras. These were dealt with, but the Rajputs of Katehar (modern Rohelkhand) continued to threaten this area. Katehar was attacked, and later Iltutmish cleared the area upto the Siwaliks. There were also hostilities with local Hindu chiefs in parts of Doab and Awadh. These areas, which were then covered by heavy forests, continued to be troublesome for outsiders for several centuries.

After settling the affairs of Bihar and Bengal, Iltutmish turned his attention towards the recapture of some of the forts, such as Bayana and Gwaliyar, which had been recovered by the Rajput rajas in the confusion following the death of Aibak. First, Iltutmish invested and captured Ranthambhor from the Chauhan successors of Prithvi Raj. This was deemed a great success because Ranthambhor was considered an impregnable fortress, and had defied many earlier invaders. However, since it was too far away from Delhi for effective control, after some time it was returned to the Chauhans as feudatories. Ajmer continued under Turkish rule.

Next, Iltutmish captured Bayana and invested Gwaliyar. The Paramar ruler of Gwaliyar resisted for over a year, but was then compelled to evacuate the fort.

Gwaliyar was made the base of plundering raids into Bundelkhand and Malwa. The Turkish governor of Gwaliyar attacked Chanderi and Kalinjar but escaped with great difficulty when on the way back, laden with plunder, he was attacked by the Rajputs.

A little earlier, Iltutmish raided Bhilsa and Ujjain in Malwa. The famous temple of Mahakali at Ujjain was destroyed, and rich plunder obtained. But little effort was made to extend Turkish dominion over the area.

iii. Estimate of Iltutmish as a Ruler

Iltutmish re-established the territorial integrity of the Delhi sultanat created by Muizzuddin and which was in danger of being split up. He defeated efforts of ambitious rivals such as Yalduz and Qubacha to divide the sultanat. In the process, he displayed a great deal of tact, patience, and far-sightedness. Thus, he bided his time till he was in a position to take decisive action. This was displayed in his dealings with Qubacha as well as Jalaluddin Mangbarani. Early in his reign he had realized that his policy must be one of steady consolidation rather than rapid expansion. He proceeded against the Khalji Maliks of Lakhnauti only when he had consolidated his position in the north-west.

It was under Iltutmish that the Delhi Sultanat can be called a truely independent state, not tied up to a foreign sovereign living at Ghazni or Ghur. Iltutmish's legal status as an independent sovereign was reaffirmed in the eyes of the Muslims when in 1229 an envoy of the Caliph of Baghdad reached Delhi with a formal letter of investitute for Iltutmish. Although it was a mere formality and recognition of an accomplished fact, Iltutmish made the visit a grand occasion.

Iltutmish can be credited with making Delhi the political, administrative, and cultural centre of Turkish rule in India. His steady presence at Delhi was a major factor in this as also the fact that Delhi became the refuge for nobles, bureaucrats, scholars, poets and religious divines from Central Asia to escape the Mongol depredations. Iltutmish beautified Delhi by setting up new buildings. The most notable example of this was the tower or minar, later called the Qutb Minar, commenced by Qutbuddin which he completed. Soon a magnificent city arose in the environs. The Hauz Shamsi, south of the Qutb Minar, and the madrasah (College or University) around it, was built by him. Iltutmish was not only a patron of men of Islamic learning and poets, he also accorded great honour to the sufi saints of his time, such as Qutbuddin Bakhtiyar Kaki.

By his military prowess, pleasing manners and liberality, Iltutmish earned the deep respect and attachment of the people of Delhi to his family, in consequence of which the right of his children to succeed him was accepted. Thus, he set up the first hereditary sovereignty at Delhi. However, his children were not successful because Iltutmish had not been able to create a well-knit and compact state. The State was still a loose structure in which the inner jealousies and rivalries of the Turkish nobles and slave officers could be kept under control only by a strong ruler.

3

STRUGGLE FOR THE ESTABLISHMENT OF A CENTRALIZED MONARCHY (1236-1290)

i. *Razia and the Period of Instability (1236-46)*

The death of Iltutmish was followed by a decade of political instability at Delhi. During this period, four descendants of Iltutmish were put on the throne and murdered. The main cause of this was acute factionalism in the Turkish nobility. As we have seen, the Turks were divided into many tribes some of which had converted to Islam, and some had not. There was acute struggle between them, as for example, between Muizzuddin and the Ghuzz Turkish tribe of Transoxiana which was non-Muslim. Even Islamized Turkish tribal groups fought against each other all the time.

Apart from the Turks, the next important ethnic group in the nobility under Iltutmish were the Tajiks (or Taziks). The Tajiks were Iranians from the Transoxiana and Khurasan regions. The Persians had settled in, and dominated the area before the Turks entered and ousted them from the region. However, the Turks were rude warriors, and knew little about the arts of administration. It was the Tajiks, many of whom had been landlords previously, who largely provided the sinews of administration. In the process, many of them had reached high offices. Thus, Nizamul-Mulk Junaidi, the wazir of Iltutmish, was a Tajik. The Turkish nobles, both free and slave, resented the pre-eminence given to the Tajiks and looked down upon them as being pen-pushers (*nawisanda*) or bureaucrats rather than warriors. Though the tribal structure of the Turks had largely broken down once they settled down in Khurasan and the neighbouring areas (Iran, Ghur, Ghazni, etc.), old tribal associations, and personal bonds were still strong. The most important personal bond was that of slavery. As we have seen, many sultans purchased Turkish slaves for the specific purpose of raising them up as warriors and administrators. Such slaves were well treated, and often trained along with the rulers' own sons.

The slave officers of Iltutmish formed an elite corp which was very proud of itself. It did not consider even the free amirs, both Turk and Tajik, as being equal to them. The later historian, Ziauddin Barani, calls these slave officers the "Corp of Forty" (*Chihalgani*). The number forty does not matter because we can identify less than 25 such persons in the list of Iltutmish's nobles.

Perhaps things could have been managed if even this "Corp of Forty" had behaved as a unified body. But as Barani says, "none of them would bow or submit to another, and in the distribution of territories (*iqtas*), forces, offices and honours they sought equality with each other."

The rise and fall of **Razia** (1236-40), a romantic figure in medieval history, should be seen against this background. She ascended the throne because a strong body of Turkish slave officers, who were *iqtadars* (governors) of Badaun, Multan, Hansi and Lahore had risen against Ruknuddin, the son of Iltutmish, who had succeeded to the throne after his father's death. Nizamul-Mulk Junaidi, the wazir of Iltutmish, also joined the rebels. Ruknuddin had become unpopular because after his accession to the throne he became immersed in pleasure, and left the affairs of state to his mother, Shah Turkan, who had been a Turkish hand-maid. As head of the Sultan's *haram* and its administration, she sought vengeance against those who had looked down upon her earlier. While Ruknuddin had gone out of the city to fight the rebels, Razia took the opportunity to go to the Jama Masjid and appealed to the people of Delhi for their support, alleging that there was a conspiracy to kill her. She succeeded, after something like a popular revolt in her favour took place.

Razia strengthened her claim by recalling that in his life time, Iltutmish had nominated her as his successor in preference to his sons. It was typical of the times that Iltutmish did not consult the theologians *before* he took this decision, but informed them about it afterwards, leaving them no option but to concur. We shall find that later on many Turkish rulers in India took decisions in the light of political circumstances, and consulted the theologians afterwards. However, the Turkish nobles, including the wazir, Nizamul-

Mulk Junaidi, did not accept Iltutmish's nomination, but at first supported his eldest son, Ruknuddin .

Although Razia succeeded to the throne it seems that she never had the solid support of any powerful group among the Turkish nobles, but depended for survival on her political skill in keeping the opposition divided. Thus, the powerful group of nobles who were governors of Multan, Lahore, Hansi and Badaun, and who had been joined by Nizamul Mulk were at first opposed to her. But she won over some of the ring leaders, and isolated Nizamul-Mulk Junaidi who had to flee.

Firmly seated on the throne, Razia set about "reorganising the administration". According to Minhaj, "the kingdom became pacified, and the power of the state widely extended. From the territory of Lakhnauti to Debal all the maliks and amirs manifested their obedience and submission." In order to have direct contact with the administration, Razia laid aside the female dress and donned the tunic and head-dress of a man. She abandoned the veil, and appeared in the darbar, and rode out on an elephant with her face uncovered. Thus, people could see her openly.

This must have led to murmurings among the orthodox sections, but there was no public opposition to it because she had the support of the people of Delhi. Soon opposition to her began in a section of the nobility at Delhi and in the provinces. This opposition began because, we are told, she had appointed a Habshi (Abyssinian), Malik Yakut, as *amir-akhur* or Superintendent of the Stables. This post, which implied control over the royal stables, including elephants and horses, was considered to be a strategic post, and one which implied that the holder was close to the sovereign. Hence, it was resented by the Turkish nobles who wanted to monopolize all the important offices in the state. There is no evidence that the appointment of Malik Yakut was a part of Razia's policy to build a bloc of non-Turkish nobles in order to off-set the power of the Turkish nobles. Nor is there any reason to believe that there was any personal intimacy between Razia and Malik Yakut. Even the charge that he had to lift Razia by the arm-pits to her horse is a later concoction because it is not mentioned by any contemporaries. Also, whenever Razia went out in public, she rode on an elephant, not a horse.

It was apparently Razia's firmness, and desire to exercise power directly which was the major cause of the dissatisfaction of the Turkish nobles with her. The first rebellion was at Lahore by its Governor, Kabir Khan. Razia marched to Lahore, and forced Kabir

Khan to submit. She then appointed him as *iqtadar* of Multan in place of Lahore. She had hardly returned to Delhi when Altunia, the Governor of Tabarhinda, rebelled. Both Kabir Khan and Altunia had been favoured by Razia, and she had little reason to expect opposition from them. She marched against Altunia, but did not know that he was in touch with a powerful group of Turkish nobles at Delhi, who wanted to overthrow her in order to clear their own way to power. Hence, when Razia reached Tabarhinda, the Turkish nobles rose in revolt, killed Yakut, and put Razia in prison at Tabarhinda. The conspirators at Delhi elevated another descendant of Iltutmish to the throne.

This virtually brings Razia's reign to a close. Her subsequent marriage to Altunia, their march on Delhi and their defeat, the melting away of her rapidly recruited soldiers, is a romantic interlude which never had much chance of success. She was murdered by dacoits while in flight.

The tragic end of Razia demonstrated the growing power of the Chihalgani Turkish nobles. The contemporary historian, Minhaj Siraj, praises Razia highly. He says that Razia was endowed with all the qualities befitting a sovereign; she was "prudent, benevolent, benefactor to her kingdom, a dispenser of justice, the cherisher of her subjects, and a great warrior." But he adds, "Of what advantage were all these attributes to her when she was born a woman?" It suited Minhaj to say so rather than blame the Turkish nobles who, as we have seen, were the principal cause of her downfall, as also that of her successors.

The period between the death of Razia (1240) and the rise of power of Balban as *naib* (vice-regent), is a period of continued struggle between the nobles and the monarchy. While the nobles were agreed that only a descendent of Iltutmish could sit on the throne at Delhi, they wanted that all power and authority should vest in their hands. As a noted modern historian, R.P. Tripathi, notes, "The chief constitutional interest in the history of the family of Iltutmish lies in the struggle between the crown and the peers for the possession of real power." At first, the nobles seemed to succeed. They appointed Bahram Shah, a son of Iltutmish, as a successor to Razia on condition that he appointed one of the Turkish nobles, Aitigin, to the post of *naib* or Vice-regent. For some time, a body of three nobles—the *naib*, the wazir, and the *mustaufi* (auditor-general) constituted itself as a kind of a governing board, reducing the monarch to the position of a figure-head. But conflict of interest among the triumvitrate, and the efforts of the ruler to reassert himself led to a struggle with the wazir in which Bahram Shah lost his throne and his life. The fate of his successor, Masud, was no different. The effort of the wazir, Nizam-ul-Mulk, to arrogate all power to himself led to his murder, and to the rise of Balban who subsequently had the monarch deposed in order to clear his own road to power.

The death of four monarchs within a brief span of six years following the death of Iltutmish denoted a serious crisis in the relationship between the monarchy and the Turkish nobles. The nobles wanted to rule while the monarch merely reigned, but they could not present a united front.

The elevation of Nasiruddin Mahmud, a grandson of Iltutmish, to the throne in 1246 was really the handiwork of Balban, though he tried for some time to take all the Turkish nobles along with him. Nasiruddin Mahmud was a suitable instrument for the nobles because he had little interest in political and administrative affairs, the fate of his predecessors being enough of a warning. He devoted all his time to prayers and religious observances, such as making copies of the Quran, or stitching caps for the devoted.

Thus, to all appearances, the nobles had won. But their victory was only of a short duration, as events showed.

ii. The Age of Balban (1246-87)

Although Balban ascended the throne only in 1266, the entire period from 1246 to his death in 1287 may be called the age of Balban because he was the dominant figure at Delhi during this time.

(a) Balban as the naib—struggle with the Chihalgani

Not much is known about the early life of Ulugh Khan, later known to history as Balban. He came from a family of Ilbari Turks who were greatly respected in Turkistan. They were ousted from the area by the heathen Turks, and Balban was sold as a slave in Baghdad, and then brought to Delhi in 1232-33 where he was purchased by Iltutmish. He was thus one of the *Chihalgani* Turks and gradually rose till he was appointed *Mir Hajib*, or the Lord Chamberlain, a post given only to important nobles. He made his mark as a brave and intrepid officer in 1246 by fighting against the Mongols who had devastated Lahore and besieged Uchch in Sindh. Following this, Balban took the initiative in carrying out a series of plundering raids against neighbouring Hindu rajas, rebellious *rais* and zamindars. In consequence, within three years he rose to the position of *"naib"* with full power to control the army and the administration. He further strengthened his position by marrying his daughter to the young sultan.

However, the position of Balban was not secure for a considerable period. The high position of Balban, and the fact that many of his relations held important posts or powerful *iqtas*, led to growing opposition on the part of the Turkish and Tajik nobles. The leader of the opposition was Qutlugh Khan, governor of Bihar, who was the senior most among the *Chihalgani* slave officers. It was due to the efforts of the Turkish nobles that in 1253 Balban was asked to quit his post as *naib*, and to repair to his *iqta*. Many supporters and relations of Balban, including his cousin, Sher Khan, who was governor of Sindh, were also ousted. Among the new appointees was Imaduddin Raihan, who was a eunuch and a Hindustani. He was appointed *Wakildar* or deputy to the king in judicial matters. The exact influence of Raihan on political affairs is not known because another Turkish noble, entitled Nizamul Mulk Junaidi, was appointed wazir. However, the contemporary writer, Minhaj Siraj, who under Raihan had lost his position of *qazi*, puts all the blame for the developments on Raihan. From his *iqta* in Nagaur, Balban continued his efforts to regain his position. He gathered much booty from a successful raid on Ranthambhor, and opened negotiations with the Turkish nobles. It seems that he also established contact with the Mongols. Soon he was able to detach many of the Turkish amirs from the side of Raihan. The sultan bowed to the strength of Balban's group and dismissed Raihan and sent him to his *iqta*. This was early in 1255. Soon, an army was sent against Raihan and he was defeated and killed. This strengthens the belief that Raihan did not have a powerful group of his own and that he was really a convenient front for powerful Turkish nobles who did not want that any one of them should attain the position of Balban.

On return to power, Balban soon settled scores with his leading opponents. He sent an expedition against Qutlugh Khan, who had married the sultan's mother, and taken her to his *iqta* of Awadh, and started behaving in independent ways. Stern action was taken against many others. To signify his new position, Balban compelled the young king to hand over to him the *chatr* or royal canopy. We have no account of the last six years of Nasiruddin Mahmud. Probably this was a period of increased factionalism which made Balban feel insecure. Hence, it seems that he decided to poison the young king. He also did away with all the royal princes so that he could himself assume the throne.

(b) Balban as the Ruler (1266-87)

The assumption of the throne by Balban at Delhi (1266) marks the beginning of an era of strong, centralized government. Balban sought to increase the prestige and power of the monarchy, and to centralise all authority in the hands of the sultan because he was convinced that this was the only way to face the internal and external dangers facing him. For the purpose, he harkened back to the Iranian theory of kingship. According to the Iranian theory, the king was divine or semi-divine in character, and answerable only to God, not to any set of intermediaries, i.e. religious figures. As such, there was a fundamental difference between the ruler and the nobles, the latter being dependent on the sultan's favour, and in no way equal to him.

These ideas, which were to some extent shared by the Hindus, had to be reconciled with the Islamic theory of sovereignty. While this was a complex matter which continued to agitate the Turks in the subsequent period as well, Balban's approach was a practical one. He underlined the theory that the sultan was the "shadow of God' (*zil-i-allah*), and emphasised it by insisting that in his court anyone presented to him had to perform the *sijda* and *pabos*, or prostration before the sovereign, a practice which, according to the theologians, was reserved for God alone. Second, he maintained a splendid court in which all the nobles had to stand in serried ranks, strict order being maintained by the *Mir Hajib* who was always an important noble. Balban himself maintained the utmost dignity in the Court. He would neither laugh out aloud himself nor allow anyone else to do so. The Court was richly decorated, with horses and elephants having jewelled trappings, and slaves and wrestlers (who were swordsmen and executioners) standing at the sides. When the Sultan moved out, he was preceded by a large posse of Sistani warriors with drawn swords which gleamed in the sun. According to the historian, Barani, Hindus and Muslims came from a distance of 100 to 200 kos to see Balban's public processions. Even the dependent rajas and *raiṣ* who visited Balban's court were deeply impressed. Barani goes on to say, "whenever the awe and spendour of the ruler do not impress the hearts of the ordinary people and the select from far and near, sovereignty and the conduct of government cannot be properly upheld." Thus, Balban's splendid court

and public processions had a political purpose. For the same reason, Balban gave up drinking even in his private assemblies though
as a Khan, he had been fond of drinking wine and gambling, and
used to hold convivial parties at his house at least three days in a
week. Balban also emphasised that it was unbecoming for a ruler
to associate with low, ignoble persons, buffoons, dancing girls etc.
Even his private servants had to observe the utmost decorum in
dress and behaviour.

Balban was not prepared to share power with anyone, not even
with the members of his family, and poisoned his cousin, Sher Khan,
for opposing him. He adopted methods fair or foul to deal with
those he considered to be his rivals. At the same time, he tried to
stand forth as the defender of the entire Turkish nobility. For the
purpose he declared that he would not give any post in the government or an *iqta*, or a post of authority in the local administration to any person belonging to a low or ignoble family. These included posts of accountant (*khwaja* or *musharif*), correspondent at
the local level, even *barids* or confidential spies. There was a deep
seated belief in those times, shared alike by Muslims and Hindus,
that only people belonging to old or noble families should be placed
in authority over the ordinary people. Contemporary writers give
free rein to this idea. However, this was almost an obsession with
Barani. Barani emphasised this by saying that since Balban claimed
to be a descendent of the Iranian hero, Afraisyab, he felt that if he
gave high government posts to the mean and ignoble, he would
prove to others that he himself came from an ignoble stock. For
Barani, a policy of excluding the mean and ignoble meant excluding the Hindus, and Hindu converts from the service of the state,
thereby strengthening the position of the immigrants and their descendants like him. How strictly such a policy of racial exclucivism
was followed by the earlier Turkish sultans in India needs a close
study. According to Barani, during the reign of Iltutmish, a survey
had been carried out as to how many persons drawn from low and
ignoble families, had been given posts of authority in the lower
administration. The names of thirty-three such persons were discovered, and they were all immediately dismissed. In fact, enquiry
had revealed that the wazir, Nizamul Mulk Junaidi, who was a
Tajik, came from a family whose ancestors had been weavers, and
that in consequence, he lost respect.

There is no means of checking the veracity of Barani's account.
That an Abyssinian like Mir Yaqut, and an Indian convert like Raihan
could reach high posts, that Nizamul Mulk Junaidi was not dis-

missed despite his weaver ancestry, and that Indian converts who were skillful and proficient in their work continued to be recommended for government service by Turkish nobles, as Barani himself states, shows that the Turkish monopoly of power was already under stress.

Barani gives two examples of Balban's attitude towards low, ignoble persons. First, when two prominent nobles proposed the name of Kamal Maihar for the post of *khwaja* (accountant) for the *iqta* of Amroha, and it was found on enquiry that he was the son of a converted Hindu slave, Balban not only flatly turned down the proposal although Kamal Maihar was reputed to be able and experienced, but gave dire warning to his officer not to propose to him in future for appointment the name of any person who was of low or ignoble birth. Explaining Balban's attitude, Barani says that it was a mandate given to him by God not to appoint any low ignoble person, and that when he saw low, ignoble persons, his body trembled (with rage).

In another case, Balban sternly refused to give audience at court to Fakhr Bawni since he was only the chief of the merchants, (*Malik-ut-Tujjar*) and it would compromise the dignity of the sovereign.

Balban tempered his despotism by laying great emphasis on justice. According to Barani, his justice and his consideration for the people won the favour of his subjects and made them zealous supporters of his throne. In the administration of justice, he was inflexible, showing no favour to his brethren or children, or to his associates or attendants. He appointed spies *(barids)* in all the cities, districts and *iqtas* to keep himself informed of the doings of the officials, and to ensure that no acts of oppression or high-handedness was perpetrated by them on anyone, including their slaves and domestic servants. Thus, when he learned that Malik Bakbak who was his confidant, and was governor of the *iqta* of Badaun, had flogged one of his servants to death in a drunken rage, and his widow appealed to the Sultan for justice, he ordered the malik to be flogged to death, and the *barid* who had not reported this matter to the Sultan to be publicly hanged. Another noble, Malik Haibat who had been his superintendent of arms and governor of Awadh had, under the influence of wine, killed a person. He was ordered to be given 500 strokes of the whip in public, and then handed over to the dead man's wife for extracting revenge for blood guilt, i.e. putting him to death if she so desired. He saved himself with great difficulty by paying her 20,000 tankas, and after that never moved out of his house for shame.

These harsh measures must have had a salutary effect, and we are told that Balban's confidential spies were greatly feared by the nobles. In his attitude to the people we see a combination of harshness and benevolence. Balban was convinced that both excess of wealth or poverty would make people rebellious. Hence, he advised his son, Bughra Khan, to be moderate in levying land tax (*kharaj*) on the peasants. When Balban was a Khan in the *iqta* under his charge, he tried to help those cultivators who had been ruined (on account of vagaries of nature, oppression by previous *iqtadars* or wars). In this way, we are told that he became famous for helping the poor and the helpless, and for making his *iqta* prosperous. As sultan, whenever the army camped anywhere, he used to pay special attention to the poor, the helpless, women, children and the old, to ensure that none of them suffered any loss, or physical harm (from the soldiers). Whenver there was a river or a rivulet or a marsh, he helped the people to cross, providing them with boats, or even his own elephants.

But Balban was extremely harsh when he found any rebelliousness on the part of the people or disturbance of the peace. We are told that following the death of Iltutmish, the Meos around Delhi had grown in numbers and boldness. Although a number of expeditions had been launched against them, they had not been successful, largely on account of the thick forests around Delhi. At this time, the Meos had become so daring as to attack the city at night, break into peoples' houses and cause them extreme hardships. People could not sleep at night for fear of the Meos, or not dare to go out of the city for visiting the various sacred tombs. Even in daytime, water-carriers and slave girls who had gone to fill water at the Hauz Shamsi were molested. All the inns in the neighbourhood had been plundered by the Meos, thereby affecting trade. In the Doab, robbers and dacoits had closed the roads to Delhi from all sides, and it had become impossible for the caravans and the traders to come and depart.

During the first two years of his reign, Balban spent a whole year in suppressing the Meos and cutting the forests around Delhi. He slaughtered a large number of Meos, built a fort, and established many *thanas* (military outposts) and assigned them to Afghans. Tax-free villages were set apart for their maintenance. Thus, Delhi was freed from the fear of the Meos.

Turning to the doab, *iqtadars* who had the requisite means were appointed to the various territories in the doab. Balban ordered the villages of the disobedient to be totally destroyed, the men were to be killed and their women and children seized as spoils of war. High ranking amirs were appointed for this task. The thick forests in the area were cut down. Similar methods were applied to the areas near Awadh. Strong forts were established, and Afghans and other Muslims with tax-free lands were settled there to maintain law and order. Thus, the roads were freed for the traders and *banjaras*. We are told that in consequence prices of cattles and domestic animals, including slaves, fell at Delhi.

Balban adopted similar measures to deal with the rebels in Katehar (modern Rohilkhand), who were plundering the villages, and harassing the people in the territories of Badaun and Amroha. These harsh methods of Balban have been called by some modern historians a policy of "blood and iron." But it would be wrong to apply this to all of Balban's policies.

A strong, centralized state needed a strong army. As it was, all medieval thinkers considered the army to be a pillar of the state. While we have no idea of the strength of the army under Balban, we are told that he tried to reorganise and expand the central army which was directly under the control of the sultan. Thus, brave and experienced maliks and sardars were appointed over the royal forces to which several thousand new *sawars* were added, care being taken to see that they were given adequate remuneration by assigning them fertile villages in *iqta*. As part of the reform process, Balban also ordered an enquiry into the position of old Turkish soldiers, many of whom had been given villages in the *doab* as *iqta* in lieu of salary. Many of the soldiers had become too old to serve, but continued to hold the villages in connivance with the *diwan-i-arz* (Department of the Muster-Master). Balban wanted to pension off the old soldiers, but withdrew his order at the instance of Fakhruddin, the kotwal of Delhi. But some improvement in the situation must have taken place.

To keep the army active and vigilant, Balban undertook frequent hunting expeditions in which thousands of hosemen, archers and footmen were employed. These expeditions were kept a secret, orders being passed only the previous night. Thus, officers and men were always kept in a state of alert. Barani praises Balban for his foresight in the matter, but foolishly puts the words to the effect in the mouth of the Mongol chief, Halaku, who had died before Balban's accession to the throne.

We have no idea about the state of the army of the nobles except that Balban appointed only able and experienced officers. Apparently, the nobles were left to recruit their own soldiers. Balban attached great importance to horses and elephants, each elephant being reckoned as equal to 500 *sawars*. While Balban had a ready supply of elephants from Bengal and Assam, the Mongol conquest of Central Asia had made it difficult to obtain horses from those areas. Hence, Balban had to fall back on Indian horses from the Siwaliks, the Punjab etc. For the army, too, recruitment of soldiers and slaves from Turkistan, Khurasan etc. had become difficult. Afghans and Indians, including Hindus, seem to have filled the vacuum. Thus, we have seen that Afghan soldiers were settled in the Doab and in the areas around Delhi. When Balban was marching to the east in order to meet the rebellion in Bengal, while at Awadh he ordered a general mobilisation, and we are told that two lakhs of men, including *sawars* (horsemen), foot-men, archers, load bearers etc. were recruited. Many of these were Hindus and Hindustanis (Indian Muslims).

Despite a large and efficient army which was kept in a state of readiness by constant exercises, Balban did not try to expand the territories of the Delhi sultanat, or raid the neighbouring kings of Malwa or Gujarat because, as Balban explained to his close associates, the "wretched Mongols were always looking for an opportunity to raid the *doab*, ravage Delhi and its neighbourhood and inflict untold suffering on his subjects."

iii. Struggle for the Territorial Integrity of the Sultanat

The Mongol threat was a major preoccupation of Balban, and the reason for not leading expeditions anywhere far away from Delhi. The Mongol threat to India during the 13th and 14th centuries shall be dealt with separately.

According to Barani, when Balban attained the throne, the dignity and authority of government was restored, and his stringent rules and resolute determination caused all men, high and low, throughout his dominions to submit to his authority. Like all generalisations, this statement also needs to be treated with caution. While the prestige and power of the Central Government increased under Balban, internal dissensions continued to raise their head. These consisted of two elements; first, the attempt of ambitious Turkish nobles and chiefs, some of them neighbours of India, to carve out an independent sphere of authority for themselves. Second was the attempt of Rajput rajas and *rais*, including big zamindars, to assert themselves, and if possible, to expel the Turks from their territories.

Among the Rajput rajas and *rais*, the most important were those from Rajasthan. In the confusion following the death of Razia, both Gwaliyar and Ranthambhor had to be abandoned by the Turks, as it was not feasible to withstand the Rajput forces. Balban recovered Gwaliyar, but his efforts to recapture Ranthambhor were not successful. From this time onwards, the Chauhans based on Ranthambhor rapidly rose in power. However, their expansionist efforts were directed against the existing rulers in Rajasthan, Malwa and Gujarat, not against the Turks. The Turks continued to hold Ajmer and Nagaur, but they had little influence in Rajasthan beyond or outside these cities.

South of the Jamuna, the Bundelkhand area continued to be ruled by different branches of Rajputs—the Chandelas, the Bhar and the Baghelas. Balban led an expedition against the Baghela chief of Rewa to clear the plain area south of Kara. His victory and the plunder he gained there has been mentioned with considerable exaggeration by Minhaj. However, the expedition had limited political significance.

North of the *iqta* of Badaun in modern West U.P., the Katehariya Rajputs, with their centre at Ahichchata, continued to harass Badaun and Sambhal. Balban's expeditions and harsh measures seemed to have removed the threat, and gradually led to the extension of Turkish influence into Katehar or modern Rohilkhand.

It will be seen that none of the Rajput efforts threatened the existence, or the essential territorial integrity of the Turkish state. However, the alleged Hindu threat was sometimes used by the rulers to counter internal dissension or differences.

Balban did lead an expedition into Malwa, but it was in the nature of a plundering expedition. The Turkish state was evidently in no position to embark on a policy of expansion at this stage.

As compared to these strifes, the attempts of ambitious Turkish officers, from within the sultanat and outside, to carve out independent spheres of authority were far more serious. Taking advantage of the Mongols threat, the Kurlugs who had been the local rulers of Ghur and Ghazni but had been outsted by the Mongols, crossed the Indus and occupied the Cis-Indus region of Koh-i-Jud or the Salt Ranges. They also tried to expand their control over Multan and Sindh. In the complex struggle, they sometimes lost control of the Koh-i-Jud to the Mongols and sometimes recovered it. The point is that the Delhi sultanat had lost all effective control over this tract. Although Lahore remained under Delhi's nominal control, the effective frontier in the north-west was the river Beas, so that the

Punjab was largely lost. In Sindh also, a number of governors raised the banner of independence, some of them even accepting a Mongol intendant *(shuhna)* as a part of their effort of gaining freedom from Delhi. However, Iltutmish, and later Balban were able to reassert control over Multan and Sindh.

In the east, Bengal and Bihar were largely under the control of the governors of Lakhnauti who sometimes tendered formal allegiance to the sultan at Delhi, and sometimes asserted their independence, according to circumstances. Some of them tried to extend their control over Kamrup (Assam), Jajnagar (Orissa) and southern Bengal (Radha). However, on a number of occasions they suffered serious reverses in their struggle with the local rulers since their resources were not sufficient for the purpose. A few of the governors even tried to extend their control from Bihar to Manikpur and Awadh. If they had succeeded, the Turkish sultanat at Delhi would have faced a split and many other internal problems.

As has been seen, Iltutmish had led two expeditions again the Khalji chief, Iwaz. His, and the subsequent efforts of the sultans of Delhi to separate Bihar from Lakhnauti rarely succeeded. Thus, in the confusion following the death of Iltutmish, another Turkish chief, Tughan Khan, became master of Lakhnauti and Bihar. He invaded Radha and made a raid on Tirhut. He even made an unsuccessful attempt to capture Awadh and its neighbouring areas. However, he was clever enough not to repudiate the allegiance to Delhi, and received from Razia and her successors conformation of his position, and honours including a *chatr* which was considered a symbol of royalty. Matters continued in this way till in his struggle against the Ganga rulers of Orissa, Tughan was put on the defensive, and requested the help of Delhi. The Orissan armies besieged him at Lakhnauti, and retreated only when it was learnt that an army led by the governor of Awadh had come to the help of Tughan Khan. The governor of Awadh removed Tughan, and himself assumed powers at Lakhnauti, but he was soon killed.

When Balban assumed power at Delhi as *naib*, he sent his slave, Yuzbek, as governor of Lakhnauti. Like his predecessors, Yuzbek also soon assumed airs of independence. Although he could not prevail against Orissa, he was successful in capturing Radha (1255). This success led to a change in his policy towards Delhi. He now assumed the title of a sultan, and the royal canopy. Taking advantage of trouble in Awadh where the governor had been ousted by Balban, Yuzbek advanced and captured Awadh, and had the *khubah* read in his name. But Yuzbek retreated on hearing rumors of an advance of Delhi armies on Awadh. Following this misadventure, Yuzbek made an attack on Kamrup. The local ruler retreated as far as he could, then turned against Yuzbek at the commencement of the rainy season. Cut off by the rising river water, Yuzbek suffered a disastrous defeat and was captured and put to death (1257).

Thus, successive Turkish officers sent from Delhi to Lakhnauti had assumed airs of independence. The worst proved to be the case of Tughril, a slave-officer, whom Balban now appointed governor of Lakhnauti. After consolidating his position, Tughril raided the territories of the ruler of Jajnagar, and amassed a lot of wealth and elephants which he refused to share with Deihi. He assumed the title of a sultan, and had the *khubah* read in his name.

News of Tughril's rebellion upset Balban greatly. He lost his sleep, feeling that events in Bengal would effect his position in Delhi. In 1276, Balban ordered the governor of Awadh, Amin Khan, to march along with his forces, and with the contingent of Hindustan to suppress the revolt. But in the engagement with Tughril many of Amin Khan's troops deserted as Tughril was lavish with money. When Amin Khan returned to Delhi, in anger Balban gibboted him and put his dead body on public display. Balban now appointed one of his chosen officer , Bahadur, to punish Tughril. But the result was the same. Bahadur fought bravely, but was defeated by Tughril. The Delhi army melted away, with many of the soldiers joining Tughril.

Thus, Balban was faced with an extremely serious situation. Two officers had been defeated, and Tughril was emerging as a rival to Balban. Balban, therefore, decided to personally lead a campaign against Tughril. To guard against all eventualities, he nominated his eldest son, Prince Muhammad, as his legal successor. However, the responsibility of runing the affairs at Delhi was given not to any Turkish noble, but to Fakhruddin, the kotwal of Delhi, with the post of *naib*. Balban took a second son, Bughra Khan, with him to Lakhnauti.

The campaign against Tughril took Balban two years (1280-82) because Tughril avoided a battle with him, retreating into the remote parts of Bengal with the hope that Balban would tire of the campaign and return. Balban relentlessly pursued Tughril till an advance guard of Balban's army surprised Tughril on a tip off from some banjaras, and killed Tughril. Balban gave savage punishment to the followers of Tughril at Lakhnauti. But when he returned to Delhi, he was dissuaded from making an example of those soldiers of Delhi who had deserted to Tughril. Perhaps, Balban's desire to

maintain the solidarity of the Turks proved stronger. Bughra Khan
was now appointed governor of the eastern part. However, it was
Bughra Khan who, after the death of Balban, set up an independent dynasty which ruled Bengal for almost forty years.

iv. Assessment of Balban

The house established by Balban lasted only three years after
his death. His son, Bughra Khan, preferred to rule at Lakhnauti,
leaving the throne at Delhi to his son, Kaiqubad, a young man of
eighteen. Kaiqubad proved to be an utter debauch, leaving all the
affairs of state to Nizamuddin who tried to kill all the Turkish officers opposed to him. In the process, Nizamuddin himself was killed.
The administration collapsed, and Jalaluddin Khalji who had been
the warden of the marches and had distinguished himself in fighting against the Mongols, was called in to help. He soon got rid of
Kaiqubad, and set up a new dynasty (1290).

Although Balban did not succeed in setting up a dynasty, by
his stern enforcement of law and order within the upper doab or
Indo-Gangetic plain which formed the essential part of his kingdom,
sternly suppressing the lawless elements, and freeing the roads for
the movement of goods and merchants, he created the necessary
basis for the growth and future expansion of the sultanat. It might
be noted that the Indo-Gangetic plain, extending upto Banaras and
Jaunpur, was one of the most extensive and productive plain
anywhere in the world, and its unification had been the essential
basis of flourishing empires in the past.

Although there is no evidence that Balban made any systematic
efforts to reorganise the system of administration, particularly at
the local or provincial levels, his tight control over the *iqtadars*, with
the *barids* informing him of all developments, imply that the revenues which were previously appropriated by the "Chihalgani" or
Turkish slave-officers for their own use, now began to be made
available to the central government. A part of these funds were
used by Balban for setting up a highly ostentatious court, as we
have noted, and the rest for strengthening the central army. Balban
did not undertake any large scale building activity at Delhi or elsewhere. In fact, in the architectural field, his period of domination
is almost a blank. Balban laid great emphasis on maintaining a large
efficient army. He advised his son, Bughra Khan, that apart from
the army half the income should be set aside as a safeguard against
an emergency.

It is difficult to estimate the efficiency of Balban's army since it was not engaged in any expansionist activities due to the fear of the Mongols. Balban did manage to contain the Mongols at the Multan-Dipalpur-Sunam line along the river Beas. But he was not able to push back the Mongols from the tract beyond Lahore, although he was faced only with second rank Mongol commanders, the attention of the Mongol rulers being concentrated on Iran, Iraq, Syria etc. Thus, it can be argued that there was no real threat to Delhi from the Mongols. However, Balban obviously could not take any chances.

More serious was the failure of Balban to control Tughril's rebellion in Bengal for six long years. The failure of two senior Turkish officers—Amir Khan, the governor of Awadh, and Bahadur, and many of their soldiers deserting to Tughril, suggests that there was growing dissatisfaction with Balban's management of affairs and his policies. The Turkish soldiers were never satisfied with their salaries, but expected to supplement these with plunder (*ghanim*). Balban's policy of consolidation provided them no such opportunity. The rebellion of Turkish officers in Sindh and, even more significantly, the attempt of two of Balban's own slaves, Yuzbek and Tughril, to become independent in Lakhnauti shows that even Balban's sternness could not put down the innate Turkish tribal desire for independence. Although Balban did finally break the power of the Turkish *Chihalgani*, his resort to a policy of poison and secret assassination of many Turkish nobles, and his exaggerated emphasis on family and ancestry rather than efficiency and ability were counter-productive. The latter not only prevented competent Indians to be appointed or rise in the service of the state, but it seems adversely effected even Turks of humble origin.

Nevertheless, Balban's achievements were greater than his limitations. He built a polity which was capable not only of sustaining itself, but had the capacity to embark on a policy of expansion as soon as the narrow constraints he had put on it were broken, and men of proven worth and efficiency were pushed forward. This was the task which he bequeathed to his successors.

4

THE MONGOL THREAT TO INDIA DURING THE 13TH-14TH CENTURIES

Although India was defended in the North and the North-West by a range of mountains, the Himalayas and their extension, the low mountains in the North-West were pierced by passes which were the traditional points of entry into India. Of these passes, the most well-known, and the most frequently used, were the Khybar and the Bolan passes. A more natural line of defence for India than these low mountains in the north-west was provided by the Hindukush mountains, which were a fairly effective barrier between Afghanistan and Central Asia in the north, while the Iranian desert provided an effective shield on the west. Afghanistan and its neighbouring areas were strategically important for India because they provided a staging centre for any invasion of India. Thus, as we have seen, attack on Afghanistan was the first stage in the Ghaznavid and Ghurian conquest of north India.

i. The Mongol Incursions (upto 1292)

After the Ghurian conquest, it might have been expected that Ghur and Ghazni would provide an effective shield against any future invasions of India. But the separation of India from Ghur and Ghazni, and the subsequent conquest of the area by Khwarizm Shah, followed by the Mongols, completely altered the strategic position. A viable defence line in the north-west could now be provided either by the Indus, or by the Koh-i-Jud (Salt Ranges) which was on this side of the Indus. We shall trace the stages by which the Mongols breached these lines of defence in course of time, and reached upto the river Beas, thereby posing a serious threat to the sultanat of Delhi.

We have seen how in 1221, Chingez loitered around the Indus for three months, after defeating the Khwarizmi prince, Jalaluddin Mangbarani. Crossing the Indus, the prince had formed an alliance with the Khokhars who dominated the tract upto the Salt Ranges. Before departing from the area, Chingez sent envoys to Iltutmish, the sultan at Delhi, that he (Chingez) had given up the project of sending his army to Hindustan and returning to China by way of Gilgit or Assam, since he had not received favourable omens from burning sheep-skins. It suggests that Chingez had contemplated the invasion of north India, but gave up the idea, either because of Iltutmish's refusal to help prince Jalaluddin, or because of a rebellion in Turkistan, which needed the attention of Chingez. It is easy to imagine what would have happened to the cities of north India if Chingez had decided to invade the country.

After the death of Chingez, the Mongols were for some time too busy in their internal affairs, and in completing the conquest of Khurasan and Iran, to bother about India. But in 1234, Oktai, who had succeeded Chingez Khan in Turkistan (also called Khitai), decided to invade Hind and Kashmir. Iltutmish advanced upto the Salt Ranges to counter this threat. On the way, Iltutmish fell ill, and returned to the capital where he died soon afterwards.

Soon after the death of Iltutmish, the former governor of Ghazni, Wafa Malik, who had been ousted by the Mongols, came to India and captured the entire tract comprising the Koh-i-Jud or the Salt Ranges. This invited Mongol attacks. The Mongols ousted Wafa Malik, and brought the entire Koh-i-Jud under their control. There was a prolonged struggle between Wafa Malik whose dynasty is called the Qarlugh dynasty, and the Mongols for the control of the Koh-i-Jud and Multan, with the sultans of Delhi intervening whenever possible. By 1246, the Qarlughs had to quit India. But by that time, the Koh-i-Jud had become a Mongol bastion, and a base for their further attacks on India.

The seriousness of the Mongol threat had become apparent to the inhabitants of Delhi when in 1240 a Mongol force under Tair Bahadur, who was the commander of Herat, Ghazni and Afghanistan, besieged Lahore. The Turkish governor was ill-prepared to stand a siege, and was further hampered because many of the inhabitants were merchants who regularly traded in the Mongol territories, and were not prepared to aid and help the governor for fear of Mongol reprisals. Also, there was little hope of any help coming from Delhi where there was utter confusion following the death of Razia. Hence, the governor abandoned the city. After capturing the city, the Mongols encountered stiff resistance from the citizens and, we are told, 30,000 to 40,000 Mongols and many of their commanders, including Tair Bahadur, were killed. The Mongols wrecked savage vengeance for this. They killed or enslaved all the citizens of Lahore, and devastated the city. Then they suddenly retreated because the Mongol Qa-an, Ogtai, had died. Although Lahore was reoccupied by Delhi, for the next twenty years Lahore remained in a ruined condition, being sacked on several occasions either by the Mongols or by their Khokhar allies.

It is not necessary for us to follow in detail the recurrent Mongol invasions of the Punjab, Multan and Sindh. It is sufficient to say that the Chaghtai Mongols who controlled Afghanistan were entrenched in the Koh-i-Jud, extended their depredations upto the river Beas which then ran north of the Sutlej, joining the Chenab between Multan and Uchch. This was the situation which faced the sultans of Delhi when Nasiruddin Mahmud ascended the throne in 1246, with Balban becoming the *naib* soon after. Although Balban wanted to adopt a bold policy, and clear the area upto the Koh-i-Jud from the Mongols, alongwith the Khokhars who were siding with them, little could be done due to the factionalism in the Turkish nobility. Hence, the frontier commanders of Multan and Sindh were left largely to their own devises to cope with the Mongols. In consequence, some of them came to terms with the Mongols, even setting themselves up as independent rulers under Mongol overlordship. Thus, Sher Khan, the cousin of Balban, who had been ousted from Sindh when Balban was displaced by Raihan, repaired to the Mongol chief, Manju Qa-an, apparently to persuade him to invade India in order to restore Sher Khan to his previous position! Nor was Sher Khan the only Turkish officer to do so. But the Mongols had already decided to conquer China, and to concentrate on the conquest of Iraq, Syria and Egypt, leaving it to local commanders to plunder as much as they could in India, on the basis of their own resources. Thus, the sultans of Delhi were lucky not to face the full brunt of Mongol power.

In order to limit the Mongol depredations, Balban adopted both military and diplomatic measures. He sent an envoy to Halaku, the Mongol Il-Khan of Iran, who, apart from the Ogtai-Chaghtai branch which dominated Turkistan and Transoxiana, was the most important figure among the successors of Chingez. Halaku sent a return embassy in 1260 which was given a grand and impressive reception by Balban. Halaku is supposed to have strictly ordered his officers not to invade India, under pain of punishment. However, this assurance need not be given too much importance because Halaku's energies, then as earlier, had been devoted to the conquest of Iraq, Syria and Egypt. He had suffered a serious set-back in 1260, being defeated by an Egyptian army which had forced the Mongols to retreat from Syria also. Interestingly, at about the same time, an envoy was received from Barka Khan, the head of the Mongol Golden Horde in South Russia, which was the most powerful group among the Mongols and which had deep enemity towards Halaku. In this complex situation, Halaku simultaneously sent his intendents (*shuhna*) to Sindh and the Koh-i-Jud areas, thus claiming over-lordship over them. Thus, the agreement also implied that the Sultans of Delhi would not try to disturb the Mongols in Sindh and in areas west of Lahore. By the time Balban ascended the throne in 1266, Halaku had died, thereby ending the nebulous agreement and goodwill between the Mongols and the ruler of Delhi. The situation on the ground had not, however, changed. Although Balban's cousin, Sher Khan, who was the warden of the marches, holding the *iqtas* of Lahore, Sunam, Dipalpur etc. acted as a shield against the Mongols, the Mongols were able frequently to cross the Beas. At the outset, Balban adopted a forward policy. After clearing the roads in the *doab*, he marched his army towards Koh-i-Jud. He ravaged the mountainous tract and its neighbouring areas, and captured large number of horses, leading to a sharp decline in the price of horses in Delhi. In 1270, he ordered the fort of Lahore to be rebuilt, and appointed architects to rebuild the city. However, soon afterwards, Balban had Sher Khan, whom he suspected of harbouring dreams of independence, to be poisoned. He then entrusted the defence of the frontier tracts to his eldest son, Prince Muhammad. Prince Muhammad was an able and energetic prince, and it appears that during the remaining years of Balban's reign, while the Mongol attacks continued, his defensive arrangements at Multan and Lahore, with the river Beas as the line of military defence, continued to hold. Barani says that the Mongols no longer dared to attack across the Beas, and that even Mongol forces of 70 to 80,000 sawars could not face the forces of Prince Muhammad from Multan, Bughra Khan from Samana, and Malik Barbak Bakatarse from Delhi. The death of Prince Muhammad outside Multan in 1285 was the outcome of a chance encounter, the prince being surprised by an advance party of the Mongols. However, rather than seeking safety in flight, he preferred to stand and die.

The death of the prince was a heavy personal blow to Balban who had designated the prince as his successor. But it did not change the ground realities as far as the Mongols were concerned.

The last Mongol attack under Balban's successors was in 1288 when Tamar Khan ravaged the country from Lahore to Multan. But the Mongols retreated as soon as they heard of the arrival of the imperial forces.

Thus, upto 1290, the Mongols dominated western Punjab, the effective frontier being the river Beas. They also continually threatened Multan and Sindh. But they did not mount any serious offensive towards Delhi. This enabled the sultanat of Delhi to survive, but only at the cost of the utmost vigilance and military preparedness.

A last invasion of India by the Mongol branch settled in Iran took place in 1192 when a Mongol army of 150,000 headed by Abdullah, a grandson of Halaku, the Ilkhan of Iran, invaded India. Jalaluddin Khalji who had just succeeded to the throne had spent a considerable part of his life in fighting the Mongols. Jalaluddin Khalji advanced with a large force. After some skirmishes, the Mongols agreed to withdraw without a fight. It seems that there was some kind of an agreement between the two. Jalaluddin had a cordial meeting with Abdullah whom he called his son, and a party of the Mongols, headed by Ulaghu, another grandson of Halaku, embraced Islam, along with 4000 of his followers. They were allowed to settle down near Delhi along with their families. The Sultan married one of his daughters to Ulaghu. These, and a band of 5000 Mongols who had entered India in 1279 became Muslims. They were called "Nau (Neo) Muslims."

These cordial relations suggest that a tacit agreement had been reached between the two sides not to disturb the status quo, leaving the Mongols in possession of West Punjab. However, changes in Mongol domestic politics created a new situation in which the Mongols for the first time posed a serious danger to Delhi.

ii. *The Mongol Threat to Delhi (1292-1328)*

The rise of the Ogtai-Chaghtai branch of the Mongols which dominated the Mongol homelands including Turkistan led to important changes in the politics of Central Asia. The Mongol chief, Dawa Khan, set out on a course of conflict with the Mongol Qa-an of Iran. Dawa Khan over-ran Afghanistan. He then extended his sway upto the river Ravi.

The first inkling of a new Mongol policy came in 1297-98 when a Mongol army of 100,000 sent by Dawa Khan crossed not only the river Beas, but the river Sutlej, and the road to Delhi seemed to lay open before them. Alauddin sent a large army under his trusted commander, Ulugh Khan, who met the Mongols near Jullundhar and completely routed them. About 20,000 Mongols were killed as they fled across the river, and many others, including officers, were captured and done to death at Delhi. This was the most convincing victory which an army of the Sultans of Delhi had gained over the Mongols in a straight fight. A similar victory was gained the following year when the Mongols captured Siwistan in lower Sindh. Zafar Khan, another favourite commander of Alauddin, proceeded against the Mongols. He won a complete victory, capturing the fort city, and bringing the Mongol commander, Saldi, in chains to Delhi.

These victories seem to have lulled Alauddin to a false sense of security as regard the Mongols. That is why he was caught unprepared when towards the end of 1299 a force of 200,000 Mongols invaded India, headed by Qutlugh Khan, the son of the Mongol ruler, Dawa Khan. The number of the Mongol soldiers may have been exaggerated, and possibly included women and children who, unlike the times of Chingez, had begun to accompany the Mongol armies. Unlike the previous times, the Mongols did not ravage the countryside or the towns on the way, their objective being to conquer and rule Delhi. Hearing of their approach, Alauddin quickly gathered an army, and took a position outside Siri, the place where he had taken residence before entering Delhi, after murdering his uncle, Jalaluddin. The Mongols entrenched themselves at Killi, six miles north of Delhi. While the two armies faced each other, Alauddin sent urgent summons to the nobles of the doab to hasten to his side with their armies. Meanwhile, many people from the environs took shelter at Delhi which became extremely crowded, and provisions became dear since the caravans of food from the doab had stopped coming.

In this situation, Alaul Mulk, the kotwal of Delhi, advised Alauddin to play a waiting game, and if possible, induce the Mongols to retire peacefully since his army consisted largely of the Hindustani soldiers who had only fought Hindus, and were not used to fighting the Mongols, and were not familiar with their tactics of feigned retreat and ambush. Alauddin rejected the kotwal's advise as being unmanly, and one which would undermine his prestige as a ruler. However, he had no intention of letting everything be decided on the outcome of one battle. Considering that time was on his side, and the Mongols, far away from their homelands, might soon fall short of provisions, Alauddin issued strict instructions to his officers, on pain of death, to stand on guard, and not to go out of their lines to attack the Mongols without his orders. However, Zafar Khan, who was itching for a fight, attacked the Mongol contingent facing him. As usual, the Mongols feigned retreat, and when Zafar Khan had gone out several miles pursuing them, an ambush party of 10,000 horses cut off his retreat, and surrounded him. According to Alauddin's orders, the rest of the army did not move out to rescue Zafar Khan who, alongwith all of his followers, died fighting bravely.

Although the Mongols won an initial victory, the firmness of Zafar Khan seems to have made an impression. Qutlugh Khan realized that he could not break Alauddin's lines, or capture Delhi. Hence, after skirmishing for two days, he retreated from Delhi and, moving rapidly, recrossed the Indus. Alauddin did not try to pursue him.

This full-scale Mongol attack on Delhi was a severe shock not only to the citizens of Delhi, but to Alauddin. He now awoke from his sleep of neglect, and undertook far-reaching measures. A protecting wall around Delhi was built for the first time, and all the old forts on the route of the Mongols repaired. Strong military contingents were posted at Samana and Dipalpur. Simultaneously, he took steps to reorganise the internal administration, and to recruit a large army. These measures, which we shall discuss separately, enabled Alauddin to meet the Mongol challenge, even though the Mongol threat to Delhi loomed over India for several more years.

In 1303, the Mongols advanced on Delhi a second time, under the leadership of Targhi. While some commentators put the Mongol force at 12 *tuman* or 120,000, the figure of 30-40,000 mentioned by Barani elsewhere appears to be nearer the mark. The Mongols had marched rapidly, meeting little resistance on the way, and expected to surprise Delhi, because they had learnt that Alauddin was away from the capital, campaigning. However, Alauddin had returned from the Chittor campaign just a month earlier. His troops needed to be refurbished. The capital had been denuded because another army had been sent to Warangal via Bengal, and had come back to the doab badly battered. Moreover, the Mongols had seized all the fords across the Jamuna so that despite royal summons no troops from the doab could reach Delhi. In this situation, Alauddin came out of Siri with all his available forces, and took up a strongly defended position, resting on the river Jamuna on one side, and the old city of Delhi on the other. He further strengthened his position by digging a ditch all round, and putting on its side planks of wood so that, according to Barani, his camp looked like a fort made of wood. The Mongols did not dare to attack this strong position, but hovered around Delhi, creating a great fear among the citizens. There was an acute shortage of both fuel and corn in the city, the caravans from the doab having stopped coming. However, the Mongols were not the same as the earlier Mongols, and their discipline seems to have become much more lax, because they came to the tanks outside Delhi, drank wine there, and sold cheap corn to the citizens, thus relieving the acute food shortage. After two months of this futile exercise, the Mongols retreated once again, without a fight.

Despite the failure of these two attempts at the conquest of Delhi, two years later, in 1305, the Mongols made a third and final desperate attempt at the conquest of Hindustan. Crossing the Indus, a Mongol army of 30,000 to 40,000 horses marched rapidly across the Punjab "like an arrow", and after burning the towns at the foothills of the Siwaliks, crossed into the doab, by-passing Delhi. However, Alauddin, whose army was much stronger than before, sent an army of 30,000 under a Hindu noble, Malik Nayak who, according to the poet Amir Khusrau, had been governor of Samana and Sunam earlier. A number of Muslim officers were placed under his command. This shows how far the social base of the Turkish sultanat had broadened since the days of Balban. Malik Nayak met the Mongols somewhere near Amroha (north-west part of modern UP), and inflicted a crushing defeat upon them. The leaders of the Mongol armies, Ali Beg and Tartaq, surrendred and were brought to Delhi, while about 20,000 Mongols were slaughtered.

This victory finally destroyed in India the aura of Mongol invincibility—something which the Mongols had lost earlier in West Asia after their defeat by the Egyptians in 1260, and the loss of Syria to them. After the death of Dawa Khan in 1306, the Mongols lost interest in the conquest of Delhi. They launched a series of attacks in the Katehar-Siwalik region, but they were all repulsed with great slaughter of the Mongols. According to Barani, whenever the Mongols attacked Delhi or the neighbouring regions, they were defeated. The armies of Islam had become so confident against the Mongols that a single soldier with a *du aspah* rank would bring in (as prisoners) ten Mongols with their necks tied with ropes. "A single Mussalman horseman would put to flight a hundred Mongol horsemen." The areas devastated by the Mongols were gradually brought under the plough once again. We are told that Lahore and Dipalpur became impassable barriers for the Mongols, "like a Chinese wall." The commander of the area, Tughlaq Shah or Ghazi Malik,

launched a series of attacks on the Mongol-held areas in West Punjab
upto the river Indus, and were so successful that in these areas
the dread of the Mongols completely disappeared from the hearts
of the people. According to Barani, the Mongols did not dare to
cross the river Indus. This, we shall see, was an exaggeration.

Thus, Alauddin not only defended Delhi and the doab from the
threat of the Mongols but created the conditions whereby the north-
west frontier of India could be pushed back from the river Beas
and Lahore to the river Indus.

These were significant achievements. However, the threat to India could not be said to have disappeared as long as the Mongols
dominated Afghanistan and the neighbouring areas. Thus, after the
death of Alauddin, the Mongol threat to India revived. In 1320,
Dalucha Khan entered the Kashmir valley with 70,000 horses, and
devastated it from end to end. All the men were killed, and the
women and children sold to slave merchants from Khitai and
Turkistan. All houses in the cities and villages were also burnt.
Fortunately, the Mongol invaders perished in a snow blizzard while
retreating from Kashmir eight months later. Shortly after
Ghiyasuddin's accession to the throne (1320), two Mongol armies
reached Sunam and Samana, and marched upto Meerut. They were
defeated with great slaughter. In 1326-27 the new Mongol Khan,
Tarmashirin, again invaded India. Ghiyasuddin Tughlaq marched
against Tarmashirin, and not only pushed him back but extended
his frontiers to include Peshawar and Kalanaur across the Indus
so as to form a better defensive line against future Mongol invasions. However, after some time, the Indian armies retreated behind the Indus which remained the frontier with the Mongols.

The boldest effort to counter the Mongol threat to India was made
by Muhammad bin Tughlaq, who shortly after his accession, recruited an army of 375,000 men for what was called the Khurasan
expedition. While the larger motives of the Sultan are a matter of
speculation, one effect of any such campaign meant the conquest
of Kabul, Ghazni and the neighbouring areas—areas which we have
described as staging theatres for the invasion and conquest of India. Muhammad bin Tughlaq's enterprise failed, like many of his
other projects, even at the planning stage. However, he was one
of the few Turkish sultans of India who seems to have possessed
a strategic insight regarding the north-west frontier of India. This
must have been so because he was a close student of Asian affairs. It was the neglect of these factors which led to Timur's invasion of India in 1399.

Thus, the Mongol threat to India lasted for almost a hundred years, gaining in intensity till it reached a climax during the reign of Alauddin Khalji. The Mongol incursions led to the virtual loss of western Punjab beyond Lahore to the Mongol during the second half of the 13th century, thereby creating a serious threat to Delhi and the doab, as in the time of the Ghaznavids. However, unlike the Rajput rulers of the time, the sultans of Delhi organized their resources, and carried out a far-reaching restructuration of their economy to meet the Mongol threat. However, they failed in the task of building a viable line of defence based on Afghanistan in order to stem such future incursions. This task was undertaken later on by the Mughals.

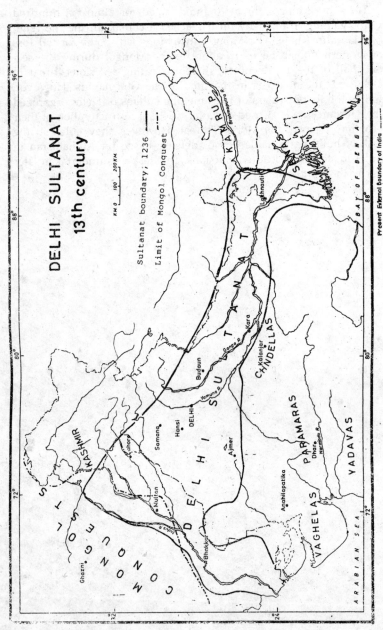

DELHI SULTANAT
13th century

KM 0   100   200 K.M.

Sultanat boundary; 1236 ————
Limit of Mongol Conquest -----

MONGOL CONQUESTS

KASHMIR

Ghazni

Multan

Bhakkor

Uchh

Lahore

Samana

Hansi

DELHI

Budaun

Yamuna R.

Ganga R.

Kara

C. Kalanjar

CHANDELLAS

DELHI SULTANAT

KAMRUP

Brahmaputra R.

Lakhnauti

ASSAM

BAY OF BENGAL

ARABIAN SEA

Anahilapatika

VAGHELAS

Ajmer

PARAMARAS

Dhara

Narmada R.

YADAVAS

72°   80°   88°   96°

Based upon Survey of India map with the permission of the Surveyor General of India.

© Government of India Copyright 1990

The territorial waters of India extend into the sea to a distance of twelve nautical miles measured from the appropriate base line.

Present External boundary of India ————

5

INTERNAL RESTRUCTURING OF THE DELHI SULTANAT AND ITS TERRITORIAL EXPANSION

The brief period of Khalji rule (1290-1320), saw important changes in the socio-economic and administrative structure of the Delhi sultanat. It also raised important questions regarding the nature of the state and polity in India.

The most important consequence of the rise to power of the Khaljis was the broadening of the social base of the ruling class. The early Turkish sultans who are called the *Ilbaris* on the basis of their tribal origin, or *Mamuluks*, i.e. slave-officers, had believed in the virtual monopoly of important posts in the state by high born Turks. The Tajiks who had formed an important part of the nobility under Iltutmish had been largely eliminated shortly after his death. The presence of an Abyssinian, Yaqut, or an Indian Muslim, Raihan, and of the Khaljis in important positions on the frontiers was more in the nature of exceptions which proved the rule. Barani says that with the accession of the Khaljis, the empire passed from the hands of the Turks, and that the people of the city of Delhi who had for eighty years been governed by sovereigns of Turkish extraction, "were struck by admiration and amazement at seeing the Khaljis occupying the throne of the Turks."

i) Jalaluddin and Alauddin Khalji's Approaches to the State

While the rise of Khaljis brought forward a new group of people to positions of power and authority, the founder, Jalaluddin Khalji (1290-96), did not follow a policy of narrow exclusivism. Many Turks and officers of Balban's time who visited Jalaluddin were given important posts and *iqtas*. Even Malik Chhajju Kishli Khan, a nephew of Balban, was appointed governor of Kara which was considered one of the most fertile and prosperous tracts. Nor were drastic punishments meted out when Malik Chhajju rebelled, marched on Delhi, and was defeated.

But even more importantly, Jalaluddin put forward by his actions the concept of a new type of a state, one which was based fundamentally on the good-will and support of the people of all communities, one which was basically beneficient and looked after the welfare of its subjects. Thus, unlike Balban, he refused to identify sovereignty with self-pride and tyranny. In the picturesque language of Barani, he believed in a policy of "not harming even an ant".

Although Jalaluddin Khalji was a pious Muslim, he considered as unrealistic a policy of forcible conversion of the Hindus or their humiliation, as demanded by some theologians. In a discussions with his close associate, Ahmad Chap, he defended the policy of allowing Hindus to worship idols, preach their beliefs, and observe practices which were the hall-mark of infidelity. Thus, they were not hindered in passing in processions outside his palace, beating drums, and to go to the Jamuna for immersing their images. Likewise, the Hindus were allowed to live a life of ease and splendour and honour even at Delhi, the centre of Islam. According to him, while by a policy of terror, fear of the government and its prestige could be established in the hearts of the people for a short time, it would mean discarding (true) Islam, or, as was said, "it would mean "discarding Islam from the hearts of the people like discarding a hair while kneading dough."

Jalaluddin Khalji's nephew and son-in-law, Alauddin Khalji, (1296-1316) who ascended the throne after treacherously murdering his uncle, did not accept the liberal, humanitarian precepts of Jalaluddin. Nevertheless, the principles enunciated by Jalaluddin had a long term relevance. In one form or another, they had to be faced by almost all his successors.

Thus, Jalaluddin's reign has a long term significance which is often ignored.

Alauddin Khalji did not accept Jalaluddin's theory of benevolence and humanitarianism, considering them to the unsuitable to the times, and signifying a weak government. He adhered more to Balban's theory of fear being the basis of good government, a theory which he applied to the nobles as well as to the ordinary people. Thus, after the outbreak of a couple of rebellions early in his reign, including one by his nephew, Aqat Khan, he decided to take harsh measures to keep the nobles under control. He revived Balban's system of spies who kept him informed of all developments, even those in the privacy of the houses of the nobles. The nobles were forbidden to associate with each other, or hold convivial parties. In fact, even for forming marriage alliances they had to seek the permission of the Sultan.

Second, he hearkened back to Balban's belief—one which the historian Barani shared, that the people should not be left enough means to harbour thoughts of rebellion. As a part of this policy he ordered that all charitable lands, i.e. lands assigned in *waqf* or *inam*, should be confiscated. Almost all the nobles of Jalaluddin's time, whom Alauddin had won over to his side by the lure of gold and positions, were uprooted, and their accumulated wealth confiscated.

Wine drinking was also forbidden and severe punishments given to those who violated these orders. However, Alauddin admitted to the Chief Qazi that buying and selling of wine did not stop.

Barani would have us believe that Alauddin Khalji's agrarian reforms were also a part of this policy of reducing the people, i.e. the Hindus to a position of destitution in order to avoid rebellions. We shall discuss this separately. Alauddin did, however, institute a new reprehensible policy. When some of the Mongol soldiers who had participated in the campaign launched against Gujarat rebelled against the policy of the state claiming 4/5 of the war spoils, Alauddin imprisoned their wives and children living at Delhi, a practice which Barani says was a novel one. Alauddin's brother, Nusrat Khan, went one step further: he gave savage punishments to the women and children of those who had rebelled against Alauddin.

However, Alauddin accepted Jalaluddin Khalji's contention that a truely Islamic state could not be set up in the specific conditions obtaining in India. In his discussions with Qazi Mughis of Delhi, as reported by Barani, he asserted that splendour and show, and award of punishments not sanctioned by *shara* or the Holy Law were inescapable in India. In fact, he went so far as to assert, "I do not know what is lawful or unlawful according to *shara*. Whatever I consider necessary for the state or for its welfare, I decree." Barani sadly concludes that Alauddin was convinced that matters concerning the state and administration were independent of the rules and orders of the *sharia*, and that while the former pertained to kings alone, the latter had been assigned to *qazis* and *muftis* (*i.e.* those concerned with justice in the courts).

During Alauddin Khalji's reign, the non-Turks were no longer kept back, and forged ahead. This was the reason why Alauddin was able to choose, and promote to the top, many non-Turks such as Zafar Khan and Nusrat Khan, and later Malik Kafur, a non-Turk slave who had been captured in Gujarat. Malik Nayak, a Hindu who had been governor of Samana and Sunam, was given command of an army with Muslims officers serving under him, which inflicted a crushing defeat on the Mongols. Large numbers of Indian Muslims also formed a part of his army.

ii) Agrarian and Market Reforms of Alauddin

Alauddin Khalji's agrarian and market reforms should be seen both in the context of the efforts at the internal restructuration of the sultanat, as also the need to create a large army to meet the threat of recurrent Mongol invasions.

The essence of Alauddin Khalji's agrarian reforms was to bring the villages in closer association with the government in the area extending from Dipalpur and Lahore to Kara near modern Allahabad. In this region, the villages were to be brought under *khalisa*, i.e. not assigned to any of the nobles as *iqta*. Lands assigned in charitable grants were also confiscated and brought under *khalisa*. Further, the land revenue *(kharaj)* in this area was fixed at half of the produce, and assessed on the basis of measurement *(paimaish)*. Barani, who is our main source of information, does not tell us about the method and mode of the measurement of the fields. On the basis of the measurements of the area under cultivation, and a standard of expected production per *biswa* (1/20 of the *bigha*), the share of the state was determined. Apart from this, no extra cesses were to be levied, except a grazing tax *(charai)* on cattle and *ghari* on houses. Both these taxes had been levied earlier and were traditional. The land-revenue was calculated in kind, but demanded in cash. For the purpose, the cultivators had either to sell the produce to the *banjaras*, or take it for sale to the local market *(mandi)*.

We do not know to what extent Alauddin's demand of half of the produce marked a rise in the land-revenue demand since we have no information about the actual incidence of land-revenue earlier, either under the Rajput rulers or the early Turkish rulers. Although the *Dharmashastras* prescribed a land-revenue of one-fourth to one-sixth which could rise to half in times of emergency, there were a lot of sanctioned taxes in addition to the land-revenue whose incidence is not known. Thus, the formula used for assigning land to nobles was *bhaga, bhog, kar,* i.e. land-revenue, cesses and taxes. These must have continued under the early Turkish rulers. Whether Alauddin merely consolidated all these taxes into one or raised the total amount payable by the cultivator is something we do not know.

Likewise, measurement was an old system, but had apparently fallen into disuse in north India. It may have been revived in some areas by earlier rulers, such as Balban, because Barani does not refer to it as a totally unknown system. However, its systematic application over a wide area was a significant contribution of Alauddin. The bringing of doab under *khalisa,* and establishing direct relations with the cultivators, did not imply that all intermediaries were removed. Since long there was a hierarchy of intermediaries in the rural areas, with the *Rai, Rana, Rawat* standing at the top. These are called chiefs. A chief sometimes controlled a considerable tract of land which was parcelled out to his clan and other supporters for collecting land-revenue. At the village level there was the village head, called *chaudhari* or *muqaddam.* As the Turkish sultanat consolidated itself in the doab, the power and authority of the *rais* and *ranas* was eroded, and some of them were displaced. In the process, there was the rise of a new set of intermediaries who operated at the pargana or *shiq* (district) level. These apparently, were the people whom Barani called *khuts* and for whom the word *zamindar* is used for the first time by Khusrau. The word zamindar began to be used widely later on for all types of intermediaries. Alauddin's agrarian reforms implied putting greater pressure for the displacement of the *rais* or *ranas.* However, we know that many of the chiefs who paid a lump-sum of money to the state as land-revenue survived into the 16th and 17th centuries. In other words, the lands dominated by such chiefs were not brought under *khalisa.*

In the area brought under *khalisa,* Alauddin tried to curb the privileges of the *khuts, muqaddams* and *chaudharis.* These sections formed the rural aristocracy and, according to Barani, were rich enough to ride Arabi and Iraqi, horses, wear weapons and fine clothes, and indulge in wine drinking and holding convivial parties. Their wealth was based on their holding the best lands in the village. Also, in a system where the village was assessed as a whole (called group-assessment), they often passed on the burden of their share of the land-revenue on to the shoulders of the weak.

We do not know what exact effect Alauddin's agrarian reforms had on different sections of rural society. Alauddin not only forced the *khuts, muqaddams* and *chaudharis* to pay the grazing and house taxes like the others, and through the system of measurement ensured that they could not pass on their burden of land-revenue on to the shoulders of the others. They were also deprived of the *khuti* charges for collecting land-revenue. Thus, in the exaggerated language of Barani, they were reduced to the level of the *balahar*, or the lowest of the low in village society, the menial! They could not afford to ride horses, wear fine clothes, or eat *pan* (the betel-leaf), and their women were forced to go and work in the houses of Muslims for wages. Since it was hardly possible for Alauddin to effect a redistribution of land in the villages, and these sections generally held the largest and the best lands, they must have continued to remain a privileged section in village society. However, we may accept Barani's statement that for fear of punishment, these sections became obedient, and would go to the collector's office for payment of land-revenue, even at the behest of a peon.

To what extent did the cultivators benefit by Alauddin's efforts to curb the exactions of the privileged sections in the village? It seems that the cultivators lost on the other hand what they gained from one. The market reforms of Alauddin affected them adversely for the policy was to leave the cultivator with so little as to be "barely enough for carrying on cultivation and his food requirements (literally, for milk and butter-milk)." We are told that the fear of the government was such that the cultivators would sell even their wives and cattle to pay the land-revenue!

While reforming the agrarian system, Alauddin tried to ensure the efficient and honest working of the machinery of revenue administration. This was not easy since with the extension of the *khalisa*, large numbers of accountants (*mutsarrif*), collectors (*amils*), and agents (*gumashtas*) had to be appointed. That this was done in a comparatively short period shows how the new rulers were able to reach out even to the small towns. Alauddin desired that the accounts of all these officials should be audited strictly by the naib wazir, Sharaf Qais, and if on the basis of the account-book of the village *patwaris*—something we hear of for the first time, even a *jital* was found to be outstanding against them, they were to be severely punished, or suffer imprisonment or even worse. Alauddin was prepared to give them sufficient wages to lead a decent life, but took a serious view of their bribe taking and corruption. Those, who did so, were to be punished severely. Barani goes on to say in his characteristic way that none of the *amils* and *mutsarrifs* could take bribes, and had been reduced to such a position by hardships, imprisonment for long periods or torture for small outstanding dues that people considered these posts to be worse than fever, and were not prepared to marry their daughters to those who held them!

Alauddin's system of measurement, of trying to limit the exactions of the local privileged sections, and of auditing the accounts
of the local revenue officials with the help of the *bahis* (ledger books)
of the village *patwaris* set up a standard and a direction which some
of his successors, such as Sher Shah and Akbar, tried to emulate.
But his effort to limit the emoluments of the privileged sections
was only partially successful. These sections were too influential,
and under Alauddin's successor, Mubarak Shah, the privileges of
the *khuts* and *muqaddams* were restored, and many of Alauddin's
revenue measures given up.

·Perhaps, a significant and lasting effect of Alauddin's agrarian
reforms was the furthering of the growth of a market economy in
the villages, and bringing about a more integral relationship between the town and the country, thus furthering the process of the
internal restructuring of the Sultanat.

Market Reforms

Although Alauddin Khalji's market reforms were oriented more
towards administrative and military necessities than internal restructuring, it would be convenient to deal with them here.

Alauddin's market reforms and their effectiveness was a cause
of wonder to the contemporaries. Medieval rulers were expected
to ensure that necessities of life, especially food-grains, should be
available to the city folk at fair or reasonable prices. This was so
because the cities were the sinews of power and authority all over
the Islamic world, the village-folk being considered backward and
immersed in their own narrow world. However, apart from imposing
periodic checks on the traders, few rulers had been able to control
the prices effectively, or for any length of time. Alauddin Khalji
was more or less the first ruler who looked at the problem of price
control in a systematic manner, and was able to maintain stable
prices for a considerable period.

Barani says that Alauddin Khalji instituted the market reforms
because after the Mongol siege of Delhi, he wanted to recruit a large
army, but all his treasures would have soon been exhausted if he
had to pay them their normal salaries. As a result of price control
and the fall in prices, we are told that he was able to recruit a cavalry
man with one horse, and pay him 238 tankas annually, and 75
tankas more for one with two horses. Barani gives us a second
reason for the market reforms. He think that it was a part of
Alauddin's general policy to impoverish the Hindus so that

they would cease to harbour thoughts of rebellion. We shall examine this while analysing his market reforms.

According to Barani, Alauddin set up three markets at Delhi, the first for food-grains, the second for cloth of all kinds, and for expensive items such as sugar, ghee, oil, dry fruits etc., and the third for horses, slaves and cattle. Detailed regulations (*zawabit*) were framed for the control and administration for all these markets.

For controlling the food prices, Alauddin tried to control not only the supply of food-grains from the villages, and its transportation to the city by the grain-merchants (*karwanis* or *banjaras*), but its proper distribution to the citizens. These undoubtedly were the three most important aspects in controlling food prices. Alauddin's first effort was to see that there were sufficient stocks of food-grains with the government so that the traders did not try to hike up prices by creating an artificial scarcity, or indulge in profiteering (regraiting). For the purpose, royal stores were set up at Delhi. It was ordered that in the area near Delhi, such as Jhain, half of the royal share, i.e. one-fourth of the produce was to be demanded in kind. The grains was first to be stored locally, then sent to Delhi.

The task of transporting food-grains from the countryside was generally carried out by *karwaniyan* or *banjaras*, some of whom had 10,000 or 20,000 bullocks. These *banjaras* were ordered to form themselves into one corporate body, giving sureties for each other. They were to settle on the banks of the Jamuna with their wives, children, goods and cattle. An official (*shuhna*) was appointed to oversee them. We are told that in normal times these *banjaras* brought so much food-grains into the city that it was not necessary to touch the royal stores.

To ensure the regular supply of food-grains to the *banjaras*, a number of Regulations were made. In the doab, and in an area of 100 kos around it which had been brought under *khalisa*, and where the land-revenue fixed at half of the produce, the local officia charged with the responsibility of collecting land-revenue were aske to be so strict that the cultivators sold their food-grains for payment of land-revenue to the merchants at cheap prices without taking them to their houses, i.e. to their storage pits.[1] If the cultivators

---

1. According to one regulation, 'the sultan ordered the whole of the *kharaj* (land revenue) of the *khalisa* towns in the doab to be demanded in kind and taken to royal stores at Delhi.' This contradicts the regulation cited above, and would have flooded the market in Delhi and deprived other towns in the area of the needed food-grains. In practice, *kharaj* seems to have been taken both in cash and kind.

could sell more, i.e. what was beyond their personal needs and for seed, they could do so. However, the local officials were asked to sign a bond that they would not permit anyone to regrate, or sell at a price higher than the official price. If anyone violated this order, the food-grains were confiscated, and the regrator, i.e. the cultivator or grocer, and the official concerned, severely punished. Barani tells us that the cultivators were not to keep more than 10 *man* of grains for themselves, but it would not have been easy to enforce such an order. All the food-grains were to be brought to the market (*mandis*) for food-grains set up by Alauddin, and sold only at official prices.

Alauddin took strict measures to see that the prices laid down by him were strictly observed. An officer (*shehna*) with an adequate force was appointed in charge of the market with strict instructions to punish anyone who violated the orders.

Barani says that in consequence the price of grains fell. Thus, wheat was sold for $7^1/_2$ jital per *man*, barley for 4 jital, superior quality rice for 5 jital, grams 5 jital etc. Calculated in terms of modern weights, these came per rupee to 88 *sers* of wheat, 98 *sers* for gram and superior quality rice. Even for contemporaries, these were very cheap prices.[1]

Alauddin also instituted a system of rationing during times of scarcity. Each grocer was issued an amount of grains from the government stores bearing in mind the population of the ward. No individual was allowed to buy more than half a *man* at one time. But this was not applied to the nobles. If they did not have villages or lands of their own, they were issued grains in accordance with the number of their dependents.

Barani says that in consequence of these measures, even during times of famine there was no shortage of food-grains at Delhi and the price of food-grains did not increase even by a *dam* or a *dirham*. This is supported by Isami, a contemporary of Barani, who says that once on account of famine, such a vast crowd of people had collected in the market for grains (*mandi*) that two or three of the weaker people were crushed to death. Alauddin ordered grain to be collected, and *sold at prices prevailing before the famine*.

The second market, the cloth-market, which also sold dry fruits, herbs, ghee, oil etc. which could be kept for a long time was called *sarai-i-adl*. Alauddin ordered that all cloth brought by the merchants

---

1. Alauddin's *man* is supposed, like the *man* in Akbar's time, to be equal to about 28 *sers*.

from different parts of the country including foreign lands, was to be stored and sold only in this market at government rates. If any commodity was sold even at a jital higher than the official price, it would be confiscated and the seller punished. To ensure an adequate supply of all the commodities, all the merchants whether Hindu or Muslim, were registered and a deed taken from them that they would bring the same quantities of commodities to the *sarai-adl* every year, and sell them at government rates.

These steps were not new, but two steps show fresh thinking. First, the rich Multani merchants, i.e. those who brought commodities from long-distances including foreign countries, were given an advance of 20 lakh tankas from the treasury, on condition that they did not sell them to any intermediaries, but sold them at the *sarai-adl* at official rates. Second, the power and responsibility for obeying these orders were given to a body of merchants themselves. We are told that thanks to these rules, so much cloth was brought to Delhi that it remained unused for years.

Finally, in order to ensure that costly cloth was not purchased by people and given to others who would take it out of Delhi, and sold in the neighbouring towns at four to five times the price, an officer was appointed to issue permits to amirs, maliks, etc for the purchase of these costly commodities in accordance with their income.

As in the case of food-grains, Barani gives us a long list of the prices of different types of cloth and other commodities. These are only indicative of the cheapness of things. Thus, for one tanka a person could buy 40 yards of coarse, or 20 yards of fine-woven cotton cloth, one *ser* of coarse sugar for 1½ jital, ½ *ser* of ghee for 1 jital, 3 ser of *til* oil for 1 jital etc.[1]

The third market dealt with horses, cattle and slaves. The supply of horses of good quality at fair prices was important both for the military department and the soldier. The horse trade was more or less a monopolistic trade, the overland trade being monopolised by Multanis and Afghans. But they were sold in the market by middle-men or *dallals*. According to Barani, the rich *dallals* were as powerful as the officials of the market, and were shameless in their dealings, resorting to bribery and other corrupt practices. The horse-merchants were in league with the *dallas* to raise the price of horses.

---

1. Alauddin's silver tanka contained about one *tola* or 250 mg of silver, 48 to 50 jitals of copper made a tanka.

Alauddin took harsh measures against such *dallals*. They were banished from the town, and some of them imprisoned in forts. Then, with the help of other *dallals*, the quality and the price of horses was fixed. Horses of first quality were priced between 100 and 120 tankas, those of the second category 80 to 90 tankas, and those of the third 65 to 70 tankas. The price of ordinary horses or *tattus* which were not used in the army was 10 to 25 tankas.

Alauddin wanted that rich men and *dallals* should not go to the horse-market, and that the horse merchants should sell the horses directly to the military department (*diwan-i-arz*). But his efforts to eliminate the middle-men were not quite successful, though Barani tells us that the prices of the horses fixed by Alauddin remained stable throughout his reign.

Similarly, the price of slave boys and girls, and of cattle were also fixed, although the need for doing so is not clear, for they were neither a necessity, nor needed for military purposes. Apparently, these prices were fixed to make life a little easier for the nobles, the richer sections including government servants, and the soldiers who had become accustomed to buy slaves for domestic and personal service. Likewise, the animals were needed for meat, transport, and for milk and milk products.

Barani says that the stability of prices under Alauddin, which was a cause of wonder, was due to Alauddin's strictness. The Sultan kept himself informed of the prices through a series of informers, even sending small boys to the market to see that the shop-keepers did not cheat them by under-weighing. In his characteristic way, Barani tells us that if a shop-keeper under-weighed, twice the amount of flesh would be cut off from his body! Perhaps, exemplary punishments would have been given in a few cases. But the scheme itself could have hardly functioned for a decade or more without the minimum support of the traders, and the wider community.

It is obvious from the foregoing that the measures were not designed to harm any *one* community. As we have seen, the merchants whose names were entered into a register, were both Hindus and Muslims. So also the Multanis and the *dallals* of the horse-merchants who were so tightly controlled that, we are told, they were fed up with their lives and wished for death. The cultivators most certainly would have been affected adversely by the low price of food-grains, and the high land-revenue.

We are told that after the death of Alauddin his market reforms vanished. Qutbuddin Mubarak Shah who succeeded him, not only released the large number of persons imprisoned or exiled from Delhi on account of various offences, he withdrew the laws which, we are told, denied freedom to people to eat, wear, speak or buy or sell what they wanted.

Barani states that the market reforms of Alauddin were applicable only to Delhi. If that was so, it was hardly necessary to control the supply of food-grains all over the doab. Also, soldiers and their families did not live at Delhi alone, but in various towns and townships (*qasbas*), from Lahore to Awadh. Barani himself suggests in a work devoted to political theory that whatever was done at the capital was generally followed in the other towns. However, we have no means of ascertaining how effective were the price controls in the towns other than Delhi.

Apparently, the regulations of Alauddin resulted in a lot of vexatious, bureaucratic controls and corruption. Perhaps Alauddin would have been more successful if he had controlled the prices of essential commodities only, or those meant for direct use by the military. But he tried to control the price of everything from "caps to socks, from combs to needles, vegetables, soups, sweet-meats to chapatis etc." Such widespread, centralised controls were bound to be violated, inviting punishments which led to resentment.

Thus, by their very nature, Alauddin Khalji's market reforms were temporary, and largely meant to tide over an emergency, or a particular situation.

iii) The territorial expansion of the Delhi Sultanat (upto 1328)

We have seen how during the previous 85 years since the establishment of the Delhi sultanat in 1206, successive sultans, far from undertaking any territorial expansion, were hard put to prevent the fragmentation of the sultanat itself, partly on account of the struggle for power at Delhi, partly on account of the attempts of individual Turkish amirs to carve out their own spheres of influence, the Mongol incursions, and the ceaseless efforts of dispossessed Hindu rajas to regain their territories. However, with the rise to power of the Khaljis, and greater openness on the part of the sultanat in recruiting as officials, administrators, and soldiers, other elements in addition to Turks, i.e. Indian Muslims and Hindus, and internal restructuring of the administration, conditions were created for the rapid territorial expansion of the sultanat.

The expansion itself took place in several phases. In the first phase, the areas not far from Delhi, such as Gujarat, Rajasthan and Malwa were brought under the control of Delhi. In the second phase, the principalities in modern Maharashtra and the Deccan were raided, and compelled to accept Delhi's vassalage. No attempt, however, was made during this phase to bring them under the direct control of the Delhi sultans. The third phase, which began during the last years of Alauddin's reign, and climaxed during the reign of Ghiyasuddin Tughlaq's reign (1320-24), saw the extention of central control over the entire Deccan. Bengal was also brought under control once again.

Thus, in a brief period of 30 years, the territorial limits of the Delhi sultanat had expanded to cover almost entire India. We shall study this process as a continuous evolving enterprise, rather than one undertaken by individually ambitious sultans.

(a) Gujarat:

Although the Turks had been trying to conquer Gujarat since the time of the Ghaznavids, their attacks had been frustrated by the Chaulaukyan rulers of Gujarat. Later, Muizzuddin M. Ghuri had launched an attack on Anhilwara, and occupied it, but could not hold it for long. However, Gujarat was far too important to be neglected by the Turks for long. Nor only was it a fertile and populous area, it was a centre for handicraft production, especially in the production of textiles. Its chief port, Khambayat (Cambay), carried on a rich trade with West Asia, as also with countries of South-East Asia and China. Apart from Jains, Hindus and Bohras, Arab merchants had been settled in Khambayat for a long time. On account of its prosperity, gold and silver had been accumulated by the rulers, and was also lodged in its rich temples. Another reason for the rulers of Delhi to covet Gujarat was that with the domination of the Mongols over Central and West Asia, and their continuous attacks on India, the supply of horses from Central Asia and Iraq had been effected. As we have seen, Balban had to content himself largely with horses of Indian breed. Control over Gujarat could ensure a regular supply of Arabi, Iraqi and Turki horses which were needed by the army, and which had been an important item of trade with Iran and Iraq etc. for a long time.

Thus, the Delhi sultans hardly needed any excuse to invade Gujarat. But such an excuse was provided when, according to tradition, the Chief Minister of the new ruler, Karan, invited Alauddin to invade Gujarat because Karan had forcefully seized his wife in his absence, and done other illegal acts. In 1299, Alauddin deputed two of his leading generals, Ulugh Khan and Nusral Khan, to lead an expedition against Gujarat. Ulugh Khan, who marched from Sindh, attacked and plundered Jaisalmer on the way. The joint forces then marched to Gujarat across Chittor, despite opposition from the Rana. Reaching Guhilwara, they thoroughly sacked and plundered it. Rai Karan was taken by surprise, and fled to Deogir. All his women and treasures, including the beautiful chief queen, Kamla Devi, were captured by the Turks. The Turks treated Kamla Devi well. She was taken to Delhi where Alauddin took her into his *haram*. Many of the other leading towns of Gujarat, including Surat, and many monastries and temples including Somnath which had been rebuilt, were thoroughly plundered. At Khambayat, neither Hindus nor Muslim merchants were spared. It was here that the slave, Malik Kafur, who later played a prominent part in the Deccan campaigns, and who was called *hazar-dinari*, i.e. bought for 1000 gold dinars, was taken by force from a Muslim merchant.

There seems to have been no serious resistance anywhere to the Turks because Karan had just succeeded and set up a new dynasty, the last ruler having died issueless. As we have seen, Karan did not enjoy much local support due to his misdeeds. After fleeing from his capital, Karan kept control over Baglana in South Gujarat where the Turks did not disturb him for some time. The rest of Gujarat passed under Turkish control, and a Turkish governor was appointed to administer it.

(b) Rajasthan

Although Ajmer had been under the control of the Turks since the time of Muizzuddin M. Ghuri, as also Nagaur and Mador, the sultans had not been able to extend their control over Rajasthan beyond these places, efforts at bringing under their control Ranthambhor, the most powerful fort in Rajasthan, having succeeded only for a brief time. Jalaluddin Khalji had invested Ranthambhor, but had to return unsuccessful, realizing the strength of the fort and the Rana's determination to resist.

After bringing Gujarat under his rule, it was necessary for Alauddin to bring Rajasthan as also Malwa under his control in order to secure his communications with Gujarat. As it was, the ruler of Mewar had opposed the movement of Turkish armies across his dominions to Gujarat. Following his example, the ruler of Jalor had also refused entry to the Turkish army. Finally, on the way back from Gujarat, the Mongols, called neo-Muslims, had risen in rebellion over the question of distribution of spoils gained in Gujarat between them and the Sultan. Although the rebellion had been suppressed, two Mongol officers along with their followers had sought shelter at Ranthambhor. The ruler, Hammir Deva, a direct descent of Prithvi Raj Chauhan, had refused to surrender the fugitives, deeming it as a matter of honour, and proud of the strength of his fort. Hence, in 1301, Alauddin ordered Ulugh Khan and Nusrat Khan, the conquerors of Gujarat, to proceed against Ranthambhor. While investing the fort, Nusrat Khan went too near while directing operations, and was killed. Taking advantage of confusion in the Turkish camp, the Rana came out of the fort, defeated Ulugh Khan in battle and forced him to retreat to Jhain, which was 12 miles away and had been the Rana's capital before he took refuge at Ranthambhor.

In this situation, it became necessary for Alauddin to proceed to Ranthambhor personally. He did so after quelling a conspiracy against him. Reaching Ranthambhor, he closely invested the fort. Although the Turks were not able to scale the walls of the fort, after the siege had lasted almost for months, there was acute shortage of food and water inside the fort. Hence the Rajputs performed the fearful *jauhar* ceremony: all the women entered the funeral pyre, and the men came out to die fighting. In this battle, the Mongols fought and died side by side with the Rajputs. The poet, Amir Khusrau, who had accompanied Alauddin, describes the fort, and refers to *jauhar* in one of his well-known poetical works.

After the conquest of Ranthambhor came the turn of Chittor which was also reputed to be one of the strongest forts of Rajasthan. Although Chittor had for long been a bone of contention between its Guhil rulers and the Chalukayas of Gujarat, it was at the time under the control of the Guhilot ruler, Ratan Singh, who had just succeeded his father. The poet Khusrau, who had accompanied Alauddin, describes the siege in detail, and says that after it had lasted for six months, Ratan Singh came out and surrendered. He was well treated, but 30,000 peasants who had taken refuge in the fort were slaughtered. Khusrau makes no mention of *jauhar* at Chittor.

Khusrau's account is supported by all the contemporaries. None of them mention the legend of Padmini which is mentioned for the first time in a literary work in the first quarter of the 15th century. It was embellished with various fanciful stories and adventures by Malik Muhammad Jaisi, a hundred years later. The story is too well-known and need not be repeated here. It has been rejected by most modern historians, including Gauri Shankar Ojha, one of the leading Rajasthan historian. The Padmini legend, therefore, need not detain us any further. It may be mentioned that after its conquest, the governorship of the fort of Chittor was given to Khizr Khan, the son of Alauddin.

After the conquest of Chittor, most of the rajas in Rajasthan, including those of Marwar and Harauti (Bundi) submitted. As it was, Mador in Marwar had been under Turkish occupation. Jaisalmer had been subdued earlier during the Gujarat campaign, as we have noted. Siwana and Jalor, adjacent to Gujarat, both of which were strongly fortified, put up stout resistance, but were occupied and plundered in 1308 and 1311.

Thus, in a period of about 10 years, entire Rajasthan had been brought under Turkish domination. However, except keeping hold of Ajmer, and of some of the powerful forts, such as Ranthambhor and Chittor, no attempt was made by Alauddin to establish direct rule over any of the Rajput states. In fact, he apparently tried to establish cordial relations with some of the Rajput rajas. Thus, according to tradition, Maldeo, brother of the ruler of Jalor, served Alauddin loyally with a force of 5000 horses, and that around 1313, Alauddin made him governor of Chittor in place of Khizr Khan.

This policy of not interfering with local administration, and befriending the Rajput rulers was later extended by Alauddin with great advantage to Deogir and to some of the other Deccan rulers.

Thus, Alauddin was the first ruler in the Delhi sultanat to put forward in a rudimentary form a Rajput policy based on recognition of mutual interests.

(c) Malwa

After the conquest of Chittor, Alauddin gave his attention to Malwa which was a rich and extensive tract with many populous cities. According to Amir Khusrau, it was so extensive that even wise geographers were unable to delimit its frontiers. Although Malwa had been invaded both by Iltutmish and later by Alauddin during the rule of Jalaluddin, and great plunder had been obtained, little effort had been made to bring it under direct occupation. Its conquest by Alauddin was both to bring under control the route to Gujarat, as also to open the way to the south.

In 1305, Ainul Mulk Multani was deputed to conquer Malwa. The *Rai* had a force of 30-40,000 horse, but it was no match for the Turkish forces. The *Rai* was pursued from Ujjain to Mandu where he had taken shelter, defeated, and killed. Unlike Rajasthan, entire Malwa was annexed, and Ainul Mulk was appointed its governor.

Thus, apart from Bengal which remained independent till the reign of Ghiyasuddin Tughlaq (1320-24), entire northern India came under the control of the sultans of Delhi. Orissa was also invaded and subdued during the reign of Ghiyasuddin, but was not annexed.

(d) Maharashtra and South India—first phase:

After successfully dealing with the Mongol invasions, and reorganizing his army and internal administration, Alauddin was prepared to undertake his most daring design, viz. raiding the Deccan states and making them subordinate to Delhi. Maharashtra and south India were known to be lands of treasures and gold. Their famed handicrafts and flourishing ports had resulted in an influx of gold which had been hoarded by generations of rulers. The country was dotted with rich temples many of which were also engaged in inland and overseas trade, and money-lending. Thus, it was an area where both money and glory could be gained. At it turned out, the enterprise succeeded beyond anyone's wildest dreams because the states in the area had been engaged in waging wars against each other in the characteristic manner, completely oblivious of developments in north India, or that the developments there could pose any danger to them.

Maharashtra

Alauddin's first contact with Maharashtra had come about in 1296 when starting from Kara, and traversing the difficult country of Bundelkhand, he had suddenly appeared before Deogir, with a force of 8,000 horse, and defeated the Yadava king Ram Chandra, and then his son, Singhana. He had returned laden with wealth, and a vague promise on Ram Chandra's part for the payment of an annual tribute.

After the conquest of Chittor and Malwa, Alauddin turned his attention towards Deogir once again. An excuse for invasion was found, though one was hardly needed in those times, that Ram Chandra had stopped paying the annual tribute during the last two to three years. According to some, this was due to the influence of his son, Singhana, who chafed at his father's subordination to Delhi.

In 1308, two armies were despatched to Deogir, one to oust Karan, the former ruler of Gujarat, from Baglana in south Gujarat which he had managed to hold on to with the help of Ram Chandra. He was defeated after a stiff fight. The armies then joined Malik Kafur who had been deputed to punish Ram Chandra. The Yadava ruler offered only light resistance, and submitted to Kafur. According to Amir Khusrau, Alauddin had ordered Malik Kafur not to injure the Rai and his family in any way. Hence, Ram Chandra or Ram Deo was honourably escorted to Delhi, Deogir remaining under the charge of his son, Singhana. Alauddin showered pearls and precious stones on Ram Deo when he entered his court. He was kept at Delhi for six months, ostensibly as a guest. According to Khusrau, "everyday his status and honour increased." He was then allowed to return to Deogir with his sons and family. At the time of his departure, Ram Deo was presented one lakh of gold tankas, given the title of Rai Rayan and a golden coloured canopy (*chatr*) which was the sign of royalty. Nausari, a district in Gujarat, was also allotted to him as a gift. It was perhaps at this time that Ram Deo gave his daughter, Jhatyapali, in marriage to Alauddin. Earlier, Deval Devi, a daughter of Rani Kamla Devi of Gujarat who had entered Alauddin's *haram* and gained influence over him on account of her beauty, was captured during the campaign against her father, Karan. At Kamla Devi's instance, Deval Devi was married to Khizr Khan, son and heir-apparent of Alauddin. Though Khizr Khan had a sad end, we can see in this a gradual expansion of Alauddin's policy of building relations with Rajput rajas.

The Southern States

The most important states in south India at the time were the Kakatiyas of Warangal (modern Telingana); and the Hoysalas with their capital at Dvar Samudra (modern Helebid in Karnataka). Further to the south were the Pandyas of Mabar and Madurai (Tamilnadu). All these powers were engaged in constant wars with each other and with the Yadavas of Deogir in territorial disputes.

Having secured a base and a reliable ally at Deogir, between 1309 and 1311, Alauddin sent two expeditions under Malik Kafur to make the southern states disgorge their accumulated wealth, and compel them to accept Delhi's suzerainty and pay an annual tribute. Alauddin had no intention of annexing any of these states and bringing them under his direct administration, since he knew that the distances, and differing conditions would make such an attempt difficult and hazardous. According to Isami, who wrote at the same time as Barani, Alauddin had instructed Malik Kafur, while leading the first expedition of Warangal, that "if the *rai* of Telang accepted subordination (to the sultan), his kingdom should be returned to him, and honoured by being granted *khilat* (robes) and *chatr* (royal canopy)." Barani says that Alauddin's instructions were: "If the *rai* gives up his treasures, elephants and horses, and promises a tribute for the future, accept the arrangement." The same instructions must be assumed to have applied to the second expedition aimed at Dvar Samudra and Mabar.

The first expedition against Warangal in Telangana (1309-10) took six months. Marching through remote and little accessible routes, Kafur reached the fort of Warangal. It had an outside mud wall which was stronger than steel, and an inside fort of stone. After a close siege, when the outer fort had been captured and the fall of the inner fort seemed inevitable, the Rai supplicated for peace, which was agreed to. The treasures surrendered were carried to Delhi on the backs of a thousand camels which were paraded before Alauddin. The Rai also agreed to pay an annual tribute.

Embolded by this success, the following year, Malik Kafur was appointed with an army to invade Dvar Samudra and Mabar. Marching through remote routes as before, and with the help of guidance provided by the Maratha sardars of Ram Deo, Kafur surprised Ballal Deva, the Hoysala ruler, at Dvar Samudra. After a close siege Ballal Deva agreed to the same terms as the ruler of Warangal. He surrendered all his treasure, and agreed to pay an annual tribute. According to Isami, Ballal Deva came to Delhi to wait on Alauddin, and was given 10 lakh tankas, a *khilat* and a *chatr*, and the kingdom was returned to him.

Kafur then moved against Mabar (Coromandal). But it was not possible to bring to battle the two Pandyan brothers, who were at war with each other. Kafur reached Patan (Masulipatanam) where he found a colony of Muslim merchants. The city was thoroughly ravaged, and none, including the Muslim merchants, were spared. Kafur devastated the temple of Chidambaram (near Madras) where he captured many elephants belonging to the Pandyan brothers. He also sacked Madurai. But he had to return without contacting the Pandyan brothers, or effecting any agreement with them. This campaign lasted a year.

These two expeditions not only brought immense wealth to Alauddin, it raised his prestige very high. Malik Kafur gained in public estimation by his skill, daring and success as a military leader. He rose even higher in the estimation of Alauddin who gave him the title of *malik naib* (regent or personal representative of the sovereign). But in the long run, it led to power going to Kafur's head, and the consequent growth of an anti-Kafur lobby among the nobles which led to his subsequent downfall and death.

The immediate political benefits of the Deccan campaigns were limited. While Deogir remained a firm ally as long as Ram Deo lived, the arrangements with the other south Indian states remained brittle. The payment of an annual tribute promised by them could hardly be ensured without continuous pressure, including military campaigns. Nor could the expeditions lead to greater trade till a greater degree of political stability had been attained. The expeditions, however, paved the way for the next step—annexation.

Maharashtra and the Southern States—Second Phase: Annexation:

Although Alauddin had made non-annexation a deliberate policy with regard to Maharashtra and the southern states, the situation developed in such a way that he had to modify this policy in his own life time. In 1315, Ram Deo of Deogir died, and his son, Bhillama, repudiated allegiance to Alauddin. Alauddin sent Malik Kafur to punish Bhillama, with instructions to send him to Delhi, and to annex the kingdom. But Bhillama escaped. Kafur occupied the fort, and tried to govern the kingdom without displacing the old Maratha chiefs. He was successful only partially, many of the chiefs asserting their independence, while a part of the kingdom remained under the control of members of the old dynasty.

This change of policy on Alauddin's part from non-annexation to annexation needs some explanation. Bhillama's rebellion alone does not appear to be a sufficient cause. Apparently, Alauddin felt that direct Turkish control over Deogir was necessary for keeping the other southern states in line by exerting diplomatic and, if necessary, military pressure on them. Thus, it was a modification, not an abandonment of the policy of non-annexation in the south.

When Mubarak Khalji succeeded Alauddin, he marched on Deogir to bring it effectively under his control. He was able to do so without meeting much opposition. He also sent an expedition against Warangal where the Rai had not paid the annual tribute for several years. The outcome of the siege was the same as before: the Rai submitted when the outer fort had been captured. On the Sultan's side, at first a demand was made for the surrender of five districts, as well as his treasure and elephants. Finally, the Rai agreed to surrender one district, and payment of an annual tribute of 40 gold bricks. This was a partial breach of the policy of non-annexation, but not its abandonment.

The abandonment of Alauddin's policy of non-annexation in the south should really be attributed to Ghiyasuddin Tughlaq, and his

son and successor, Muhammad bin Tughlaq. Immediately after his
accession, Ghiyasuddin ordered his son, Ulugh Khan later known
as Muhammad bin Tughlaq, to invade Warangal where the ruler,
taking advantage of the confused situation at Delhi, had stopped
paying tribute. An army was deputed from Delhi which, after resting
at Deogir, proceeded to invest Warangal. After six months siege,
the fort was about to fall when rumours of the king's death at Delhi
led to a confusion in Ulugh Khan's camp. Taking advantage of the
flight of some of the nobles, the Rai attacked and compelled Ulugh
Khan to fall back on Deogir.

After the rumours of the king's death had been successfully
scotched, and with the help of a new army from Delhi, Ulugh Khan
renewed the campaign against Warangal the following year. This time
no quarter was given to the Rai. He was compelled to surrender, and
sent to Delhi. But on the way he committed suicide. The entire
Telangana was now annexed. It was divided into nine districts, and
officials were appointed to govern them, and a year's land-revenue
collected. The name of Warangal was changed to Sultanpur.

The conquest of Mabar followed the conquest of Telangana. Thus,
Madurai, the capital of Mabar, was captured in 1323. It seems that
earlier, Malik Kafur had left a Muslim garrison at Madurai, the
Pandyan capital, but its effectiveness is not known. The area had
also been raided by Khusrau Khan, an officer of Mubarak Khalji.
Thus, the Tamil area had been in a state of confusion. The expedition sent during the reign of Ghiyasuddin Tughlaq reinstalled a
Muslim governor at Madurai and the entire Mabar area was brought
under the control of Delhi.

Finally, in 1328, following a rebellion by Gurshasp, a cousin of
Muhammad Tughlaq, who took refuge with the ruler of Kampil in
south Karnataka, Muhammad bin Tughlaq sent an army, and the
Karnataka was also annexed.

Thus, in a brief space of twelve years, the entire south upto the
borders of Malabar had been brought under the direct administration of Delhi. Only some areas, including Dvar Samudra, remained
under the control of their own rulers. Events soon proved that this
was a hasty and ill-considered step. The rapid incorporation of such
a vast area, so far away from Delhi and with a different administrative set up and different socio-cultural outlook and traditions,
strained the resources of the sultanat to the limit, and soon a process of its disintegration began.

Thus, the territorial expansion of the Delhi sultanat brought forward new opportunities, as also new challenges.

6

PROBLEMS OF A CENTRALISED ALL-INDIA STATE—GHIYASUDDIN AND MUHAMMAD BIN TUGHLAQ (1320-1351)

The last years of Alauddin Khalji were disturbed by a painful disease, and intense struggle for power among the nobles. Malik Kafur, the *malik naib* or vice regent who had the complete confidence of Alauddin, gradually eliminated his opponents, and to clear his way to power had Khizr Khan, the heir apparent, imprisoned and then blinded. After Alauddin's death (1316), Kafur elevated a minor son of Alauddin to the throne, and assumed all powers. But Kafur was overthrown in a month's time, and another son of Alauddin, Mubarak Khalji, ascended the throne. In order to gain popularity, Mubarak Khalji abolished all the agrarian and market control regulations of Alauddin. However, he tried to maintain the position of Alauddin in the Deccan and Gujarat by sending expeditions there. Barani condemns Mubarak Khalji for being a homosexual and a pervert, though these "vices" were not unusual among the Turkish warrior class. The main criticism of Barani was of the sultan giving undue favour to a group of new Muslims, the Baradus, whom he calls "ignoble". The Baradus, who belonged to a warrior caste, forged ahead under their leader, Khusaru Malik, who assassinated the young Sultan, and assumed the throne himself (1320). The Khalji dynasty thus came to an end. Barani accuses the Baradus and their Hindu supporters of starting idol-worship in the palace, of insulting Islam and of strengthening the ways of infidelity day by day. Modern research does not support these charges. The Baradus did not try to monopolize power, and received the support of a sizeable section among the Alai nobility and the Muslims of Delhi. The standard of rebellion against them was raised by Ghiyasuddin Tughlaq who was the warden of the marches against the Mongols, and was an experienced warrior. The Baradus could hardly stand against him in battle, and within two month, they were defeated and dispersed. The new ruler, Ghiyasuddin Tughlaq was, however, destined to rule only for a short time. After setting the administration to order, and appointing his son, Ulugh Khan, to restore the Imperial position in Warangal, and sending a noble to deal with a rebellion in Gujarat, Ghiyasuddin marched on Bengal to reduce it to submission. As is well-known, on his return from the successful campaign, a pavilion erected by his son, Ulugh Khan (Muhammad Tughlaq), to welcome him, crashed and crushed, him to death (1325). Modern research does not support the idea that it was due to an intrigue on the part of the prince, or was the effect of lightening. The crash of the hastily erected building may have been due to the parading of captured elephants.

i. Problems and Approaches

As has been pointed out in the previous Chapter, Ghiyasuddin Tughlaq, and his son and successor, Muhammad bin Tughlaq, rejected Alauddin's policy of non-annexation of distant states and of being content with their formal submission and sending tribute regularly. Barani tells us that both Ghiyasuddin and Muhammad bin Tughlaq were highly ambitious. Muhammad bin Tughlaq was not prepared to leave a scrap of territory in India which was not subordinate to him and under his control. Thus, during their rule, the direct control of Delhi was extended to Warangal (Telingana), Mabar (Coromondal), Madurai (Tamil Nadu), and Dvar Samudra (Karnataka) upto the southern tip of India. Whenever a territory was annexed, Muhammad Tughlaq would appoint a set of revenue officials to assess it. It was with their help that the accounts of distant provinces and tracts were audited in the office of the wazir, "in the same (detailed) manner as the villages and towns in the doab." (Barani).

Such a rapid expansion of the directly ruled territories, and such a high degree of centralisation, had their own pitfalls which Muhammad Tughlaq was to realize later.

There are two other aspects which have a bearing on the character of the state with which Barani and other contemporary historians were concerned. The first was the question of the welfare of the people. Though Barani praises Alauddin Khalji for his control of the market and (wrongly) lauds him for crushing the Hindus, he criticizes him for his policy of "excessive bloodshed, harsh and tyrannical behaviour, and inflicting hardships on others in order to get his orders obeyed." In contract to this, he praises Ghiyasuddin Tughlaq for his concern for the welfare of the people and his policy of moderation so that "the country might not be ruined by the weight of taxation, and the way to improvement be barred.. The Hindus were to be taxed so that they might not be blinded by wealth, and so become discontented and rebellious, nor, on the other hand, be so reduced to poverty and destitution as to be unable to pursue their husbandry."

Almost for the first time, we see a recognition of the importance of agriculture and handicrafts on the part of the state, and the need to continuously expand cultivation. Thus, the policy of welfare and humanitarianism put forward by Jalaluddin Khalji was reiterated and sought to be revived by Ghiyasuddin Tughlaq in a more positive manner. He extended this policy of mildness and generosity to the noble families of the time of Alauddin and his son, Kaiqubad. Many of these were leading lives of poverty and neglect. They were given posts and *iqtas*. The revenue-free lands held by theologians, some of them for long periods, were examined and many of them reduced. Those who had received large sums of money as gifts from the previous regime were called to audit, and most of them forced to return the sums.

Regarding the question of the relationship between state and religion, Ghiyasuddin Tughlaq, though a strict Muslim in his observance of religious practices such as the regular and public prayers, fasting during the month of Ramazan etc., did not accept the narrow interpretation of the *shara* regarding the humiliation and impoverishment of the Hindus advocated by some theologians. Muhammad Tughlaq also was strict in himself observing the injunctions regarding prayers, fasting etc., and was strict in seeing that others observed them also. He was a learned man, and had a deep understanding of many branches of knowledge such as philosophy, mathematics, *tibb* (medicines), religion etc. He was interested in Persian and Hindi poetry, and had read widely. Barani's criticism, which we may treat as a compliment, was that he was a "rationalist", that is, he would not accept anything except by logical proof. This meant that while he did not reject the essential articles of the Muslim faith, he was not prepared to accept many traditions and practices merely on the basis of faith. Barani accuses Muhammad bin Tughlaq of combining in his person the traditions of prophethood (*nubuwat*) with sultanat, i.e. of trying to combine spiritual and political authority. This charge has no basis, except that Muhammad Tughlaq refused to accept the spiritual authority of many theologians and mystics. It might be recalled that Barani also accuses Alauddin Khalji of wanting to set up a new religion, merely because he was not prepared to blindly accept the authority of the *shara*. Though not a believer in mysticism, Muhammad Tughlaq respected the sufi saints, and was the first sultan to visit the tomb of Muinuddin Chishti at Ajmer. He also built mausoleums over the tombs of many sufi saints, including Nizamuddin Auliya at Delhi.

That Muhammad Tughlaq was a man of an open mind, and not a blind dogmatist is also demonstrated by his associating with *jogis*, and Jain saints such as Raj Shekhar and Jinaprabha Suri. While in Gujarat, he visited some of the Jain temples there, and gave them grants. He is also known to have associated himself with some Hindu festivals, such as Holi.

Barani's criticism of Muhammad Tughlaq's faults of character cannot, however, be dismissed out of hand. He is accused of being hot and hasty in character, with an excessive reliance on his own judgement, without heeding the advice of others. Hence, many of his innovations were ill-considered, or launched without "adequate preparations". Barani, and the Moroccan traveller, Ibn Battutah, also accuse Muhammad Tughlaq of giving excessive rewards and punishments, and of appointing mean, low-born people to high offices.

ii. Experiments and Reforms

The problems and approaches we have outlined above should be helpful in understanding the many experiments and reforms which Muhammad bin Tughlaq launched, and for which he is so well-known. Muhammad bin Tughlaq was keen to tone up the administration, and bring about uniformity in its functioning. Towards this end, according to Ibn Battutah, he issued large numbers of orders *(manshurs)*. However, only a few of these appear to have been taken up seriously, or to have made an impact. These have been listed by Barani, and may be divided into two: (a) administrative and political measures, and (b) economic and agrarian reforms. Of course, each influenced the other, so that no rigid demarcation can be made between them.

(a) Administrative and Political Measures: Exodus to Deogiri

One of the most controversial step taken by Muhammad bin Tughlaq early in his reign was his so-called transfer of capital to Deogiri which was renamed Daultabad, and the alleged orders of the sultan ordering a mass transfer of the people from Delhi to the new capital. A careful analysis of the contemporary and later sources show that Barani grossly exaggerated when he alleges that the steps led to the ruination of Delhi which, till then, had equalled the leading cities of the Islamic world, Cairo and Baghdad. Some others have alleged that the step was taken by the sultan to punish the people of Delhi who had become hostile to him. However, there is evidence that the step was not taken by Muhammad bin Tughlaq in a pique, but was the result of considerable thought, and had been carefully prepared for.

The motive of the step taken by the sultan has been set out by Barani himself, viz. that it was central to all parts of the empire. As we have seen, during the reign of Ghiyasuddin and the early years of Muhammad bin Tughlaq, the direct rule of Delhi had been extended to cover almost the entire south. Since the days of Alauddin, Deogiri had been the virtual base of operations in the Deccan. Muhammad bin Tughlaq had spent a number of years in the south, both as a prince and as a ruler, campaigning, and was familiar with Deogiri which had a pleasant climate, being surrounded by hills. He wanted to have a second capital in the south so that he could control it more easily. According to a 17th century author, Ferishta, some of the councillors of the sultan suggested Ujjain in Malwa which had been made his capital by Raja Vikramaditya for the same reason. But the sultan preferred Deogiri, both because he was more familiar with it, and because it was already one of the great cities of India.

The decision to make Deogiri a second capital was apparently taken in 1327 when Muhammad bin Tughlaq passed Deogiri after his journey to the Karnataka to suppress the rebellion of his cousin, Gurshasp. In preparation for the new step, he planted trees on both sides of the road and at a distance of every two miles (a *karoh*) set up halting stations. Provision was made for food and drink being available for the travellers at the station. Land was allotted from the income of which the staff working there could draw their salaries. We are told that at each station, a sufi saint was stationed, and a *khanqah* (hospice for the saint) built. Soon afterwards the sultan's mother was sent to Deogiri or Daultabad. The sultan's mother was accompanied by many nobles, leading men of the city, and the entire royal house-hold including slaves, servants, and treasures. Sometime afterwards, the sultan summoned all the sufis,[1] ulema and grandees of Delhi. This is placed in the year 1328-29.

It is clear that no mass exodus of the population at Delhi was ordered. However, it seems that a good deal of pressure was exerted upon the people to migrate, the royal orderlies even inspecting their houses for the purpose. Those travelling to Daultabad were divided into caravans for purposes of convenience. The journey was long, and undertaken during the hot months, so that many people died on the way. Full preparations had been made for welcoming those who reached Daultabad. The city had been divided into wards (*mohallas*), with separate quarters for troops, the nobles, the civil servants, the judges and the learned men, the merchants and artisans. Mosques, markets, public baths etc. were built in each mohalla. The Sultan purchased the houses and dwelling of those at Delhi who had migrated and wanted the government to do so. Liberal grants were made to people, both at the time of their departure at Delhi and at their arrival at Daultabad where free boarding and lodging was provided to them.

Nevertheless, most of the migrants were not happy. They had got used to Delhi where many of them had lived for more than a hundred years, and which they regarded as their home. That many of the Turks had started looking upon India with love and affection is obvious from the writings of the poet, Amir Khusrau. For them, Daultabad was an alien land, full of infidels.

Meanwhile, Delhi was not deserted. Coins struck at Delhi, two Sanskrit inscriptions in *baolis* (sunken wells with steps) built by some wealthy Hindus in the environs of Delhi at this time prove it. But, we are told, many of the houses had been shut up, and the bad characters in the city started looting them. Hence, Muhammad bin Tughlaq invited sufis, learned men and others living in neighbouring cities to move to Delhi. In 1334, when Ibn Battutah visited Delhi, it was fully settled.

Nor was there any question of the capital being shifted from Delhi. Rather, Daultabad became a second capital, as coins struck at Daultabad testify. However, the Sultan's ambitious project soon struck a reef. In 1334-35, there was a serious rebellion in Mabar (modern

---

1. The author, Yahya bin Sirhindi, says all the Saiyyids and sufis (mystics). But Ibn Battutah tells us that all sufis were called Saiyyids in the Delhi Sultanat.

Coromandal in Tamilnadu). The sultan marched to the south to suppress the rebellion. While he was at Bidar, there was an out-break of bubonic plague in which many of his soldiers perished. Muhammad Tughlaq himself was taken ill, and retreated to Daultabad. Rumors spread of the sultan's death, and soon the en-tire south, including Mabar, Dwar-Samudra (Karnataka), and Warangal (Telingana) were lost to the Delhi sultanat. Thus the *raison d'etre of keeping Daultabad as a second capital disappeared.* It was around this time, i.e. between 1335-37, that the Sultan permitted the peo-ple at Daultabad to return to Delhi.

Thus, the exodus to Daultabad proved to be a costly failure, and brought misery to many people. However, its effects were felt large-ly by the upper classes, not by the people of Delhi. It is not clear why Muhammad bin Tughlaq ordered the sufis, clergymen and the learned people to migrate to Daultabad. Perhaps he felt that he or the state could not function in an atmosphere where mystics and men of Islamic learning were not present. He might also have felt that by their example, the sufis and the men of learning would spread Islam, and the hold of the sultan there become more secure. What-ever may have been his motives, one long-term effect of Muhammad bin Tughlaq's exodus to Daultabad was that many of the sufis and men of learning decided to stay back at Daultabad, so that in course of time it became a centre of Islamic learning. But the beneficiaries of this were not the sultans of Delhi, but the Bahmani rulers who established their rule in the area soon afterwards.

The Khurasan and Karachil Expeditions

Although the Khurasan and Karachil expeditions, and the recruit-ment of a large army by Muhammad bin Tughlaq, are mentioned by Barani separately, we may take them together as they were in-terconnected.

The Khurasan expedition was closely connected to events in Cen-tral and West Asia, and with Muhammad bin Tughlaq's desire to make Sindh and the Punjab safe at all times from the danger of recurrent Mongol invasions. After the death of Chingez Khan, one branch of his descendants, the Chaghtai branch, had dominated Turkistan and Transoxiana, while another branch, led by Halaku, had captured Iran, Iraq etc. Ghur, Ghazni, Afghanistan etc. which provided access to India was a bone of contention between the two. However, both the branches were in decay at this time, the condi-tions in Transoxiana being unsettled after the death of Tarmashirin whose invasion of India in 1326-27 has been mentioned earlier. We are told that Muhammad bin Tughlaq wanted to overthrow the descendants of Chingez. Khurasan was used vaguely to describe the area, and Barani adds Iraq and sometimes Trans-oxiana to it. To realise his objective, Muhammad bin Tughlaq invited and gave lavish grants to some of the leading men of those areas. He also raised a large army of 370,000 soldiers. They were paid by the grant of *iqtas* but, Barani says, no care was taken about enforcing the brand of the horses, or the description of the soldiers, or testing their swordsmanship. They were kept idle for a year, and then dispersed since it was not possible to pay them any longer.

The rapid raising of the army and its nature suggests that it was not meant to be a major enterprise, and perhaps only aimed at extending the sultan's control over Kabul, Ghazni, etc. Muhammad bin Tughlaq's interest in the area is shown by the fact that after the failure of Tarmashirin's invasion (1326-27), he frequently sent money to the government of Ghazni, and almost took the qazi of Ghazni into his pay, a fact which Barani deplores. However, conditions were not ripe even for this limited enterprise, and hence it was abandoned.

The Qarachil expedition (1333) is placed soon after the Khurasan expedition. This expedition was apparently aimed at the Kulu-Kangra region of Himachal. However, Barani quite wrongly links it to the Khurasan expedition and says that its conquest would have enabled him to capture horses (from Turkistan), and provide an easier road to Transoxiana! Some later writers, such as Badayuni and Ferishta, call it the expedition to China and Himachal. Medieval ideas of geography were very vague, and these historians thought that Khitai or old China was just across the Himalayas. As it was, the expedition proved a failure. The commander of the Delhi armies advanced too far into the mountains so that his retreat was cut off by the defending forces, and almost the entire army of 10,000 was destroyed. However, this expedition was not a total failure because, after some time, the ruler of the area patched up a treaty with Muhammad bin Tughlaq, agreeing to pay him a certain sum of money for the use of the territory lying at the foot hills. He also accepted the sultan's overlordship.

(b) Economic and Agrarian Reforms

Token currency: One of Muhammad bin Tughlaq's ambition was to reform the coinage and, according to a modern historian, Dr.

Ishwari Prasad, from his mints in different parts of the empire, various kinds of coins were issued which were unequalled in the artistic perfection of their design, execution and finish. An experiment which Muhammad bin Tughlaq launched after the exodus to Deogiri in 1329-30, was the token currency which has been little understood and much condemned.

He issued coins of copper and brass which were to exchange as equal with silver and gold. The idea of a token currency is known to everyone in the modern world, but it was a novelty in medieval times. However, it was not a totally new thing. Paper currency in China was known. The Mughal ruler, Kublai Khan, had introduced in the first year of his reign in 1260 a paper currency called the *chan* which had lasted throughout his reign till his death in 1294. It had been accepted by everyone including foreign traders. This fact was widely known, and it is referred to by Barani to explain the background of Muhammad bin Tughlaq's action.[1] Later, in 1294, an Iranian king, Qai Katu, had tried to introduce the paper *chan* in his country, but it had led to serious disturbances, and had to be discontinued after eight days.

There has been a great deal of controversy regarding the motives of the sultan in introducing the token currency. According to Barani, it was part of his ambition to conquer all the inhabited quarters of the world for which a huge army was needed and a large treasury to pay them. Thus, it was for the purpose of supplementing the treasury. But Barani contradicts himself when he goes on to say that the sultan's treasury had been exhausted by his reck less grant of gifts and awards. However, shortage of gold and silver could not have been a major reason for the step because, when the experiment failed, the sultan called in the token coins, and paid gold and silver in exchange for them.

The experiment failed largely because the sultan was unable to prevent forging of the new coins. Barani in his picturesque language says that the 'house of every Hindu became a mint'. Perhaps, what he implied was that the gold-smiths who were Hindus knew how to make alloys of copper and brass coins, and did so. The state suffered a big loss because the *khuts* and *muqaddams* in the rural areas paid the land-revenue in the copper and brass coins, and purchased arms and horses with the same currency. Soon, there was such an abundance of these new coins that their value depre-

---

1. This is referred to in the Rampur copy of Barani's *Tarikh-i-Firuz Shahi*. In the later revised edition which became popular, this reference is omitted.

ciated rapidly and they became "as worthless as stones and pot-sherds". Trade and commerce began to be disrupted. Hence, in anger, Muhammad bin Tughlaq cancelled his orders, and redeemed the token coins by gold and silver coins. This could have been done only for the coins issued from the royal mints. The token coins issued by Muhammad bin Tughlaq were both in copper and brass. None of the earlier sultans had issued any coins in brass which was an alloy of copper with tin and zinc etc. According to an eminent modern historian, Professor Muhammad Habib, Muhammad bin Tughlaq had issued coins of bronze which had distinct inscriptions in Persian and Arabic to mark the new coins. Confusion arose because ordinary people could not easily distinguish between these and the forged coins. The forged coins brought by people for redemption, but not accepted by the government, lay heaped in mounds outside the fort for a long time.

The experiment if successful, would have led to an expansion of India's trade and commerce because there was a world wide shortage of silver at the time. This is reflected in the reduction of the silver content of the tanka by Muhammad bin Tughlaq from 178 to 140 grains early in his reign. The failure of the token currency must certainly have affected the treasury adversely. But it was not too serious a blow, or upset public life. It was given up by 1333, three years after its introduction. Thus, no issues of the token coins are available after 732 *hijri* or 1332-33. The token coins are not mentioned by Ibn Battutah who came to Delhi in 1334. This shows that the the entire episode had been speedily forgotten.

Agrarian Reforms

The failure of these three experiments—the exodus to Deogiri, the failure of the Khurasan expedition, and the withdrawal of the token currency as also the disastrous result of the Karchil campaign must have affected the public reputation of the Sultan, as also his treasury. However, the resources of the empire were still vast, and the loss to the treasury must have been quickly made up. But it seems to have encouraged the practice of letting out big tracts of land on revenue-farming terms *(muqata)*—a development to which we shall revert later on.

Meanwhile, certain agrarian measures of Muhammad bin Tughlaq, epidemics, and a famine which lasted for six to seven years and affected large parts of the *doab* and Malwa, created serious public distress, and a widespread peasant uprising.

We are told that Ghiyasuddin had replaced Alauddin's system of measurement for the fields by sharing of the produce. This was advantageous to the peasant because it made allowance for a total or partial failure of crops. According to Barani, the Sultan's policy was that increase in the incidence of taxation was to be gradual, and such that it did not affect the prosperity of the peasantry. Instructions were issued to the officials to see that cultivation increased from year to year, and that the revenue also increased proportionately. We do not know what he actually charged from the cultivators, but there seems no reason to believe that he reduced it to one-fifth, as argued by some modern historians.

When Muhammad bin Tughlaq came to the throne, he attempted a substantial increase in the scale of the land-revenue demanded from the cultivators. Barani says that he increased it from "one to ten or one to twenty". This was only a figure of speech, and should not be taken literally to mean either increase from ten to twenty times, or one in ten or twenty, i.e. ten to five per cent. Barani elsewhere uses the words "one to hundred", or "one to thousand" to convey a sense of considerable increase. We are told that new cesses were levied, and the old cesses—grazing tax *(charai)*, and house *(ghari)* tax were collected in a rigorous manner, the cattle being branded and the houses counted. Worse, when assessing the yield of a field, not the actual produce, but the standard yield was taken into account. Further, when commuting the state's share into cash, not the actual but the officially assumed prices were used.

These measures, we are told, led to the destruction of the peasantry and to an agrarian uprising which affected a large area near Delhi and the *doab*. Barani says that the Hindus, i.e. the peasants set fire to the grain heaps, and drove away cattle from their homes. Thus, "Whole regions were devastated. Cultivation was totally abandoned." The Sultan adopted the usual methods to suppress rebellion. Thus, *shiqdars and faujdars* (revenue collectors and military officials) were ordered to lay waste and plunder the country. In consequence, many of the *khuts and muqaddams* were killed, or took refuge in forests. The Sultan's troops surrounded the jungles and killed everyone whom they found within the jungle. Thus, the entire area from Kannauj to Dalmau was laid waste.

The range and extent of this agrarian rebellion need some explanation for we must remember that Alauddin Khalji had raised the land revenue in the doab to half, given no concessions to the *khuts* and *muqaddams*, and insisted on measurement which put he cultivators in a position of disadvantage when the rains failed, wholly or partially. Yet the *khuts* and *muqaddams*, or the peasants had not risen in rebellion. Fear of drastic punishment by Alauddin is no answer, for Muhammad bin Tughlaq was no less severe. Even if we imagine that Barani exaggerated, as he often does, the reality of a wide-spread peasant rebellion cannot be denied. Does it mean that Muhammad bin Tughlaq had, in effect, raised the land revenue to more than half, the share demanded by Alauddin? If that was so, Barani, who was critical of Muhammad bin Tughlaq, would have said so. A possible explanation is that unlike Alauddin, Muhammad bin Tughlaq was not able to keep a tight control over the local revenue officials. Hence, in the name of realising the standard produce on the basis of officially accepted prices, many of them must have indulged in gross oppressions. Barani says, when peasants of distant regions heard of the ruin and destruction of the peasantry, and fearful that the same orders may be applied to them, they also rose in rebellion. However, this may have been an exaggeration for we do not hear that the rebellion spread to areas outside the *doab*.

Barani says that the contraction of cultivation in the doab, the ruin of its peasantry, the reduction in the number of grain-carriers (*banjaras*), and the failure of the grains to reach Delhi led to a famine. The rains, too, failed. Hence, the prices of grains rose very high.

To cope with the famine, relief camps were opened at Delhi, food-grains arriving from Awadh where there was no famine. Muhammad Tughlaq also advanced agricultural loans (*sondhar*) to dig wells and to buy seed and implements.

It seems that the famine began in 1334-35 and lasted for seven years. During this period, Muhammad bin Tughlaq found that the atmosphere of Delhi had become pestilential. Hence, the entire imperial camp moved to a place on the Ganges 80 kms away. This place was called Swarga-dwar ('Gateway to Heaven"), and the Sultan lived there for two years, food-grains being dispatched to him from Awadh. Many notable people from Delhi also moved to the areas where there was no famine.

After returning from Swarga-dwar, Muhammad Tughlaq conceived of a grand design to extend and improve cultivation. A Diwan called 'Diwan-i-Amir-i-Kohi' was set up to take charge of a territory 30 *kroh* by 30 *kroh* (roughly 100 kms, by 100 kms). He planned to extend cultivation in the area so that "one span of land would not remain uncultivated." The intention was to bring barren (*banjar*) land under cultivation, not uncultivable *(usar)* land, as Barani asserts. Simultaneously, whatever was being cultivated would be improved.

In the words of Barani, "thus wheat would be sown instead of barley, and sugarcane instead of wheat", and "grape and date would be planted instead of sugarcane."

Thus, the scheme had two aspects; one, to extend cultivation, and second, to improve the crops. Both would have led to the realisation of higher land-revenue. To implement the scheme, 100 *shiqadar* were appointed. They were honoured, and given horses, and large sums of money for giving agricultural loans *(sondhar)*. We are told that in this way, 70 lakh tankas and more were advanced by way of *sondhar*. Afif, who wrote in the time of Firuz Tughlaq, puts this figure still higher, at two crores.

Barani says that the entire scheme failed, and during three years, not a thousandth or hundredth part of wasteland was brought under cultivation. He ascribes this to the fact that the persons chosen to implement the scheme were incompetent. He calls them "greedy, impecunious men, without hope of salvation." Apparently, they had no understanding of local conditions, and spent the money meant on loans for their own expenses and needs.

If Muhammad bin Tughlaq had come back from his Gujarat expedition after suppressing the rebellion there, these men would have had to pay a heavy price. However, Muhammad bin Tughlaq died, and his successor, Firuz Tughlaq, wrote off the loans.

Nevertheless, the scheme cannot be called a total failure. The idea of extending and improving cultivation with the help of agricultural loans became a standard practice with later sultans, and became a part of the agricultural policy of the Mughals. Thus, both Alauddin Khalji and Muhammad bin Tughlaq helped in the evolution of an agrarian policy which matured fully under the Mughals.

iii. Rebellions and Changes in the Ruling Class

In order to present the image of a ruler who was confused, went from one project to another which emptied his treasures, and the consequent discontent and outbreak of rebellions which the sultan was unable to control, Barani has lumped together all the rebellions which took place in Muhammad bin Tughlaq's vast empire during a period of 26 years. However, in order to assess the true extent of Muhammad bin Tughlaq's successes and failures, we may divide his reign into three unequal parts, the first two consisting of ten years each, and the third of the remaining five to six years of his reign.

During the first phase (1224-35), Muhammad bin Tughlaq was engaged in consolidating the vast kingdom he had inherited. The only expansion was the conquest of Kampil in south Karnataka following Muhammad bin Tughlaq's march to crush the rebellion of his cousin, Gurshasp. There were rebellions in Multan and Lakhanauti, which were crushed. There was also a rebellion in Sindh (Sehwan) which was brought under control after some time. Despite the failure of his schemes of exodus to Deogiri, Khurasan and Karchil expeditions, and the token currency experiment, the Sultan's prestige remained high, as Ibn Battutah testifies. According to him, the ruler of Delhi was one of the four most powerful rulers of the world at that time, the other three being China, Iraq and the king of Uzbeks.

The second decade (1236-45) began badly with a rebellion in Mabar, and famine in the doab. The failure of the Mabar campaign where epidemic played a role, led to the loss of all the other southern states. Bengal was also lost. The Sultan made little effort to recover these distant areas, either because he lacked the resources in men and money, or because he felt that the control and direct administration of these areas from Delhi was an impossible task in the given circumstances. The only area which he considered important, and to which he held on to was Daultabad.

During the period, there were a series of rebellions in north India, and also in the Daultabad region which can be linked either to the discontent of the old nobles, or grasping revenue policies. What are called the *sadah* nobles also became disaffected during this period. Perhaps, the most important rebellion of the old nobles was by Ainul Mulk, who had been a close friend and associate of the Sultan, and been made governor of Awadh. He had provided the sultan with provisions while at Swarga-Dwar and had suppressed a rebellion at Kara (near Allahabad). Muhammad Tughlaq became suspicious of the growing popularity of Ainul Mulk who had also given shelter to some revenue defaulters. Hence, he issued orders for his transfer to Daultabad, which was the occasion of the rebellion. Although Muhammad bin Tughlaq ultimately pardoned Ainul Mulk, the conflict showed the deep division between the Indian and foreign elements. Ainul Mulk was an Indian, and the bulk of the forces of the wazir who was an enemy of Ainul Mulk were foreigner—Persians, Turks and Khurasanis. These divisions were aggravated further because Muhammad bin Tughlaq gave great patronage to foreigners whom he called *"aziz"* or friend, (pl. *aizza*) and to whom he gave lavish gifts.

Among the foreigners to whom Muhammad bin Tughlaq gave patronage were Mongols. Many of these had come to India as soldiers or lower grade officials. The lower grade officers came to be called *sadah*. *Sadah* or hundred (centurian) was the term used in the Mongol military for one who commanded a hundred men. But in India, the word *sadah* began to be used as a territorial divisions, to signify a hundred villages. This, apparently, was the basis of the pargana which emerges as an administrative unit around this time. The *sadah* amirs were, however, not all Mongols. Afghans and others were also to be found among them.

Muhammad bin Tughlaq's approach towards the nobility was, however, not based on racial, or on narrow religions considerations. He welcomed not only those families which had been settled in India for long, and had served previous rulers but also admitted to the service persons from the artisan or other classes/castes despised by the Turks, such as gardeners, barbers, cooks, weavers, wine-distillers, musicians, etc. Some of these were converts, and some were Hindus. Thus, Barani mentions Kishan Bazran Indri who was made governor of Sehwan (Sindh). Barani says that these people were given high status, offices and territories to govern. Thus, Najba, a singer, was given charge of Badaun, then Gujarat and Multan; Aziz Khammar, a wine-distiller, was given charge of Malwa. Their elevations to high posts was deeply resented by the old nobles, and by the *aizza*. It is not that these people were incompetent, or were still carrying on their old family/caste professions. They had evidently risen on the basis of merit. But they were not soldiers. Hence, they failed whenever they had to deal with rebellions. Barani not only severely critices Muhammad bin Tughlaq for appointing these low, ignoble people, but pours scorn on "the clerks and grain-merchants (*bania*) who could not distinguish the front (reins and accoutrements) of a horse from its tail."

Thus, Muhammad bin Tughlaq's nobility was very heterogeneous in character, and could not be an instrument on which the sultan could lean in times of difficulty. Even though the low-caste appointees, and many Turkish and Hindustani nobles, remained loyal, the Mongol and Afghan *sadah* amirs behaved differently. Muhammad bin Tughlaq also tried to induct into the administration members of the religious classes, especially the sufis. Towards this end, he even entered into matrimonial relations with some of them. However, most of the sufis wanted to keep aloof from the state, and did not welcome this. In anger, Muhammad bin Tughlaq gave drastic punishments and executed some of them. Barani says that he put many theologians (*ulema*), shaikhs, saiyyads, sufis and *qalandars* (wandering saints) to death. In retaliation, and for his association with the *yogis* etc., the qazis issued a *fatwa* making it legal for anyone to rebel against the Sultan. In order to counter this propaganda, Muhammad bin Tughlaq decided to seek a formal rescript from the Caliph, making his rule legal in the eyes of the orthodox. He found out that a relation of the Caliph of Baghdad who had been killed by Halaku, the Mongol chief, in 1258, was living at Cairo. Representatives of the Caliph, and a descendant of his, reached Delhi in 1339, and were given a lavish reception. Muhammad bin Tughlaq went so far as to substitute the name of the Abbasid caliph in his coins. Later, he also received a formal rescript (*manshur*) from the Caliph. But all this could hardly change the attitude of the orthodox elements towards him.

Some of the rebellions which took place during this period, such as the one at Kara, and another at Bidar, was because the Sultan had given the area on contract (*muqata*) to some persons on the basis of their promising large sums of money which, however, they failed to collect from the peasants. In the process, they tried to squeeze the local officials or the *sadah*. Rebellions in Malwa and Gujarat later on were also connected to this phenomenon.

Despite the Sultan's concern with these repeated rebellions, they were contained. The Sultan remained at Delhi during this period. That his prestige remained high is shown by the embassies he received during this period from leading countries, such as China, Egypt, Khurasana, Iraq, Transaoxiana, and even some African countries.

It was during the third phase (1346-51), that a series of rebellions broke out at Kulbarga and Malwa. A more serious rebellion broke out later at Gujarat, and at Bidar by Hasan Kangu. Muhammad bin Tughlaq decided to lead in personal the campaign against Gujarat because of its economic and strategic importance, although the rebellion was led by low grade *sadah* amirs. In his absence, Daultabad was lost and the Bahmani kingdom born. Muhammad bin Tughlaq remained in Gujarat for two-and-a-half years, spending the later years campaigning in Saurashtra and then moving to Thatta (lower Sindh) in pursuit of the rebel, Taghi, a former slave of his, who had been given shelter by the Jam of Thatta. Amazingly, in this rather futile campaign, he accepted the help of 5000 Mongols sent by Altun Bahadur, the ruler of Transoxiana. Muhammad bin Tughlaq died before reaching Thatta. Meanwhile, a council of regency set up by him functioned at Delhi. There were no rebellions in the north during the Sultan's prolonged absence.

Despite his many limitations, Muhammad bin Tughlaq bequeathed a large empire with a functioning administration to his successor. While his rash and hasty temperament, his suspicious nature, and giving excessive punishments added to his difficulties, his main problems arose from an empire which had become too large, and in which he tried to impose a uniform and highly centralized system of administration. Some of his experiments and reforms also had a long term significance. His experiment with a token currency was a bold step, but one which was much beyond his time. He did, however, indicate a direction for agricultural expansion and growth. Finally, he tried to take the first faltering steps towards a composite ruling class consisting of Hindus and Muslims. Even more importantly, he tried to rise above the narrow limitations of caste, inducting into service not only people of land-owning classes, but men belonging to low, or artisan classes.

7

REASSERTION OF A STATE BASED ON BENEVOLENCE—DISINTEGRATION OF THE DELHI SULTANAT

The long reign of Firuz Tughlaq (1351-88), a cousin of Muhammad Tughlaq, who succeeded him after he left the army in a state of disarray at Thatta, is a watershed in the history of the Delhi sultanat. Firuz Tughlaq tried to revive the tradition of a state based on benevolence, and the welfare of the people which had been sought to be established by Jalaluddin Khalji, as we have noted earlier. Firuz pursued a policy of conciliation, of trying to win over the sections—nobles, administrators, soldiers, clergymen, peasants etc. which had been alienated by Muhammad bin Tughlaq for one reason or another. After a number of military expeditions, which were not significantly successful, Firuz gave up warfare, and made the state more an instrument of development and welfare. Unfortunately, during the latter part of his reign, Firuz became more and more narrow in his understanding of religion. Lacking a broad philosophical base such as Muhammad Tughlaq had, he interpreted religion in a narrow sense, and indulged in acts of bigotry and oppression, against sections of both the Hindus and the Muslims. This weakened rather than strengthened his concept of a benevolent state. Finally, Firuz undertook a series of administrative reforms which brought him popularity in the immediate context, but weakened the central government in the long run.

i. Firuz's Concept of Benevolence, and Peoples' Welfare:

Firuz Tughlaq spells out his basic concept of benevolence in the *Fatuhat-i-Firuz Shahi*, a book which he is supposed to have written but of which only a portion is now available. Mentioning that in the past times, much "Muslim" blood had been shed, and varieties of tortures been used which he describes, such as cutting of hands, feet, ears and noses; plucking out the eyes, breaking bones, burning and flaying people alive etc., Firuz goes on to say that he had resolved that during his reign "no Muslim blood shall be shed without just cause or excuse, that there shall be no torture, and that no human beings shall be mutilated."

Firuz's orders in the matter covered both Muslims and non-Muslims, though Firuz prefaces his orders by saying that as a good Muslim, his concern was to prohibit all practices contrary to the Muslim holy law, the *shara*. The *shara* did, of course, sanction cutting off the hands and feet of robbers, and punishment for retaliation for a crime committed against an individual. We do not know if Firuz's prohibitions extended against such punishments. Perhaps, his orders were restricted to political, and in some cases, financial offences.

Firuz says that the purpose of giving drastic punishments in previous times was "to terrorise the people so that fear of the government gripped their hearts and the tasks of government were carried out (undisturbed)." Firuz asserts that the fear and prestige of the government did not decline by abrogating drastic punishments. In other words, people were drawn to the government without fear of punishment.

The basic concept of benevolence, that the state was to be based on the willing acceptance of the people, rather than fear or threats of violence, had wider implications, especially in a society where the large majority consisted of non-Muslims.

As a part of his policy of conciliation, Firuz publicly destroyed the documents on the basis of which advance of money amounting to two crore tankas had been made to officials by Muhammad bin Tughlaq in order to expand and improve cultivation in the doab, but most of which had been misappropriated. In a somewhat childish manner, Firuz Tughlaq asked those who had been punished by Muhammad bin Tughlaq by their eyes, noses, hands and feet being cut off, to write letters of good-will which were put in a box and deposited at the head of Muhammad bin Tughlaq's tomb.

Likewise, no large scale punishments were given to those who had joined Ahmad Ayaz, the favourite of Muhammad bin Tughlaq, in putting up a rival prince on the throne at Delhi while Firuz was at Thatta. If Firuz had his way, he would have excused even Ahmad Ayaz, but his leading supporters would not permit it. However, no attempt was made to recover the jewels and gold which Ahmad Ayaz had distributed to gather a following—a practice which was in sharp contrast to what Ghiyasuddin Tughlaq had done at the time of his accession, adopting harsh methods to disgorge funds from those who had benefitted from the liberality of Khusrau Malik.

Another step taken by Firuz Tughlaq was to restore the rent-free lands (*inam, idrar*) granted to theologians, the learned and the weaker sections but which had been resumed by the previous rulers and included in the royal crown-lands (*khalisa*). We are told that these grants were, in fact, increased.

It was due to these mild methods that in the exaggerated language of Barani, "the administration became stable, all the tasks of government became firm, and all men, high and low, were satisfied, and the subjects, Muslims and Hindus, made content, and everyone busied himself in his own persuits."

All contemporary writers refer to the general prosperity in Firuz Shah's long reign of 40 (lunar years), and the cheapness of commodities. Shams Siraj Afif, the biographer of Firuz, says that while food grains were cheap during the reign of Alauddin due to his strict regulations, there was all round cheapness in Firuz Shah's reign without any effort on his part! This prosperity was, according to him, shared by everyone, including traders and artisans, because production and wages increased from year to year. Referring obviously to previous practices, we are told that regulations had been made that "brocades, silks and goods required for the royal establishments were to be purchased at the market price, and the money paid." Remarking that all homes were replete with grains, property, horses and furniture, and no women was without her ornaments, Afif goes on to say that there was such all round prosperity that even poor men could marry off their daughters at a young age! The obvious implication was that the girls were no longer needed to supplement the family income.

Regarding the peasants or the *raiyat*, Afif says that he was told that previously "it was the practice to leave the *raiyat* one cow and take the rest." Firuz tried to rectify this situation by abolishing all taxes not sanctioned by the *shara*, and by preparing a new valuation (*jama*) which was based on produce, not measurement. We shall discuss this when we take up Firuz Shah's administrative and agrarian reforms.

Firuz Shah's benevolent and humanitarian efforts extended to repairing and rehabilitating the mosques and the *madrasas* attached to them. The grants (*idrar*) of the teachers were raised from 100-200 tankas to 400 or 500, or 700 or even 1000 tankas. Likewise, the students who earlier did not receive even 10 tankas as stipends, were given grants of 100 or 200 or 300 tankas.

Similarly, many sufi *khanqahs* which had been repaired were rehabilitated and villages assigned for their upkeep. Grants were also made to the old men and women, widows, orphans and the physically handicapped. An attempt was made to set up a kind of an unemployment bureau for the unemployed, and to provide state help for the marriage of girls of respectable families. These measures were largely meant to benefit Muslims, especially those among them who were living at or near Delhi. A reform which was of more general benefit was Firuz Tughlaq's setting up a hospital (*darus-shafa*) at Delhi for free treatment for all. Although Delhi had a number of hospitals from the time of Muhammad bin Tughlaq, the extension of state patronage to hospitals must be considered a positive factor.

In the medieval context where warfare and violence were almost the norm, the emphasis on the principle of benevolence, even though with limitations, was a valuable contribution for which Firuz must be given credit.

ii. Military Expeditions of Firuz and the Impact of their limited success.

When Firuz Tughlaq ascended the throne at Thatta in 1351, the Sultanat was faced with a crisis. The southern states, which had been brought within the ambit of the Sultanat by Ghiyasuddin and Muhammad bin Tughlaq, had fallen away, followed by the loss of Daultabad. There were rebellions in Gujarat and Sindh. Bengal, too, had once again asserted its independence.

Neither by temperament nor by training was Firuz Tughlaq cut out to be a great warrior or military leader. He did, however, lead two campaigns to Bengal, raided Orissa and Nagarkot, and led a campaign into lower Sindh. None of them added to the territories of the Delhi sultanat. At the same time, nor did the territories of the Delhi sultanat diminish further.

Bengal Campaigns

The two Bengal campaign of 1353-54 and 1359-60 were aimed at recovering Bengal which had declared independence of Delhi. On both occasion, Firuz led a large army which was joined by local *rais*, such as the powerful *rais* of Gorakhpur and Champaran.

On account of their support, the armies of Delhi swelled to 90,000 horse. On both occasions, the Bengal sovereigns, Haji Ilyas during the first expedition, and his son, Sikandar, during the second, retreated, taking shelter at Ikdala which was a strong fort surrounded by a broad moat linked by a canal to a river nearby. On both occasion, Firuz was unable to storm the fort. Considering the fort to be impregnable, and unwilling to wait outside it any longer in view of the approaching monsoon which would have made all roads impassable and the climate, unhealthy Firuz opened negotiations for peace. After exchange of costly presents, *status quo* and a policy of mutual peace was agreed upon. Afif's story that Firuz refused to attack the fort because it would lead to further bloodshed, and the dishonouring of Muslim women was, perhaps, the official explanation put out.

Jajnagar (Orissa) and Nagarkot Campaigns:

On his way back from Bengal during the second expedition, Firuz halted at Jaunpur, and from there marched on Orissa. The purpose of the expedition was to reassert Delhi's overlordship over the region which had been subjugated following the expedition of Prince Muhammad bin Tughlaq, during the reign of Ghiyasuddin Tughlaq. The ruler had also withheld tribute when Bengal asserted its independence from Delhi. Worse, he had sided with the ruler of Bengal in his conflict with Delhi. Firuz's march became almost a pleasure hunt because the Orissa ruler avoided conflict. Ultimately, a truce was patched up, with the Orissa ruler agreeing to pay regular tribute including a certain number of elephants which were highly valued by Firuz. The return journey was uneventful, except that Afif tells us that Firuz wandered about, lost in the jungles for six months before returning.

After a stay of four years at Delhi, Firuz decided to undertake a campaign against Nagarkot in Kangra which was reputed to be one of the strongest forts in the country. Perhaps, it was also considered to be an occasion to compensate for the hardly successful campaigns in Bengal. At first, Firuz had decided to move against Daultabad, and moved upto Bayana for the purpose. But wiser counsel had prevailed. The Rai of Nagarkot retreated, and shut himself in the fort which was besieged by the invading forces. The countryside was, as usual, put up to plunder. After six month of siege, the two sides entered into negotiations. The Rai made a personal submission, and Firuz placed his hand on the shoulder of the Rai, bestowed on him robes of honour and a *chatr*, and sent him back, laden with presents. In return, the Rai accepted the Sultan's overlordship as before, and sent many offerings and horses of priceless worth.

There is no reference to the destruction of any temples during this expedition. In fact, Afif mentions that Firuz visited the Jwalamukhi temple which was on the way to Nagarkot, but he indignantly refutes the rumour "put out by some Hindus that during the visit he (Firuz) held a golden umbrella over the idol (in fact, the flame)." No attempt, however, was made to desecrate it.

The Thatta Campaign (1365-67)

The last campaign in which Firuz spent two-and-a-half years was a campaign against Thatta in lower Sindh to punish its local rulers, called Jam and Bahbina. The precise purpose of the campaign is not clear. We are told that the governor of Multan had many complaints against them—hardly sufficient for Firuz himself undertaking to punish them. Perhaps, the campaign was concerned with the recurrence of Mongol activities. The previous year, a Mongol army had reached upto Dipalpur, but retreated on the arrival of armies from Delhi. Jam and Bahbina were suspected to be in close touch with the Mongols. Firuz must apparently have feared that Mongol control over lower Sindh would endanger Punjab, and also disrupt the trade down the river Indus.

Some modern historians have dubbed the Thatta campaign as the most mismanaged campaign. Firuz Shah marched with an army which was supported by a flotilla of 5000 boats, itself an index of the amount of river trade along the Indus. Arrived at Thatta, Firuz encountered stiff resistance which he had not expected. Meanwhile, three-fourths of the horses died due to an epidemic, and there was acute shortage of food in his camp. With defeat staring him in the face, Firuz retreated to Gujarat, but lost his way in the Rann of Kutch due to the treachery of his guides. After great sufferings, the army reached Ahmedabad. Two crores were taken out of the treasury to re-equip the army, but many soldiers took advantage of the situation to return to Delhi. Firuz considered it counter-productive to try to stop them. But when he returned to Thatta with his reduced forces, he was unable to capture the two parts of the city which were situated on opposite sides of a broad river. Hence, he asked the wazir, Khan-i-Jahan, to send reinforcements. It was only after their arrival that Jam and Bahbina entered into negotiations and submitted. They were treated with honour, and taken with Firuz to Delhi. In their place, lower Sindh was assigned to a son of the Jam, and to Tamachi, the brother of Bahbina.

After his return from Thatta, Firuz decided not to lead any further campaigns, but to devote himself to peace. A last effort was made when Firuz announced his decision to invade Daultabad, but he allowed Khan-i-Jahan to "dissuade" him from an enterprise which would lead to shedding of further Muslim blood!

Firuz's love of peace, and his reluctance to shed Muslim blood have little to do with the limited success of his various military expeditions, and show his incompetence as a leader. However, these failures themselves became a blessing in disguise. Deterred from undertaking any more military adventures, he now presided over a state which was territorially more cohesive and managable. Even in its reduced size, it was by no means small, consisting more or less of the territories bequeathed by Alauddin Khalji at the time of his death (but excluding Daultabad annexed during the last few years of his reign). Firuz was lucky that unlike the previous rulers, he did not have to face recurrent Mongol attacks on his territories.

Thus, Firuz was able to concentrate on the tasks of consolidation and development which brought an unprecedented level of prosperity, at least to the central areas of his empire.

iii. Reorganisation of the Nobility and the Administration

As we have noted, Firuz was keen to conciliate all sections, including the nobility. He wanted a nobility which was stable and cohesive. There had been a lot of instability in the nobility since the death of Iltutmish, successive rulers trying to constitute a new nobility loyal to them. The efforts of Jalaluddin Khalji and Ghiyasuddin Tughlaq to take a kinder attitude towards the earlier nobility had been frustrated. Firuz Tughlaq tried to cherish the nobility which had remained loyal to Muhammad bin Tughlaq. Thus, he appointed Khan-i-Jahan Maqbul who had been trained by Muhammad bin Tughlaq as the wazir, and left much of the work of the administration to him. Other senior nobles, such as Tatar Khan, were also honoured.

Unlike Muhammad bin Tughlaq, Firuz had no special fondness for foreigners. He made this clear at the outset when many foreigners from Herat, Sistan, Aden, Egypt etc. had been camping at Thatta, waiting to hear from Muhammad bin Tughlaq offering them employment, or asking them to meet him. They were given travelling money by Firuz, and asked to go back. At the same time, Firuz did not try to induct into the nobility men from the lower classes, either Muslims and Hindus, whom Barani had denounced as "mean and ignoble."

Firuz awarded extremely high salaries to the nobles. He gave to his Khans and Maliks for their personal income, salaries of 4,00,000 tankas; 6,00,000 tankas, and 8,00,000 tankas. His wazir, Khan-i-Jahan, received a salary of 13,00,000 tankas, and additional grants were given for each son or daughter born to him. These salaries were given in terms of grants of *iqtas*. Right at the beginning of his reign, Firuz had a new valuation (*jama*) of the income from the lands made. This *jama* was not revised during the rest of his reign. The nobles, therefore, were the beneficiaries of any extension and improvement of cultivation which took place in their holdings during the period.

Finally, Firuz tried to give to his nobility a hereditary character. In his *Fatuhat*, Firuz says, "When a person holding an office died, I transferred his office and his dignities to his son, and the status, perquisites and dignities of the office were not reduced in any way." We have some examples of the application of this law of heredity, the most notable example being that of Khan-i-Jahan Maqbul whose son, Jauna Khan, succeeded him in his office as wazir after his death in 1368-69. However, this was done when Jauna Khan asserted that Firuz had given a written undertaking, apparently at the time of Khan-i-Jahan's accession, that the post of wizarat would remain in his family as long as he reigned. Another such case was that of Zafar Khan, governor of Gujarat, who died in 1370-71 and was succeeded in his post and title by his son, Darya Khan. But Darya Khan was ousted from the post soon after. The rule of heredity was not applied by Firuz to any of the other senior posts. Perhaps, what Firuz implied was that the *iqta* of any incumbent would not be transferred, but granted to his sons after his death. Such an attempt had recurred whenever there was any weakness in the central government, for it strengthened the position of the nobles *vis-a-vis* the Sultan.

Next to the nobility, the army was the next most important element in the administration. Like the nobility, Firuz wanted to have an army which was drawn from elements which had a tradition of soldiering, and which had a long term stake in the stability of the state. Hence, he ordered that the soldiers of the central army should be paid not in cash, but by grants of villages (*wajh*) in the neighbourhood of Delhi and the doab. He thus conceded the demand put forward by the Turkish soldiers and partly conceded by

Balban, but sternly rejected by Alauddin Khalji. We are told that eighty per cent of the central army were paid by means of grants of villages (*wajh*). The rest which included irregular (*ghair-wajahi*) soldiers were to be paid in cash from the treasury or by assignments on the *iqtas* held by the nobles. However, the soldiers could obtain only a part of the grants from the *iqtas* held by the nobles.

In order to emphasize the hereditary and family character of soldiering, Firuz ordered that if an army man died, his village would go permanently to his son; if he had no son to his son-in-law; if he had no son-in-law, to his slave, and if he had no slave, then permanently to his women. Later, Firuz issued an order that if a soldier became old, he could be deputized by his son, if he had no son by his son-in-law, if he had no son-in-law by his slave. "The veteran may thus remain at home at ease, and the young ride forth in their strength."

It is hardly possible to defend these measures. Even then, an attempt to create a corp of families whose profession would be soldiering might have succeeded if Firuz had not undermined the system of *dagh* or branding of horses to ensure that sub-standard horses were not produced for service. Normally, horses had to be produced for branding within a year. But many soldiers were not able to do so and, at the instance of the deputy muster-master, Firuz granted them an extension of 51 days, and then, another two months. Even this was waived on the ground that the soldier had to go to the village at the instance of the officers to collect their salaries. Adopting a wholly wrong view of generosity, Firuz once even gave a golden tanka to a distraught soldier so that he could bribe the clerk to pass his sub-standard mount before the year ended!

In the later part of his reign, Firuz seems to have realised that by his mistaken view of generosity, he had undermined the efficiency of the central army. Hence, he ordered the great *iqtadars* and officers to capture slaves whenever they were at war, and to pick out and send the best of them for the service of the court. This was extended to chiefs who, according to practice, sent annual presents to the ruler. In this way, 180,000 slaves were collected. While some of them spent their time in reading and in religious studies, and 12,000 of them became artisans of various types and were dispersed into many parganas, a large central corp of slaves was brought together as an armed guard. This was in addition to the central army of 80,000 horse. A separate muster-master, a separate treasury and a separate diwan was set up for this corp of slaves who consisted mostly of converted Hindus.

The efficiency of the corp of slaves was not tested in battle by Firuz, but to the extent that it was a counter to the power of the nobility and the standing army, it created a duality in the administration, and went counter to Firuz's attempt to provide stability by depending upon a cohesive nobility and an army drawn from a band of military-minded families. It was, therefore, no surprise that conflict between the two erupted even before Firuz closed his eyes.

In the field of general administration, Firuz was fortunate in having an able and energetic officer in the person of Khan-i-Jahan Maqbul whom the Sultan used to call 'brother', and to whom the Sultan extended full support. He went so far to say that he (Khan-i-Jahan) was the real sultan. On his part, Khan-i-Jahan never exceeded his powers, and kept the sultan fully informed. He was also scrupulously honest. Although he did take presents from the governors of provinces, he entered them in the royal treasury. He was also strict in collecting government dues. His powers, however, were restricted by the Auditor (*mustaufi*) and by the Accountant-General (*mushrif*) both of whom had direct access to the Sultan. Sometimes, it led to bitter disputes in which the sultan mediated.

Another powerful noble at Firuz's court was Bashir Sultani, the *Ariz-i-Malik* (Muster-Master). He had been a slave of Firuz and accumulated a lot of money by dishonest means. Khan-i-Jahan shielded him for his corrupt practices. When Bashir died, he left 13 crores. Firuz confiscated nine crores on the ground that Bashir had been his slave, and distributed the rest among his sons.

The tasks of administration were continued with reasonable efficiency after the death of Khan-i-Jahan by his son, Jauna Shah, or Khan-i-Jahan II. But Khan-i-Jahan II was ambitious, and tried to build a party of his own supporters while the powers of Firuz gradually declined with advancing age. This was another cause of conflict after the death of Firuz.

iv. Developmental Activities—Agrarian & Urban

Firuz Tughlaq carried forward the traditions of Muhammad bin Tughlaq in the field of agricultural development. At the outset of his reign, he appointed Khwaja Hisamuddin Junaid to settle the revenues afresh. The Khwaja toured the country for six years with a team of officials, and made a new valuation (*jama*). The amount, six crores and seventy-five lakhs tankas, was fixed on the basis of "inspection", i.e., rough estimation, and was not altered during the rest of Firuz Tughlaq's reign. Although the standard share to be paid by the cultivator is nowhere stated, the basis of assessment was not measurement but sharing. This meant that the benefit of any growth (or decline) would be shared by the peasant and the State. Since the bulk of the land-revenue had been granted to the nobles as *iqta*, they were likely to be the principal beneficiaries of any development. As we shall see, this is exactly what happened.

In between his Bengal campaigns, Firuz founded the city of Hissar-Firuza (modern Hissar), and decided to dig two canals to bring water to the city from the Sutlaj and the Jamuna. These canals which were about 100 miles long, joined together near Karnal and provided plenty of water to the city of Hissar. We are told that previously the area was so arid that merchants coming from Iraq and Khurasan had to pay four jitals for a pitcher of water. But now the peasants could cultivate two crops, the spring (*kharif*) and winter (*rabi*). This canal which had become choked up, was repaired by Akbar. Later, in the time of Shah Jahan, it was extended upto Delhi. In the 19th century, the British repaired and extended it, and it became the basis of the Western Jamuna Canal. In Firuz's time, the entire tract of land along the canal was irrigated, and led to the expansion of cultivation in the old villages, and new villages came up. Other canals were also dug by Firuz. Contemporary writers give details of six of them. Most of these canals were in the present Haryana area. One canal also carried water to the city of Ferozpur—south of Delhi founded by Firuz. Afif says that the entire areas from the river Sutlej to Koil (modern Aligarh) became fully cultivated. In the words of Afif, "there were four villages to every kos (two miles) in the area, as in the *shiq* of Samana." An effort was also made to improve the cropping pattern in the area so that wheat and sugar-cane began to be cultivated in place of inferior crops.

It was perhaps the prosperity of this area, and the resulting affluence of the nobility, which is reflected in the writings of Barani and Afif. Of course, other sections, such as the peasants, the artisans, and traders of the area also benefited. But in places distant from Delhi, such as Sindh, according to a contemporary, grain-prices were unstable and wages of the artisans extremely high. We have no information of the situation prevailing in other areas.

Firuz also benefited from the agrarian prosperity of this region. He brought together a set of learned men and *mullahs* who decreed that for his pains of digging the canals and bringing water, the sultan was entitled to an extra charge of 10 per cent or *haqq-i-sharb*. This was levied from the old, villages where cultivation had grown, and was a part of the personal income (*khalisa*) of the sultan. The normal land-revenue of the new villages was also part of the sultan's personal income which amounted to two lakh tankas. This was distributed by the sultan in charity to the religious divines and learned people.

Besides canals, Firuz also built many dams (*bunds*) for purposes of irrigation. He was also very fond of planting orchards, and is supposed to have planted 1200 gardens around Delhi, after paying the price to those in whose property or tax-free (*inam*) lands they lay. The gardens included 30 which had been commenced by Alauddin. We are told that most of the orchards grew black and white grapes and also dry fruits, and that the sultan's income from these was 180,000 tankas.

In the latter years of his reign, Firuz tried to bring the agricultural taxation system in line with the *shara*. Thus, he abolished all the taxes not sanctioned by the *shara*. Twenty-one such taxes which were abolished have been listed by contemporaries. These included the *ghari* (house tax) of which we hear during the time of Alauddin. Many others were cesses on produce payable at the market. It is difficult to say how far the abolition of these taxes benefited the peasants, or how effective the abolition was, because many of them had to be abolished by Akbar, and again by Aurangzeb!

As part of his policy of levying only taxes sanctioned by *shara*, Firuz insisted upon payment of *jizyah* by the non-Muslims. Although *jizyah* was levied by the earlier rulers, it was treated as a part of the land-tax (*kharaj*), and was indistinguishable from it. Firuz was the first ruler who collected *jizyah* as a separate tax apart from land-revenue. To some extent, it replaced *ghari* or house tax which was also a tax on individuals.

Firuz built a number of towns around Delhi, two of them, Hissar-Feroza and Ferozpur having been mentioned earlier. He also built or renovated Jaunpur in East UP, and built a new capital, Ferozabad, along the Jamuna. Only the fort, now called Kotla Feroz Shah, has survived from this town. The eastern part of this town extended up to the Ridge, the town itself being five kos or ten miles, including some parts of what later became Shahjahanabad, or the present Old Delhi. The many towns which Firuz built reflected a felt need. They reflected the agricultural development of the area which needed new towns (*qasbas*) as their grain-markets. The new towns also became centres of trade and handicrafts, some of the 12,000 slaves trained as artisans being posted in these towns.

Thus, Firuz's concept of development, both agricultural and urban, was strikingly modern.

Firuz was also a great builder. He set up a public works department which repaired many old buildings and mausoleums. Thus, he repaired the Qutb Minar a storey of which had been destroyed by lightening, and restored the Mosque and the tombs of Iltutmish and Alauddin near it. He also repaired the Shamsi Tank (south of Qutb Minar), and the Hauz-i-Alai (present Hauz Khas), the water-channel to which had been choked.

Firuz Tughlaq also had two Ashokan pillars transported from Meerut and its neighbourhood, installing one of them at the Kotla at Firozabad, and another at a hunting lodge on the Ridge. He also built many inns for the use of the travellers.

Firuz mentions his orthodox measures in the *Fatuhat*, but does not mention having forbidden wine bibbling. Interestingly, Afif lists the wine department as one of the departments (*karkhanas*) of the state. Firuz was also fond of music and songs to which he listened during the festivals of the two Ids and after the Friday prayers—a practice which he continued till the end of his reign. He also celebrated Shab Barat with great pomp. These were practices which were banned as being anti-Islamic by Aurangzeb later on.

However, as Firuz grew older, he became narrower, even bigoted in his religious approach. Although he was reputed to be a disciple of the liberal sufi saint, Fariduddin Ganj Shakar of Ajodhan, the warrior saint Salar Masud Ghazi appeared to him in a dream when the Sultan visited his tomb at Bahraich in 1374-75. Much moved, the Sultan had his head shaved as a mark of submission to him. Many nobles followed suit. Thereafter, the Sultan decided to forbid all practices which were against the *shara*, banned all taxes not sanctioned by *shara*, and warned the revenue officials not to realise any such taxes. He also ordered all paintings with human figures erased from his palace, and forbade the use of gold and silver vesseles for dinner. He also banned clothes of pure silk or pure brocade, or where human figures had been painted.

One of the worst instance of bigotry on the part of Firuz at this time was that he publicly burnt a brahman on the charge that he openly conducted idol-worship at his house in which both Hindus and Muslims participated, and that he had converted a Muslim woman. He also insisted on collecting *jizya* from the brahmans who had been exempted from this tax till then. He refused to relent even though the brahmans from the four cities of Delhi went on hunger strike. Finally, the Hindus of the city agreed to pay themselves the brahmans' share of the *jizyah*. We do not know whether this arrangement was extended to other towns.

In the *Fatuhat*, Firuz says that while the Hindus who paid *jizyah* were protected people, and their property was safeguarded as also freedom of worship, they had started to build new temples which was against teh *shara*. He had such temples razed. He includes in this a temple in village Malwa near Delhi on the ground that the Hindus had built a *hauz* (tank) where a festival was held to which Hindu men and women and even Muslims used to go. Similarly, he destroyed new temples built in the villages of Salehpur and in gasba Gohana.

In his eagerness to serve the *shara*, Firuz inflicted death penalty on the leaders of the Ismaili group of Shias. He also inflicted a similar punishment on a number of Muslims who in a sufistic manner, had gone against the orthodox beliefs. In his orthodoxy, he even banned Muslim women going to the tomb of saints outside Delhi, as it would expose them to licencious people.

There is, however, no evidence to show that despite individual acts of intolerance, Firuz went agaisnt the concept of broad religious freedom granted to the *dhimmis* or Hindu subjects. Nor can the age of Firuz be considered one of growing intolerance. In fact, this was the age when the largest numbher of Sanskrit works on music, medicine etc. were translated into Persian. Hindu chiefs were treated with respect by Firuz, and three of them were even allowed to sit on the floor in his Court, which considered a rare honour. Firuz established an office *hajib-i-hinduan* or an office probably to deal with the Hindu office holders coming to the court from the provinces.

Nevertheless, Firuz's occasional acts of intolerance, and the importnace given by him to theologians and men of religion, to the exclusion of others, tended to strengthen the position of the orthodox ulemas, and to that extent, weaken the concept of a benevolent policy based on peoples' welfare and broad religious freedom. Firuz also reversed the trend towards a composite ruling class, consisting of Muslims and Hindus, a trend which had been started by Muhammad bin Tughlaq. This was resumed in a cautious manner by the Lodis, but was adopted in a real sense only with the coming of Akbar.

v. Disintegration of the Delhi Sultanat—Its causes:

Even before Firuz Tughlaq closed his eyes, the Sultanat of Delhi began to disintegrate. First there was a struggle for power between Prince Muhammad, the eldest surviving son of Firuz, and the wazir Khan-i-Jahan II. Irince Muhammad managed to win over Firuz to his side, and ousted Khan-i-Jahan. He was given all the paraphenalia of royalty by Firuz, and made joint-sovereign. However, this was not to the liking of the slaves of Firuz, who numbered almost 100,000. In the struggle that followed, Firuz foolishly sided with the slaves, and Prince Muhammad was ousted. Soon, Firuz died (1388), and a struggle for the Crown began between his sons and grand-sons. The corp of slaves tried to play the king-maker but failed, and were defeated and dispersed. A number of princes sat on the throne for a brief time till Nasiruddin Mahmud succeeded in 1394. He managed to remain on the throne till the Tughlaq dynasty was displaced in 1412. Meanwhile, provincial governors had begun to assert their independence, the first to do so being the governor of Gujarat. The Khokhars of the Punjab followed suit, followed by Malwa and Khandesh. Soon after, Khwaja-i-Jahan, the wazir of Nasiruddin Mahmud, got the privilege of governing all districts from Kannauj to Bihar. Thus was the kingdom of Jaunpur born. During this time, various Hindu chiefs had started withholding land-revenue, so that a wit observed "The orders of the king of the world (title of the Sultan of Delhi) extend from Delhi to Palam."

The disintegration of the Delhi sultanat was completed by Timur who sacked Delhi and the neighbouring areas in 1398-99. Although Timur's son had conquered Uchch and Dipalpur in 1396-97, and besieged Multan, no effort had been made by the rulers of Delhi to meet this threat, or resist the invasion of Timur. As is well known, Timur not only spread death and destruction at Delhi and its neighbourhood, but, according to his usual practice, carried away a large number of slaves including Indian stone-cutters and masons etc. to beautify his buildings at Samarqand. He also annexed the districts of Lahore, Dipalpur, and Multan to his kingdom. This provided a basis for Babar's claim later on. Apart from this, Timur's invasion had little political consequences.

*****

No individual sultan can be held responsible for the downfall of the Delhi sultanat. As we have seen, regional factors of disintegration were strong in medieval India. There were also numerous powerful chiefs who either had a clan-following of their own, or had strong links with particular areas. They were always ready to rebel when they found any weakness in the Central government.

The Turkish sultans tried to counter these elements of disintegration first by collecting a corp of slaves, and creating a nobility completely dependent on the sultan. The main instrument of this

devise was the *iqta* system. However, the sultans found it difficult
to control the powerful and ambitious nobles even among this limited
group, many of whom wanted to carve out their own independent
spheres of authority. Thus, it was always difficult to control governors of distant places such as Bengal, Sindh, Gujarat, Daultabad
etc. Attempts of successive sultans to have a nobility based on racial antecedents (Balban), or personal loyalty checked by spies
(Alauddin Khalji) or a dispersed nobility (Mahmud bin Tughlaq)
failed. Hence, it is no surprise that Firuz's attempt to build a small
nobility based to a large extent on the principle of heredity also
failed.

In this situation, religion was hardly of help because the main
conflict, once the Sultanat had been established, was not between
Hindus and Muslims, but between Muslims and Muslims. The slo-
gan of religion was, however, used to justify the plunder of the
Hindu rajas, and of the peasantry as a whole.

The recruitment of the army also created a problem. Once the
sultans of Delhi had been cut off from West and Central Asia, they
could no longer hope to recruit Turkish and other soldiers from
that area. They had, therefore, to fall upon (a) Afghans many of
whom had settled in India; (b) descendents of Turkish soldiers who
had come to India, mainly at the time of occupation; (c) Mongols
and Muslims converts; and (d) Hindus belonging to what might
be called the martial communities (Rajputs, Jats etc.). Each of these
sections had their own problems. Firuz tried to give preference to
the descendents of Turks and Mongols by giving them a hereditary
character. He also recruited converted Muslims in his corp of slaves.
Neither proved a success. The hereditary soldiers proved inefficient,
and the corp of slaves selfish and disloyal. Each of these groups
were also antagonistic to each other.

Another problem facing the sultans was that of succession. Even
when the nobles were willing to accept that the successor to a successful ruler should be drawn from his progeny, there was no rule
whereby the eldest son could succeed. This led to struggles for succession in which ambitious nobles found an opportunity to further
their own interests.

8

GOVERNMENT AND ADMINISTRATION UNDER THE DELHI SULTANAT (13TH—14TH CENTURIES)

The machinery of administration as it evolved under the Delhi sultanat was derived from the Abbasid and following it, the Ghaznavid and the Seljukid systems of administration. It was also influenced by the Iranian system of administration, and the situation in India and Indian traditions. Both West Asia, including Iran, and India had a long tradition of rule by a monarch assisted by a council of ministers. Hence, we find that some of the departments of government, or even officers, were old institutions under a new name. However, the Turks were also able to evolve a number of new institutions and concepts which provided a basis for centralization of power and authority of a type which had not existed in India earlier.

i. The Sultan

According to a number of thinkers, the institution of monarchy was not an Islamic institution, but one which emerged gradually due to circumstances. The original Islamic concept of government in Islam was that of the Imam who was chosen by the faithful, lived a life of simplicity, and combined in his person both political and spiritual authority. The collapse of the Abbasid Caliphate led to the rise of sultans who were only secular leaders. In course of time, the post of the sultan began to be elevated. He was not only the pivot of administration, commander-in-chief of the armed forces, and the ultimate court of appeal in all judicial cases. He was the centre of society and politics, and held a magnificent court.

He had great prestige and was the source of honour and patronage so that a large number of persons, including scholars, musicians, poets, religious divines etc. flocked to his court. This aura
of power and prestige made many thinkers to ascribe divine attributes to the king. According to Hindu ideas, the ruler was 'a
God in human shape.' Iranian ideas, which deeply influenced Islamic thinking on the subject, also made the office of the king divine. According to Barani, the heart of a monarch was a mirror of
God, that is, it reflected the wishes of God so that the actions of a
king could not be questioned. It was in order to emphasize these
aspects that Balban assumed the title of *Zill-Allah* (shadow of God),
and introduced the ceremonies of *sijda and pabos* (prostration on
the ground, bending down to touch one's feet), ceremonies which,
according to the *shara,* were meant only for Allah.

Two questions arise: was the medieval sultan an autocrat without any limitations on his powers; second, what was the institutional basis of the centralization achieved by the Turkish rulers in
India? It has been rightly pointed out that unrestricted individual
despotism is a myth in the sense that in a civil society every individual, howsoever powerful, had to take into account the opinions,
aspirations and ambitions of the group around him without whose
support he could not function. He had also to ensure at least the
passive support of the population. But the point at issue is whether there were any institutional limitations on an individual ruler.
According to both Hindu and Muslim thinking, religion was the
major institutional check on misuse of power by a monarch. The
ruler was required to subserve the broad purposes prescribed by
religion, and to function within the ethical and moral norms prescribed by it. According to some thinkers, a ruler who violated these
norms could be removed from power by the people, supported and
backed by the religious leaders. But there was no complete agreement in the matter, some thinkers leaving the matter in the hands
of God. In practice, while the ruler paid obeisance to the
Dharamashastras, or *shara* in the case of a Muslim ruler, he was given
a wide latitude with regard to his political functions. On balance,
while a number of unrestrained tyrants did arise from time to time,
the moral influence exercised by religion on political authority should
not be understimated.

In the western world, apart from the Church, the major institutional check on royal absolutism was a hereditary nobility. Such a
hereditary nobility did not exist in the case of the Turks. The ruler
was free to appoint anyone as an amir, and vest him with vast

military and administrative powers. The basis of this was the *iqtadari* system. This system which can be traced back to the Seljukids, seems to have subsequently become universal in all the Islamic states which arose. As we have seen, this gave the grantee considerable administrative and military power, but he did not acquire any hereditary rights in land, and could be transferred by the sultan almost at will. A change of dynasties always meant a large scale removal of the former *iqtadars*. Thus, when Jalaluddin Khalji, after his accession to the throne, enquired about the old nobles, it was found that many prominent nobles of Balban's time were living in poverty and want, following their removal from offices and the loss of their *iqtas*.

Another institution which, for some time, augmented the power and authority of the sultans was the institution of slavery. This gave even greater opportunity to the sultans to advance those individuals whom they liked and who were completely dependent on them. But the conflict between the *Chahalgani* Turkish slave-officers and the others after the death of Iltutmish eroded it as a political system, and it gradually fell into disuse. It was revived by Firuz Tughlaq, but on balance, its role was more negative than positive. Personal slavery continued, but it had little political role. Hence, the political importance of slavery during the Delhi sultanat should not be over emphasized, except in the early phase.

The unprecedented personal power which many sultans, such as Balban and Alauddin Khalji were able to gain, was limited by two factors. There was no universally accepted basis of succession among rulers in Islam. The principle of election had been whittled down to justify nomination by a successful ruler. However, this depended upon the nobility, and the military capacity of the person nominated. Since there was no established system of primogeniture (the eldest son succeeding), even nomination left the field open for rival claimants. In a number of cases, all such claimants were brushed aside, and one of the nobles, seen to be energetic and efficient, elevated himself to the throne, and was accepted by the other nobles. This system did, to some extent, weaken the prestige and authority of *monarchy* since any competent military officer could hope to acquire it in favourable circumstances. But, on balance, the problem of succession did not weaken the Turkish *system of government*, except for short periods, since a weak successor was always replaced by an efficient and energetic one.

Struggle for power with the nobility was a second limiting factor. But this issue had been largely resolved by the time Balban rose to supreme power. The rebellions of the nobles under Muhammad bin Tughlaq were due to specific factors which have already been discussed. Thus, despite all its problems, the monarchy remained the pivot of power and governance during the sultanat period.

The Ministries

In his task of governance, the sultan was assisted by a number of ministers. The number of such ministers or the departments of government they headed was not fixed. In a passage, Barani, speaking in the name of Balban's son, Bughra Khan, advises his own son who was ruling at Delhi not to depend on any *one* advisor, though the wazir was principal among them. He speaks of four prominent advisors, mentioning four departments. However, the number four was only indicative. The number of departments could and did vary, and in practice the monarch could seek advice from anyone in whom he had confidence. Thus, Fakhruddin who was merely the *kotwal* of Delhi, had the confidence of Balban and then of Alauddin Khalji. The ministers did not form a council, there being no concept of joint responsibility. Each minister was chosen by the ruler, and held office during his pleasure. While the wazir was considered the principal advisor of the ruler and he did often exercise a broad supervision over the entire machinery of government, he was specially charged with the management of finances.

The Wazir

Much has been written about the role, powers and qualifications of the wazir. According to Nizamul Mulk Tusi, who was wazir under the Seljukids, and whose book, *Siyasat Nama*, exercised enormous influence on Muslim political thinking, the wazir had to be an *ahl-i-qalam*, i.e. a man of learning rather than a warrior. He had also to be a man of wide experience, wisdom and sagacity because his views could be sought by the ruler on any subject. Also, he had to be a man of tact because he had to control the nobility without alienating it.

Powerful wazirs not only supervised the entire administration, but also led military campaigns. This was inevitable as long as the military character of the state was emphasized. But 'under a powerful ruler, the wazir exercised such power as the ruler allowed'. Muslim political thinkers tried to generalize this situation by saying that there was two types of wazirs, the *wazir-i-tafwiz* who had unlimited powers except to appoint his successor, and the *wazir-i-tanfiz* who merely carried out the wishes of the ruler. But this did not solve the problem at issue. The ruler wanted a wazir who was influential enough to relieve him from the day to day burdens of government, but not powerful enough to eclipse or displace him. To resolve this problem, a number of experiments were made. Sometimes no wazir was appointed, or his duties were bifurcated, or offices were created to rival him, or even to put him into shade. Broadly speaking, these experiments covered the thirteenth and the first quarter of the 14th century, the wazirs emerging to power and influence with the rise of the Tughlaqs.

Iltutmish's wazir was Fakhruddin Isami, an old man who had served in high offices at Baghdad for thirty years. He was soon succeeded by Muhammad Junaidi, who had the title of Nizamul Mulk. Muhammad Junaidi was a powerful person. However, his opposition to Razia cost him his office and his life. After the death of Razia, Muhazzab Ghanavi emerged for some time as a king maker. But he suffered an eclipse with the rise of Balban to power. As the most powerful noble, Balban claimed, and was granted the post of, *naib-us-sultanat*, or deputy to the sultan. As such, Balban exercised all the power, the wazir remaining under his shadow. When Balban became the ruler after displacing Nasiruddin Mahmud, he abolished the post of *naib-us-sultanat*. Balban was too dominating a person to allow any powerful wazir to emerge. Though Balban did appoint a wazir, Khawaja Hasan, he seems to have remained a titular wazir since he had little idea of revenue affairs. The power of the wazir were further cut down by Balban appointing Ahmad Ayaz, his favourite, as the Muster-Master (*Ariz-i-Mamalik*) who was responsible for the payment, and maintenance of the efficiency of the army. Balban also appointed a deputy wazir.

The office of the wazir remained under eclipse till the end of Alauddin Khalji's reign. Khwaja Khatir who had been a deputy wazir during the region of Balban and was a revenue expert, was re-inducted as wazir by Jalaluddin Khalji, and continued for some time under Alauddin Khalji. But he was soon replaced by Nusrat Khan, the sultan's brother, who was a noted warrior of his age. When Nusrat Khan died, the post of wazir was given to Malik Kafur, a favourite of the king and a leading general. He combined the post of wazir with the post of *naib-us-sultanat*. After the death of Alauddin, as *naib* Malik Kafur tried to act as king maker, but was replaced by Khusrau Malik who also took the post of *naib*, and then ascended the throne.

Thus, the post of *naib* had come into bad odour and the Tughlaqs discontinued it on coming to power. Later, it was revived in the 15th century by the Saiyid rulers under the title *Wakil-us-sultanat*— a post which continued with some ups and downs till the time of the Mughals.

Tughlaq rule is the period of the high water mark of the institution of wizarat in India. After some experimentation by Ghiyasuddin Tughlaq, Muhammed bin Tughlaq appointed Ahmed Ayaz with the title of Khan-i-Jahan as wazir. Khan-i-Jahan was an elderly person, and had worked as deputy in the department of public works during the reign of Ghiyasuddin Tughlaq. He was considered to be a rigid but competent officer. The Sultan had so much confidence in him that he was left in charge of the administration at Delhi when the sultan was out campaigning, or pursuing rebels. He remained wazir throughout the long reign of twenty-eight years of Muhammad bin Tughlaq, though we do not know his actual influence on Muhammad bin Tughlaq and his policies. He did not try to, or was not allowed to build a group of his supporters so that he failed miserably when, on Muhammad bin Tughlaq's death, he tried to prop up his own nominee on the throne at Delhi.

Firuz Tughlaq appointed as wazir Khan-i-Jahan Maqbul, a converted Tailang brahman who had been deputy to the previous wazir. That an orthodox ruler like Firuz could appoint a converted Hindu to such a high post shows how far the Delhi sultanat had travelled from the time of Balban. The wazir was competent, and Firuz could depend on him to deal with all the affairs of state when he was out campaigning, as for example in Bengal, or Orissa. But it would be wrong to think that Firuz himself took no interest in administration, and that Khan-i-Jahan Maqbul was all in all. Thus, when there was a sharp conflict between the wazir and his auditor-general, Ain-i-Mahru, and the wazir tried to transfer the auditor-general, Firuz intervened, and an amicable arrangement was arrived at. It has been rightly argued that Khan-i-Jahan's success lay in managing Firuz rather than act as a rival centre of power.

When Khan-i-Jahan Maqbul died in 1368-69 after serving as wazir for eighteen years, he was, according to agreement, succeeded by his son, Jauna Khan, who was also given the title of Khan-i-Jahan. Khan-i-Jahan II was equally, if not more competent than his father. But he was no military leader, and failed in the conflict for succession which began even during the life time of Firuz. He was captured, and executed. However, the charge that he wanted to set up his own nominee on the throne is not accepted by many modern historians, such as R.P. Tripathi.

Under the Tughlaqs, the wazirs not only had great prestige, they received very high salaries. In the reign of Muhammad bin Tughlaq, while the highest grandee, a Khan, received many lakhs of tankas annually as pay, Khan-i-Jahan received a salary, which was equal to the income of Iraq. Under Firuz, Khani-Jahan Maqbul received 13 lakhs tankas as pay over the above the expenses of his army and servants. In addition, each of his sons received a *wajah* (salary) of 11,000 tankas, and his sons-in-law even higher, 15,000 tankas each. That was how Khan-i-Jahan Maqbul could present 4 lakh tankas every year to the Sultan.

The *diwan-i-wizarat* or the internal structure of the wazir's department gradually developed. Even during Abbasid times, there used to be a *mushrif* who supervised expenditure, and a *mustaufi* who was perhaps incharge of income. There also used to be a treasurer. These posts were continued in India under Iltutmish who also appointed a deputy (*naib*) to the wazir to provide relief to him in his heavy duties. With the appointment of an Ariz-i-Mamalik under Balban for looking after the army, the civilian character of the wazir's department was further emphasised. However, the wazir did not emerge as the head of civil administration till the rise of the Tughlaqs. Even then, in a military age, any noble, including the wazir was expected to be able to lead a military campaign if asked to do so. Thus, there was no clear distinction between civil and military duties, except in the case of religious and judicial officers.

With the bringing of the doab under direct administration (*khalisa*) by Alauddin Khalji, the revenue department expanded rapidly, and hundreds of collectors (*amils, mutsarrif etc.*) were appointed. To control them, a new department, *diwan-i-mustakharaj*, was created. This department fell into bad odour because of the harshness it often exercised in taking accounts, and collecting 'arrears' from the collectors. It seems to have been abolished after Alauddin's death. But the collectors remained, and in Muhammad bin Tughlaq's time, an attempt was made to give them a new shape. They were now to be more or equally concerned with agrarian development. Hence a new department, *diwan-i-kohi*, under a separate amir was set up. As we have seen, this also ended in failure.

The structure of the revenue department developed fully under Firuz. The duties of the *mushrif* and the *mustaufi* were clearly defined, the former being primarily incharge of income, the latter of

expenditure. The chief *mushrif* and the chief *mustaufi* were high officials directly appointed by the sultan, though they were subordinate to the wazir. This system of checks and balance was not to
the liking of the wazir, and the Sultan had sometimes to intervene
and mediate.

Firuz also set up a department of slaves under a separate officer, and a separate department of *imlak* for the direct income of the
sultan.

Diwan-i-Arz

The special responsibility of the Ariz-i-Mamalik was to recruit,
equip and pay the army. The *Ariz* was *not* the commander-in-chief of
the army, the sultan himself being the commander-in-chief. But the
Ariz was invariably a leading noble, and a warrior in his own right.
The Ariz is asked to be the friend and well-wisher of the soldier, and
to look after him like his own son. The office of the Ariz existed
under the Abbasids, and is mentioned in the *Siyasat Nama*. It
probably existed under Iltutmish because we are told by Barani that
Ahmad Ayaz Rawat-i-Arz who was appointed Ariz-i-Mamalik by
Balban, had held this post for thirty years under the Shamsi rulers.
Balban gave more importance to this post than that of the wazir. So
much so that Ahmad Ayaz declared. "Let all those assembled hear:
I am the (chief) defender and assistant of the system of government
and administration."

However, it was under Alauddin Khalji that the functioning of
this office was properly organized, with the introduction of the branding system (*dagh*) for horses so that horses of inferior quality were
not presented, an efficient cavalry force being the main element on
which the Turkish rulers depended. We have also seen how Alauddin
used the control of the market to ensure that good quality mounts
were made available to the state at fixed and reasonable prices.
He also introduced the system of descriptive roll (*chehra*) of the
soldiers so that servants and other untrained and unreliable persons were not put up in the muster to draw fictitious salaries. This
system continued till the time of Firuz, though it could not be a
guarantee against all fraud. This was recognised by Firuz when he
gave a gold coin to a soldier so that he could bribe a clerk to pass
his inferior quality mount.

The *Mir-Hajib* or superintendent of the royal stables, a post held
by Malik Yaqut during the reign of Razia, and the *Darogha-i-Pil* or
Keeper of the royal elephant stables, were considered important

officers till the office of the Ariz had been organized. We hardly hear of the nobles who held these posts thereafter.

We do not know how precisely the army was recruited, and the type of training provided to soldiers. According to Ibn Battutah, who came to India during the reign of Muhammad bin Tughlaq, when anyone wanted to be enrolled in the army of the governor of Multan as an archer, his strength was tested by giving him bows of different stiffness. If he wanted to be enrolled as a trooper, a target was set up which he had to hit with his lance, and to lift a ring from the ground with his lance while the horse was on the gallop. A mounted archer had to hit a ball on the ground while galloping his horse. This must have been part of a general system. The training mentioned above must have continued after recruitment.

It seems that there was a central force of which the royal body-guard was a part. We do not have any precise idea of the strength of this force. We are told that Alauddin Khalji's army consisted of 300,000. Muhammad bin Tughlaq's army was larger. Not all this force could have been stationed at Delhi. The bigger *iqtadars* who administered large areas apparently recruited their own forces. The chiefs had their own forces. Both of these could be brought under the royal standards in case of need. Thus, when Balban led the campaign to Bengal, the Hindu chiefs of the eastern parts were asked to join with their forces, while Balban recruited an additional force of 200,000 men from the region. Being largely cut off from West Asia after the rise of the Mongols, the Turkish rulers had to rely increasingly on Indian Muslims and Afghans for their armies. Thus, the army of the Turkish rulers was a mixed up, consisting of descendants of the original Turkish soldiers, Afghans and Hindustanis (Indian Muslims), supplemented by Hindu contingents of the chiefs.

It was an onerous burden to pay such a large army. Apart from extraction of land-revenue from the cultivators, plundering the neighbouring countries was a time-tested system which the Turks also followed, but giving it the title of "*jihad*", or holy war. From the time of Alauddin Khalji, the soldiers were paid in cash. The salary of 238 tankas for a soldier with one horse fixed by Alauddin was a low one. What it was later on we do not know. Obviously, the strength, efficiency and loyalty of this central force played a major role in the stability of the Delhi Sultanat.

The *Ariz* was thus a very important officer who put limits on the powers of the wazir. In consequence, none of the succeeding wazirs could become powerful military leaders who could put their own nominee on the throne, or succeed the ruler on the throne. This situation arose only when the system of administration broke down due to internecine warfare, as after the death of Firuz, and the invasion of Timur.

Diwan-i-Insha

The *Diwan-i-Insha* was *not* the foreign office. In those days, relations between states were not so continuous as to need a separate office, or minister of foreign affairs. The wazir was expected, however, to keep track of developments in neighbouring countries, and to keep the ruler informed. Formal epistles or letters were sometimes despatched to neighbouring rulers and towns to register a new succession to the throne or announce a major event, such as a victory. These letters which were sometimes written in a grand manner with a great literary flourish, were drafted, copied and despatched by the *Diwan-i-Insha* which was headed by a *dabir*, or *dabir-i-khas*. The Dabir was also responsible for drafting orders and communications to the important *iqtadars*, and neighbouring rajas. The post was an important and responsible one, ensuring close proximity to the ruler. As one who enjoyed the sultan's confidence, the *dabir* could be a rival or a check to the wazir. The post of *dabir-i-khas* was sometimes a stepping stone to the post of wazir.

Diwan-i-Risalat

The *Diwan-i-Risalat* is one of the four major ministries mentioned by Barani. But the functions of this office were not mentioned by him, and there has been a sharp division of opinion among modern historians about its duties. Some call it a ministry of foreign affairs, others as a department for control of prices and public morals, and still others a department of hearing public grievances. From its title—the word *risalat* being derived from rasul or a prophet, it apparently had a holy character. One of the functions of medieval states was to grant stipends of rent-free lands *(imlak)* to Muslim scholars and divines, the learned, and the recluse etc. The chief person incharge of this ecclesiastical department was either the Sadr-i-Jahan, or the Wakil-i-Dar who was also called Rasul-i-Dar.

Apart from the post of Sadr-i-Jahan, another important post was that of the Chief Qazi or Qazi-ul-Qazzat who was the head of the judicial department. Sometimes, the posts of Sadr-i-Jahan and Chief Qazi were combined.

Apart from granting stipends and revenue-free lands, the Sadr's department was also responsible for the appointment of *muhtasibs*, or censor of public morals. These officials were meant to check gambling, prostitution and other vices, as also to ensure that Muslims did not publicly violate what was prohibited in the *shara*, such as wine-drinking, or not observing what were considered obligatory duties, such as *namaz* (public prayers), *roza* (fasting during the month of Ramzan). They were also to check weights and measures, and to keep a broad check on prices. All this fell within the ambit of the *diwan-i-risalat*.

The duties of the *diwan-i-risalat* could be added to or separate offices created. When Alauddin was concerned with the control of the market, he appointed *shuhnas* to control the different markets, and a prominent noble was deputed to supervise their work. This was called the *diwan-i-risalat*. After the death of Alauddin, and the disappearance of the market controls, we do not hear of this department.

Firuz Tughlaq who augmented the stipend and *imlak* (revenue free lands) of the scholars, theologians and the students, was also concerned with abolishing the injunctions prescribed by *shara* for disfiguring people by cutting off hands, ears, nose etc. in punishment. He also wanted to have the reputation of being a humane ruler. He separated the office of sadr and chief qazi. He also set up a separate department of public grievances, which he called *diwan-i-risalat*. This was headed by a prominent noble, apparently the *wakil-i-dar*. Even the wazir and princes could apply to this department for redressal of grievances.

Thus, the *diwan-i-risalat* had different forms under different rulers, but its basic function of giving stipends and revenue-free lands to the deserving and the needy seems to have continued all the time.

ii. Court and the Royal Household

In a situation where the sultan was the centre of power, the organisation of the court and of the royal household became matters of prime importance. However, unlike the Mughals, there was no single officer in charge of the court and the royal household during the Sultanat.

The most important officer concerned with the royal household was the *wakil-i-dar*. He controlled the entire royal household and supervised the payment of allowances and salaries to the sovereign's personal staff which included the royal kitchen, the wine department and the royal stables. He was even responsible for the education of the princes. The courtiers, the princes, the sultan's private servants, even the queens had to approach him for various favours. As such, the post was of great importance and sensitivity, and was bestowed only to a noble of high rank and prestige.

Another officer of high importance connected with the court and the royal household was the *Amir Hajib*. He was also called *barbek*. He was master of ceremonies at the court. He marshalled the nobles in accordance with their ranks and precedence. All petitions to the Sultan were presented through him, or his subordinates, called *hajibs*. The post was so sensitive that sometimes princes of blood were appointed to it.

Another important officer connected with the royal household was the *barid-i-khas*, or the head of the intelligence department. Spies or *barids* were appointed to different parts of the empire. It was their business to keep the sultan informed of all the developments. This was the main weapon used by Balban and Alauddin Khalji to control and demoralise the nobles.

There were many minor officials such as the head of the hunt, the officer in charge of royal parties *(majlis)* etc. whom we may pass over. Two departments which, however, may be noted is the *Karkhana* or royal stores and the Public Works department. The Karkhanas were responsible for the storing and manufacture of all the articles required by the Sultan and the royal household. This included food and fodder, lamps and oil, clothes, furniture, tents etc. Firuz Tughlaq gave great importance to the *karkhanas*, and many slaves were trained to become good artisans in these departments. Robes of silk and wool which were distributed to the nobles twice a year by Muhammad bin Tughlaq were manufactured in the royal *karkhanas*. Each *karkhana* was supervised by a noble of rank, and was assisted by a large staff of accountants and supervisors.

From the time of Alauddin Khalji, great importance was given to the department of public works or *diwan-i-amirat*. But the prince of builders was Firuz Tughlaq who not only repaired many old buildings, including sarais, mausoleums etc. but dug canals, and built many new towns. A separate department, therefore, was set up under Malik Ghazi who was called Mir-i-Imarat.

iii. Provincial and Local Government

Our knowledge of the structure and working of the provincial and local government under the sultanat is rather limited. To begin with the sultanat was a loose structure made up of military commands. There was hardly any single direction, and the commanders were busy subduing the various Hindu chiefs, and extracting money from them for supporting the army. In such a situation, the question of a uniform civil administration over all parts of the dominion hardly arose. But this gradually changed, the Khalji rule forming the phase of transition.

During the Khalji period, we hear of *walis* or *muqtis* who were commanders of military and administrative tracts called *iqtas*. There was no clear definition of provinces. A number of iqtas could be grouped together to form a province, called *khitta* or *vialayat*. The exact powers of the governor, called *muqti,* varied according to circumstances. In larger provinces, they could appoint their deputes (*naibs*) for various regions or posts. The governor of Lakhnauti was almost independent, and declared himself a sultan more than once, and military campaigns had to be launched to subdue him. However, it does not appear useful in the context of India to divide them into governors of unlimited or limited powers, as some jurists have done. As the process of centralization of power proceeded in India, provincial governors had to submit to increasing central control unless they were prepared to be treated as rebels.

To begin with, the *muqti* had complete charge of the administration of the *iqta* including the task of maintaining an army with which he could be asked to join the sultan in case of need. He was expected to defray the cost of the army, meet his own expenses and to make financial contributions to the sultan. But the basis of this was not clear. Later, from the time of Balban, the *muqti* was expected to send the balance (*fawazil*) of the income after meeting his and the army's expenses. This means that the central revenue department had made an assessment of the expected income of the *iqta,* and the cost of the maintenance of the army and the *muqti's* own expenses. This process became even stricter in the time of Alauddin Khalji. Even more, the *muqtis* were now expected to follow the system of revenue assessment Alauddin had instituted in the doab in the areas called *khalisa,* income from which went straight to the royal treasury, and was used for paying cash salaries to the soldiers.

As the central control grew, the control over the *muqti's* administration also increased. The *naib diwan* (also called *khwaja*) in charge of revenue administration began to be appointed from the centre. A *barid* or intelligence officer was also posted to keep the sultan informed. But it seems that the *muqti* appointed his own troops, keeping a *naib ariz* at the centre to represent him. It is not clear who appointed the qazis. Appeals from the qazis, and against the conduct of the governors could be made to the sultan. The governor could, however, give revenue-free lands to scholars out of his *iqta*.

Under Muhammad bin Tughlaq, we hear of a number of persons who were appointed governors on revenue-farming terms. This attempt to maximise the income was a step back for it implied elimination of central control over revenue affairs. But it seems that such persons were not required to maintain troops for the service of the centre, these being placed under a separate officer. This duality of functions did not work and was apparently given up by Firuz.

According to Barani, there were 20 provinces in the Sultanat when it did not include the south. As compared to the provinces (*subahs*) of Akbar's time, these were smaller. Thus, out of the modern U.P., the middle doab was divided between Meerut, Baran (now Bulandshahr) and Koil (now Aligarh), and another three were in the north-west. Provinces in the Mughal sense really began under Muhammad bin Tughlaq. Under him, the number of provinces covering the entire country upto Malabar according to an Arab writer, Shihabuddin al Umar, was twenty-four.

We do not know whether there were any units equivalent to the modern district or division below the provinces. We hear of *shiqs* and *sarkars* in the Afghan histories dealing with the Lodis and the Surs. But these accounts were written during Akbar's time, and we are not certain that these were not, in fact, administrative units of a later time. We do, however, hear of parganas, *sadis* (unit of 100), and *chaurasis* (unit of 84). The *sadis* and *chaurasis* were collections of villages. The number of villages could vary. Perhaps, a chaudhari who was a hereditary land-holder, and an amil or revenue collector were posted there, especially if the area was under *khalisa*. We hear of *khuts* and *muqaddams*. The former was the zamindar of one or more villages, while the latter was the village headman. The patwari was also a village official because we are told that Alauddin Khalji had the account books of the patwaris examined in order to detect frauds by the *amils* and *mutsarrifs* who were dealt with very harshly.

Thus, a rudimentary system of government, some of it inherited from the earlier Hindu rulers, continued down to the village level.

In this way, gradually a new centralised form of government emerged. The first step was the consolidation of the central government. As the central government became stronger and more confident, it tried to extend its direct control over the regions and the countryside, which, in turn, implied reducing the powers and privileges of the chiefs who dominated the countryside. This led to a prolonged struggle, and no clear forms had emerged by the time the Delhi sultanat disintegrated. This was a task which was taken up by the Mughals later on.

9

ECONOMIC AND SOCIAL LIFE IN NORTH INDIA UNDER THE DELHI SULTANAT

There has been a considerable difference of opinion among scholars regarding the impact of Turkish rule on the economic and social life of North India beginning with the 13th century. One view was that the Turks wrought such damage to the economic life and the social and cultural fabric that it could only be repaired after a long time and, to some extent, only under the Mughals. In other words, the entire period of Sultanat rule was painted in dark colours, so much so that it was argued that there was a decline of population in northern India during the period! A second opinion was that since Indian society had hardly changed over the millenia, the negative aspects of Turkish rule were soon overcome, and that after some time the Turkish rulers emphasised justice and protection of the people rather than conquest. Hence, the even tenor of life was continued as far as the mass of the people were concerned, the effect of Turkish rule being felt mainly by the former ruling section—the Rajputs, and their close associates and beneficiaries, the brahmans. It was argued that in this way, there was change only at the surface.

In recent times, a new view of Indian history has emerged which emphasises change rather than continuity. Thus, it traces the various phases of social development from the time of the Vedic Age. It is argued that along with periods of growth, decline and stagnation, there have been important structural changes in Indian society during its long history. We need not discuss here the early period of Indian history. The period following the decline of the Gupta empire in north India is seen as one during which towns and long distance trade declined, gold coins virtually disappeared and even the silver currency was debased. At the local level, the power of the landed elites increased not only on the economic and social life, but over the administrative processes of the state. The word "feudal" has been used for this system, even though some of the characteristic features of European feudalism, the manor system and vassalage, were absent.

The establishment of Turkish rule in north India led, according to an eminent modern historian, Muhammad Habib, to far-reaching changes in society and economic life. According to him, the new Turkish regime released social forces which created an economic organisation considerably superior to the one that had existed before, that it led to the expansion of towns, and to important alternations in agrarian relationships. We shall examine these views in the following pages.

A. Economic Life

i. Agricultural Production

There were hardly any elements of change in the rural economy during the Sultanat period. Ibn Battutah, who travelled all over India, has left us a detailed account of the food-grains and various other crops, fruits and flowers produced in the country. Most of them are familiar to us, with rice and sugar-cane being produced in the east and south, and wheat, oil-seeds etc, in the north. Cotton was grown widely, as also barley, sesame and other inferior crops. Ibn Battutah says that the soil was so fertile that it produced two crops a year—the familiar *rabi* (winter) and *kharif* (monsoon) crops. Rice was sown three times a year. Some of the crops were the basis of village industries, such as oil-processing, making jaggery, indigo spinning and weaving etc. Maize, red chillies and tobacco which were introduced during the 17th century or later are, of course, missing.

During the 14th century, under Muhammad bin Tughlaq and Firuz Tughlaq, there was a marked development of gardens. Firuz Tughlaq is said to have built 1200 gardens in the neighbourhood and suburbs of Delhi, 80 on the Salora embankment, and 44 in Chittor. These gardens led to the improvement of fruits, especially grapes. Thus, we are told that wine, apparently grape-wine, used to come to Delhi from Meerut and Aligarh. Dholpur, Gwaliyar and Jodhpur were the other places where improved methods of fruit culti-

vation and gardening were adopted. Special attention was paid to
the improvement of pomegranates at Jodhpur. Sikandar Lodi declared that Persia could not produce pomegranates which were better
than the Jodhpur variety in flavour.

However, the fruits produced in these orchards were meant mainly
for the towns, and for the tables of the wealthy. They may, however, have produced some employment, and added to the avenues
of trade.

Regarding implements, although they are hardly mentioned, we
may assume that there was no change in them till the 19th century. We have no idea of the productivity of the soil. It may have
been higher because of more extensive manuring by cattle which
were plentiful, as testified to by the fact that *charai* based on the
number of animals was an important agricultural tax. Also, *banjaras*
had thousands of oxen for their journeys. The peasants had more
land per head because of a much smaller population. Forests were
also much more extensive. However, on account of social constraints,
we hear of landless labourers and menials in the villages. Most of
the land was rain fed, though digging of wells and making of *bunds*
(embankments) for storing water for irrigation were considered holy
acts, and the state took an active part in building and preserving
them.

An extensive system of canals was set up for the first time by
Firuz during the second half of the 14th century. As we have mentioned earlier, he cut two canals from the Jamuna, and one each
from the Sutlej and the Ghaggar. But these mainly benefited the
areas around Hissar in modern Haryana. Other smaller canals in
Sindh and the Punjab are also mentioned.

Rural Society

The contemporary sources are almost silent on the subject of rural
society. This deficiency can be made up, to some extent, by taking
recourse to information available in Sanskrit, Apabhramsh and some
of the south Indian languages. Although the information on village life available in these sources deal with the period from the
9th—10th centuries onwards, they provide us a background, and
enable us to understand better the changes and continuities in village life under the Delhi Sultanat.

From the writings of the 12th century Jain writer, Hemachandra,
we can divide the village folk into four categories, i.e. (i) the pro-
duce-sharing peasants or share-croppers for whom the words *karshak*

or *ardhikas* (receivers of a half share) are used; (ii) plough-shares and field labourers for whom various words such as *halavakaka, kinasa* and even *karshak* are used. These two sections constituted the lowest, most dependent peasantry. It seems that the word *karshak*, literally meaning the tiller of the soil, was a generic word for the lower peasantry which formed the largest group in the villages. Following them came the sections (iii) whom some modern writers have called free peasants, but for whom the word owner-proprietor may be more appropriate. In later times, they were called *malik-i-zamin* (owners of the land) or *khud-kasht* (owner cultivators). They were entitled to inherit the land they claimed by descent. They also owned their huts or houses, and had the use of the village commons. They were often organised on a caste basis. Lastly (iv) there were the villages artisans: the cobbler, the rope-maker, the watchman, etc. Some of the village artisans, such as the cobbler and field-labourers belonged to the *svapach* (untouchable) category. The word low or *adhama* is generally applied to them.

The commentators cn *Dharma Shastras,* and other writers are agreed about the harrowing poverty and wretched life of the mass of the toiling peasantry. The *Padma Purana* describes the miserable life of the *karshaks* and that they were so much oppressed by the rulers of the time as to be unable to even support their families. The poverty of the peasants and field-labourers is contrasted with the luxurious life of the landed aristocracy, the *samantas*.

It will thus be seen that village society was highly unequal. The growth of a cash nexus which became more rapid under the Sultanat increased the disparities further. While the agrarian policies of the Sultans were meant to ensure a steady income for the ruler and the officials who administered the state, their policies also had an impact on the rural society and economy. This is an aspect which we have to infer because the medieval chroniclers were hardly concerned about it.

The Revenue System

We have little idea about the agrarian policies and practices before the arrival of the Turks in north India. The cultivators were required to pay a large number of cesses which were subsumed under the broad categories of *bhaga* (land revenue), *bhog* (cesses), and *kar* (extra cesses). However, it is difficult to calculate the share of the produce they comprised, individually or collectively, nor how much of it went to the ruler, and how much to his subordinates or to the local landed elites. The traditional share of the produce payable by the peasants, according to the *Dharamashastras*, was one-sixth, but we hear of kings in south India demanding one-third, or two-thirds of the produce. We also hear of a Chola king who had authorised his feudatories to collect half of the produce. In actual practice, the land revenue demand must have depended upon what the peasants could be made to pay.

. There was hardly any change in the structure of rural society during the 13th century. The early Turkish rulers depended on the Hindu chiefs to pay the land-revenue, leaving it to them to collect it from the peasants according to the existing practices. This, again, gives us no idea of the actual land-revenue that was demanded from the cultivators. The general approach of the Turkish ruling class is indicated by Barani who wrote almost a hundred years later. According to him, Balban advised his son, Bughra Khan, not to charge so much land-revenue (*kharaj*) as to reduce the peasant to a state of poverty, nor so little that they become rebellious on account of excess of wealth. We have no idea how this was implemented in practice. In general, it was designed not to interfere with the existing village set up.

The 14th century saw a number of new developments, as we have noted in the earlier chapters. Alauddin Khalji raised the land-revenue demand to half in the upper Doab region upto Aligarh, and in some areas of Rajasthan and Malwa. This area was made *khalisa*, i.e. the land-revenue collected there went directly to the Imperial treasury. The land-revenue demand was based on the measurement of the area cultivated by each cultivator. Further, except in the area around Delhi, the cultivators were encouraged to pay land-revenue in cash. Alauddin tried to ensure that the cultivators sold their grains to the *banjaras* while the crops were still standing in the field, i.e. without transporting them to their own stores so as to be sold later when more favourable prices might prevail. However, this had to be modified in practice because we are told that many of the cultivators themselves brought their grains for sale in the local *mandi*. These could only have been the rich cultivators.

Alauddin's agrarian measures amounted to a massive intervention in village affairs. Thus, he tried to operate against the privileged sections in the villages—the *khuts*, *muqaddams*, and *chaudhuris* and, to some extent, the rich peasants who had surplus food-grains to sell. The *khuts* and *muqaddams* were suspected of passing their burden on to the weaker sections, and not paying the *ghari* and *charai* taxes. In Barani's picturesque language, the *khuts*, and *muqaddams* became so poor that they could not wear costly clothes and ride on Arabi and Iraqi horses, and their women were obliged to work in the houses of Muslims. Barani, no doubt, exaggerates. But the attempt to take away all the inherited privileges of the *khuts* and *muqaddams*, or of the upper sections of the landed nobility and to appoint an army of *amils*, most of whom proved to be corrupt, to supervise revenue collection was not liable to succeed.

We are told that Alauddin's revenue measures collapsed with his death. But we do not know whether it implied that the system of measurement was abolished, as also the demand for half of the produce in the *khalisa* areas of the doab. The restoration of the privileges of the *khuts* and *muqaddams* implies that the state no longer tried to assess the land-revenue on the basis of the holdings, i.e. area cultivated by each individual, but assessed it as a lump sum, leaving the assessment of individuals to the *khuts* and *muqaddams*. This was also a recognition of the economic and social power wielded by the *khuts* and *muqaddams* in the country-side.

Ghiyasuddin Tughlaq took the definite step of replacing the system of measurement by sharing in the *khalisa* areas. This was considered a step towards providing relief to the cultivators because while under measurement the risk of cultivation of crops had to be largely borne by the cultivator, under sharing both the profit or loss were shared by the cultivator and the state. Ghiyasuddin took another important step. In the territories held by the holders of *iqtas*, i.e. outside the *khalisa* areas, he ordered that the revenue demand should not be raised on the basis of guess or computation, but "by degrees and gradually because the weight of sudden enhancement would ruin the country and bar the way to prosperity." Barani explains this policy of moderate increases by saying that the revenue demand in the areas of the *iqtas* should not be increased by "one in ten or eleven". This phrase does not mean that the increase may be one-tenth or one-eleventh. Nor does it mean that the land revenue should be one-tenth, or the theoretical minimum of one-fifth, as some modern historians have assumed. Barani nowhere mentions the scale of the revenue demand, either in the *khalisa* areas of the doab, or in the *iqtas*. Perhaps, the traditional demand in the ares outside the *khalisa* areas remained one-third as before.

Muhammad Tughlaq tried to revive Alauddin's system and to extend it all over the empire. His measures led to a serious peasant uprising in the doab. The reason for this, it seems, was that in assessing the land-revenue on individuals, not the actual yield but the artificially fixed standard yield was applied to the area under measurement. Further, when converting the produce into cash, not the actual prices but official standard prices were applied. There was also harshness in levying the tax on cattle and houses. Thus, the actual incidence of land-revenue demand rose considerably, to half or even more.

Like Alauddin Khalji's agrarian reforms, Muhammad Tughlaq's measures were also designed to curtail the privileges of the more affluent sections in village society, especially the *khuts* and *muqaddams*. But his measures also hurt the average cultivator. This may explain why there was a serious uprising against his measures in the doab.

Muhammad Tughlaq then tried to reverse direction. In the doab which was the directly administered area (*khalisa*), he tried to improve cultivation by changing the cropping pattern, replacing inferior crops by superior crops. The main inducement for this was granting loans (*sondhar*) for digging wells, etc. This policy could only have succeeded with the co-operation of the richer cultivators, and the *khuts* and *muqaddams* who had the largest land-holdings, as well as the means. However, it failed because the officials appointed for the purpose had no knowledge of local conditions, and were only interested in enriching themselves. Firuz met with greater success by providing water to the peasants of Haryana by his canal system, levying an extra charge of 10 per cent, and leaving it to the peasants to cultivate what they wanted.

All in all, it would appear that the land-revenue under the Sultans, especially during the 14th century, remained heavy, hovering in the neighbourhood of half, and that there was a definite effort to reduce the power and privileges of the old intermediaries, the Rais, Rawats etc., with the *khuts* and *muqaddams* forging ahead. This was the first time that such a high magnitude of land-revenue was assessed and collected from a large and highly fertile area for several decades. Both the administrative methods adopted, and the centralisation of such large, liquid resources in the hands of the ruling class had important consequences, both for rural life and for the urban manufacturers, trade and commerce.

Firuz Tughlaq's rule is generally considered a period of rural prosperity. Barani and Afif tells that as result of the Sultan's orders, the provinces became cultivated, and tillage extended widely so that not a single village in the doab remained uncultivated. The canal system extended tillage in Haryana. According to Afif, "In the houses of the *raiyat* (peasantry) so much grain, wealth, horses and goods accumulated that one cannot speak of them." He goes on to say how none of the women folk of the peasantry remained without ornaments, and that "in every peasant's house there were clean bed-sheets, excellent bed-cots, many articles and much wealth." Obviously these remarks applied largely to the richer sections among the peasants and the rural, privileged sections—the *khuts, muqaddams* etc. Thus, rural society continued to be unequal, with imperial policies siphoning off a large share of the rural surplus. However, there was some limited success to the efforts to improve the rural economy even though the benefit of these was reaped largely by the privileged sections in rural society.

ii. Non-Agricultural Production

We do not have any detailed account of the economic resources of the country during the Sultanat period, and it has to be supplemented by the account provided by Abul Fazl in the *Ain-i-Akbari*, written towards the end of the 16thy century. Briefly, the most important manufactures pertained to textiles, metallurgy, building activities, mining and other ancillary activities, such as leather-work, paper-making, toy-making, etc.

Textiles

Textile production was the biggest industry of India and goes back to ancient times. It included the manufacture of cotton cloth, woollen cloth silk. Cotton cloth itself could be divided into two categories— the coarse (*kamin*) and the fine (*mahin*). The coarse cloth, which was also called *pat*, was worn by the poor and the *faqirs*. It was often manufactured in households in the villages, but was also produced in some regions, such as Awadh, from which it was imported into Delhi. Cotton cloth of a little superior quality was called calico (*kirpas*), and was widely used. Cloth of fine variety included *muslin* which was produced at Sylhet and Dacca in Bengal, and Deogir in the Deccan. This was so fine and expensive as to be used only by the nobles and the very rich. According to Amir Khusrau, Deogir cloth was so fine that a hundred yards of it could be put through a ring. The fine clothes included those which were embroidered (*zardozi*) painted, or of gold work (*zarbaft*). Gujarat also produced many variety of fine cotton-stuff. Barbossa tells us that Cambay (Khambayat) was the centre for the manufacture of all kinds of finer and coarse cotton cloth, besides other cheap varieties of velvets, satins, tafettas or thick carpets.

Various varieties of cloth was both painted, and printed by using blocks of wood. Thus, the 14th centrury Sufi Hindi poet, Mulla Daud, talks of printed (*khand chaap*) cloth. Apart from the manufacture of cloth, other miscellaneous goods such as carpets, prayer carpets, coverlets, bedding, bed-strings, etc. were also manufactured in other parts of Gujarat.

The production of cloth improved during the period because of the introduction of the spinning-wheel (*charkha*) which is attested to in China in the first century AD. According to a modern historian, Irfan Habib, the spinning wheel is attested to in Iran in the 12th century by some well-known poets. Its earliest reference in India is in the middle of the 14th century. Thus, it apparently came to India with the Turks, and came into general use by the middle of the 14th century. We are told that the spinning-wheel in its simplest form increased the spinner's efficiency some six-fold, in comparison with a spinner working with a hand spindle.

Weaving was improved by providing additional straddles on the loom. Block printing (*chhāp*), mentioned by the Hindi poet Mulla Daud in the 14th century, also became more wide-spread.

An old device which became widespread during the period was the bow of the cotton-carder (*naddaf, dhunia*) which speeded up the process of separating cotton from seeds.

Silk was imported from Bengal where silk worms were reared. However, a greater supply of silk yarn, including raw silk, was imported from Iran and Afghanistan. There was much use of silk cloth, and of cotton and silk mixed at Delhi and its neighbourhood. The silk of Cambay (Khambayat) was among the costly items of cloth controlled by Alauddin Khalji. The *patolas* of Gujarat with many fancy designs were highly valued. Gujarat was also famous for its gold and silver embroidery, generally on silk cloth.

Wool was procured from the mountainous tracts, though sheep were also reared in the plains. The finer qualities of woollen cloth and furs were largely imported from outside, and were almost exclusively worn by the nobles. However, the shawl industry of Kashmir was well established. Muhammad Tughlaq sent Kashmir shawls as a present to the Chinese emperor. Carpet weaving also developed under the patronage of the Sultans, with many Iranian and Central Asian designs being incorporated.

Mention may be also made of the dyeing industry. Indigo and other vegetables dyes were responsible for the bright colours of which both men and women were fond. The dyeing industry went hand in hand with calico-painting. The tie and dye method was of old standing in Rajasthan, though we do not know when hand-printing using wooden blocks was introduced.

We do not know much about the organisation of the textile industry which gave employment to a large number of people. Then as later, spinning was considered to be women's work, and was carried out in the homes. Even slave-girls were used for this purpose. Weaving was also a house-hold industry, carried out in towns or in some of the villages. The weaving material was purchased by the weavers themselves, or supplied to them by merchants. The luxury items were, however, generally produced in the royal workshops or *karkhanas*. Thus, we are told that in Muhammad Tughlaq's *karkhanas*, there were 4000 silk workers who wove and embroidered different types of robes and garments. Firuz Tughlaq had recruited and trained a large number of slaves to work in his *karkhanas*, and in the parganas.

Metallurgy

India had an old tradition of metal-work as testified to by the iron-pillar of Mehrauli (Delhi), which has stood the ravages of time and weather over centuries. Many idols of copper or mixed-metals also testified to the skill of the Indian metal-workers. Indian damascened swords and daggers were also famous all over the world. Large scale use of the iron-stirrup and armour for horses and soldiers led to a much larger production of metallurgical goods. Another practice which became wide-spread was the technique of tin-coating (*qalāi*) so that cheap copper utensils can be used for cooking. Vessels of bronze and copper, including inlay work, produced in the Deccan had a steady demand in West Asia. The high quality of the Sultanat coinage is also an evidence of the skill of the Indian metal workers. The gold and silver-smiths of India were known for the fine pieces of jewellery produced by them for which there was an insatiable demand from both women and men.

Building Industry

The building industry was a major means of employment. There had been a spurt of temple building activity in north India from the 10th century, as witnessed by the temples at Khajuraho in Bundelkhand, at Dilwara in Rajasthan and other places in Orissa and Gujarat. The Turkish sultans, too, were great builders. They introduced a new style of arch, the dome and the vault, and a new mortar, the "gypsum and lime" lime mortar for cementing. They built cities, forts and palaces, the remains of many of which are still visible. It seems that there was a great spurt in brick making, and more and more people began to live in brick and stone houses, though the poor continued to live in mud houses, with thatched roofs. As stone cutters, the Indian craftsmen were unrivalled. Amir Khusrau proclaimed that the mason and stone-cutters of Delhi were superior to their fellow craftsmen in the whole Muslim world. As is well known, Timur had taken masons and stone-cutters of Delhi to build his capital, Samarqand. We have no idea of the number of people engaged in building industries. Barani tells us that Alauddin Khalji employed 70,000 craftsmen for the construction of his buildings. Both Muhammad Tughlaq and Firuz were great builders. Firuz not only established a number of new towns, but had many old buildings, including mausoleums repaired. Enamelled tiles were introduced in India during the period. Hindu Rajas and chiefs also patronised building-artisans, and a number of new towns, such a Jodhpur in Rajasthan, were built during the period. Wood work of excellent quality was carried out throughout the country, with doors, seats, bed-stands for domestic use being made.

Other Crafts including Paper-making

Another crafts which was widespread in India was leather-working, based on the large cattle wealth in the country. This was largely organised on a caste basis. Superior quality saddles were produced for a large number of horses in the stables, or gifted to nobles. Gujarat produced exquisite mats of red and blue leather, decorated with birds and beasts, or inlaid work.

A new industry which arose during the period was paper-making. Although known to China in 100 A.D., knowledge about paper technology reached Samarqand and Baghdad only in the 8th century. The Arabs introduced a new technology, using rags and ropes instead of the mulberry trees and the bark of trees. There is no evidence of its use in India before the 13th century, and the earliest paper manuscript in India available to us is from Gujarat dated 1223-24. Paper making undoubtedly meant a great increase in the availability of books.

Other crafts included salt-making, quarrying for stone and marbles, and extraction of iron and copper ore. There was also diamond mining in Panna and in south India, as also diving for pearls from the sea. Ivory working was another important craft.

iii. Trade:
(a) Domestic Trade

During the Sultanat period, as during the earlier period, India remained the manufacturing workshop for the Asian world and adjacent areas of East Africa, with brisk and well-established domestic trade. India's position was based on highly productive agriculture, skilled craftsmen, strong manufacturing traditions, and a highly specialised and experienced class of traders and financers. We have noted the growth of towns and a money nexus in north India following the Turkish centralisation which led to improved communications, a sound currency system based on the silver *tanka* and the copper *dirham*, and the re-activation of Indian trade, especially over-land trade with Central and West Asia.

Domestic trade may be divided into local trade between the villages, and with the *mandis* and district towns; and long distance trade between metropolitan towns and regions. Trade between district and metropolitan towns fell between the two. Local trade involved the sale of crops for the payment of land-revenue and to feed the towns which were growing in size and number. The sale of crops was primarily the responsibility of the village *bania* who also provided the peasants with such necessities as salt and spices, and raw iron for use by the village blacksmith. Sometimes, the rich cultivators themselves took their surplus produce to the local *mandis*—a practice which Alauddin Khalji tried to encourage to prevent hoarding at the village level. The *mandis* were supplemented by local fairs where animals were also sold, animals being a necessity for field operations, local transport, milk etc. We have no means of assessing the volume of this local trade. It undoubtedly played a vital role in the economic life of the country. However, local trade did not generate enough wealth to make the traders engaged in it wealthy enough to lead a life of ease and plenty. Thus, the much reviled village *bania* probably did not have a standard of living higher than that of a rich peasant.

At the other end of the spectrum were the rich traders and financers, the *sahs, modis* and *sarrafs*. Their trading activities were geared both to the movement of bulk commodities within the country, as well as to cater to the demand for luxury goods required by the nobility living in the big cities. The bulk commodities included food-grains, oil, ghee, pulses, etc. with some regions having a surplus and some others a deficit. Thus, rice and sugar which were surplus in Bengal and Bihar were carried by ships to Malabar and Gujarat. Wheat which was surplus in modern east U.P. (Awadh, Kara/Allahabad) was transported to the Delhi region. But transport of bulk commodities overland was expensive, and was carried on mainly by the *banjaras*, who moved with their families along with thousands of bullocks. Perhaps, the operations of the *banjaras* were financed by the rich merchants, the *sahs* and the *modis*, though we do not have enough information on the subject. Expensive but bulky commodities, like fine quality textiles, were carried on the backs of horses or in bullock carts. The movement of these good was in caravans or *tandas*, protected by hired soldiers because roads were unsafe on account of both wild animals and dacoits.

The building of the road from Delhi to Deogir by Muhammad bin Tughlaq illustrates the manner in which road communication were sought to be improved. Thus, trees were planted on both sides of the road, and a halting station (*sarai*) was built every two miles (*karoh*) where food and drink was available. In Bengal, an embankment was made so that a part of the road to Lakhnauti which had remained under water during rains could become passable.

Regarding the commodities transported in long distance trade, apart from the bulk commodities, textiles were the main item. We have already referred to *muslin* from Bengal and Deogir, and fine textiles from Gujarat. Horses, both foreign and domestic, were also an important item of import. Indigo, spices, ungents, drugs, leather-goods were other important items. Shawls and carpets from Kashmir were in demand at Delhi. So were dry fruits. Wine was imported from abroad, and also produced at Meerut and Aligarh in the Gangetic doab.

Regarding the financing of long distance trade, the *hundi* system must have continued. The *modis* and *sarrafs* were the main means of operating and financing the *hundi* system. Although there was no system of banking as such, the village *bania* at the village level, and the *modis* and *sarrafs* at the national level were the main means of providing finance for agricultural operations and trade. According to an eminent modern historian, K.M. Ashraf, the interest charged on loans was 10 per cent per annum for big loans, and 20 per cent on small or petty sums.

(b) Foreign Trade

India had an old tradition of trade with West Asia and extending through it to the Mediterranean world, as also to Central Asia, South-East Asia and China both by over-seas and over-land routes. The overland routes lay through the Bolan pass to Herat, and through the Khyber pass to Bokhara and Samarqand, and also by the Kashmir routes to Yarkand and Khotan for onward transmission to China. These trade routes were sometimes disrupted due to the outpouring of nomadic hordes from Central Asia, such as the Hun eruption during the 6th-7th centuries, and the Mongol onslaught during the 13th century. The rise and fall of empires also effected the safety of these trade routes. However, the traders proved to be extremely hardy and skillful in overcoming these obstacles. Also, the nomads quickly realised the value of permitting trade to flow, and tax it to their benefit. Thus, the Mongols not only permitted trade but, when not at war, themselves traded in camels and horses, arms, falcons, furs and musk. Although Balban had difficulties in getting horses from Central Asia on account of the Mongols, this must have been temporary because Alauddin Khalji had no such difficulty. With the establishment of the Mongol empires, and the security of roads, trade with China and West Asia became easier than ever before. The effect of the destruction of flourishing cities such as Samarqand and Bokhara by the Mongols should not, therefore, be overestimated. With the gradual assimilation of the Mongols to Islam, conditions for trade improved further during the 14th century. However, over- land trade concentrated on commodities which were light in weight but high in value because of the high cost of transportation. Hors- es were the most important commodity imported overland into In- dia. There was a steady demand for Arabi, Iraqi and Central Asian horses in India for the needs of the army, the cavalry being the principal instrument of warfare. They were also valued for pur- poses of show and status. Hence, the careful regulation of sale and purchase of horses was a priority for the state. The other commodities imported into India included camels, furs, white slaves, velvet, dry fruits and wines. Tea and silk were imported from China, though silk was also imported from Persia, the mulberry tree and silk co- coons having been introduced there during the 13th and 14th cen- tury by the Mongols. The exports from India included cotton tex- tiles, food stuffs such as rice, sugar and spices. There was a con- tinuous export of slaves from India for whom the demand in the Islamic world was quite considerable.

The principal centre for overland trade from India was Multan. Lahore had been ruined by the Mongols in 1241, and was not able to regain itself till the reign of Muhammad Tughlaq. Multan was also the entry point of all foreigners, including traders who were all called Khurasanis. It is difficult to estimate their number, but in wealth they appear to be inferior to the Multanis. However, the foreign merchants, especially the Arabs, were more active in Gujarat and Malabar in overseas trades. Indians, both Hindus (Agrawal and Maheshwari) and Jains and Bohras were also active in this trade, with colonies of Indian traders living in West and South-East Asia. Bengal also carried on trade with China and countries of South- East Asia, exporting textiles, and importing silks, spices etc. Ma Huan, who came to Bengal in the early part of the fifteenth century, men- tions that "wealthy individuals who built ships and go to foreign countries to trade are quite numerous."

B. Social Life

i. The Ruling Classes (a) The Nobility

The most important class which emerged in northern India during the 13th century was the ruling class consisting of the nobles. Generally, the nobles have been divided into three categories, the Khans being the highest category, followed by Maliks and Amirs. However, this categorisation was never very clear. To begin with, people holding junior posts in and around the court, such as *sarjandar* (commander of the king's personal forces), *saqi-i-khas* (in-charge of water and other drinks etc.), as also those holding the posts of *sipahsalar, sar-i-khail* (junior commanders of military forces) were called amirs. Later, the word amir began to be used in a loose sense to signify a person of wealth and influence in the government. The most important categories remained the Maliks, and the Khans. All the top posts in the government were held by persons belonging to these categories. In the lists of nobles given by Minhaj Siraj and Barani, only Maliks are mentioned. The category of Khan was the result of Mongol influence among whom the Qa-an (Khan) was the commander of 10,000 troops. In the Delhi Sultanat, the word 'Khan' was only used to give a special status. Thus, Balban was given the title of Ulugh Khan. The nobles were also dignified by being given other titles, such as Khwaja Jahan, Imad-ul-Mulk, Nizam-ul-Mulk, etc. They were also awarded various privileges (*maratib*), such as robes of different kinds, sword and dagger, flags, drums, etc. These were greatly valued because they often signified status, and closeness to the Sultan. Horses and elephants with costly trappings were also awarded to them on special occasions.

We do not have any precise idea of the number of nobles in office at any one time. Minhaj Siraj gives a list of 32 Maliks under Iltutmish which included 8 princes who were displaced Central Asian rulers. Perhaps, the term *Turkan-i-Chahalgani*, or the corps of forty Turks used by Barani is a reflection of the number of top nobles. For Balban's reign, Barani gives a list of 36 Maliks excluding qazis. The number of top nobles rose to 48 under Alauddin Khalji, out of which 7 were relations, including sons. From this, we may conclude that till the Sultanat suddenly expanded after the death of Alauddin Khalji, the number of top nobles or Maliks in the country was quite small. As we have seen, even among this small group of nobles, there was bitter factional fighting. In this struggle, mutual relationships, ethnicity etc. played a role. The Turks considered themselves superior to all others such as Tajiks, Khaljis, Afghans, Hindustanis etc. The Turks ousted the Tajiks after the death of Iltutmish, and established a virtual Turkish monopoly over high offices. This was broken with the rise of the Khaljis. Under the Khaljis and the Tughlaqs, Indian Muslims forged ahead, largely on the basis of personal efficiency. However, foreign blood, or descent from a well-known foreign family continued to have considerable social value and esteem, as the Moorish traveller, Ibn Battutah, testifies.

We do not have much knowledge about the social origin of the high grandees. During the early phase, there was considerable social mobility among the nobles, and people from a wide social background, who had the capacity to attract and maintain a military following (*jamiat*) or who caught the eye of the Sultan, could, with luck, rise to the position of a Malik. Many of the nobles had, in fact, started their career as slaves, and slowly climbed the social ladder. This open character of the nobility continued to a large extent during the 13th century on account of the rapid rise and fall of dynasties, resulting in large scale displacement of nobles belonging to the previous regimes. Thus, in the 13th century we hardly hear of families whose members continued to hold the position of high grandees for more than one generation.

During the 14th century, with the rise of the Khaljis, and then of the Tughlaqs who ruled for almost a hundred years, the social character of the nobility broadened, and it became more stabilized. With the breaking of the Turkish monopoly of high offices, the zone of recruitment to the nobility broadened. Many Khaljis, Afghans and Hindustanis were admitted to the nobility. No attempt was made to exclude the Turks. However, according to popular perception, even when a noble lost his power and position, the tradition of former dignity and social honour were handed over to his descendants who believed that their restoration to former power was only a question of time and opportunity.

Along with the clergy, these sections constituted what were called *ashraf* (pl. of *sharif*) or the respected sections. According to contemporary thinking, the state had a special responsibility towards these sections, not only in matters of employment, but for giving pensions to the widows, even providing funds for the marriage of their unmarried daughters.

Generally speaking, there was a broad division among the *ahl-i-saif* or men of the sword, and the *ahl-i-qalam* or the literati. The latter were chosen for judicial and clerical posts. The *ulema* also fell in this category. As long as administration was tantamount to a military exercise for realising land-revenue from recalcitrant chiefs, *muqaddams* and peasants, the literati had to be kept away from administration, although it was urged that the wazir should come from the class of the literati. In general, the nobles looked down on the literati, and considered them unfit for administrative or political matters. Thus, Alauddin Khalji not only rejected the advice of Qazi Mughis to try and arrange a compromise with the Mongols, but ridiculed him for offering advice on military and political matters although he was a *nawisanda* (clerk), and the son of a *nawisanda*!

The emergence of a class of *ashraf* from whom the nobility was expected to be recruited gave it a measure of social stability, but also heightened stratification in Muslim society. The counterpart of the *ashraf* were the *ajlaf* or *kam-asl*, i.e. the lower, inferior classes consisting of citizens, professionals and working sections, such as weavers, peasants, and labourers. While such social gradations had existed among the Muslims in West and Central Asia, they became even more rigid and pronounced after their coming to India which had a tradition of stratification on the basis of heredity, i.e. caste.

Arising from this deep social division was the belief that only persons belonging to the 'respectable' classes had the right to occupy high offices in the state. Hence, there was widespread resentment among the upper classes when Muhammad Tughlaq appointed to high offices, apparently on the basis of their efficiency, Hindus and Muslims belonging to the 'inferior' classes or castes, such as wine-distillers, barbers, cooks, gardeners, shop keepers (*bazaris*) etc. The experiment failed for a variety of reasons. Firuz Tughlaq earned high praise and approval when he chose as nobles only those whose ancestors had been in the service of the king or belonged to the 'respected' classes. That the prejudice was not against 'Hindustanis' as such but against the so-called inferior classes, whether Hindustani Muslim, is borne out by the fact that Firuz's wazir, Khan-i-Jahan, who was a converted *brahman*, was acceptable to all sections of the Muslims. This was in stark contrast to the Baraduis or Parwaris, wrongly considered to be low-caste converts, who had come to the top for a brief time after the death of Alauddin Khalji, and have been sharply denounced by Barani.

We are told by Barani that during the time of Balban when, apparently, the nobles did not have much ready cash in their hands, whenever they wanted to hold a *majlis* or a convivial party, their agents would rush to the houses of the Sahs and Multanis to borrow money, so that all the money from their *iqta* went to them as repayment, and gold and silver was to be found in the houses of the merchants alone. This situation seems to have changed with the coming of Alauddin Khalji and the growth of a new centralised system of land revenue administration which began with him, and continued under the Tughlaqs. In the new system of revenue administration, there was an emphasis on payment of land-revenue in cash. This applied not only to *khalisa* territories, i.e. reserved territories income from which went to the central treasury, but even in areas assigned as *iqta*. Thus, when Ibn Battutah was appointed a judge and given a salary of 5,000 *dinars*, it was paid for by assigning him 2½ villages, the annual income of which came to that sum. We now also hear of nobles being assigned large salaries. Thus, a Malik was paid between 50,000 to 60,000 tankas; an amir 30,000 to 40,000 tankas, a *sipahsalar* got 20,000 tankas. These salaries were even higher under Firuz Tughlaq. Thus, Khan-i-Jahan Maqbul got 13 lakh tankas over and above the expenses of his army and servants, and separate allowances for his sons and sons-in-law. Other nobles got salaries ranging from four to eight lakh tankas per year.

This implied unprecedented centralization of the rural surplus in the hands of the central elite. The high emoluments not only implied great affluence for the nobles, but possibility of hoarding of wealth. When Malik Shahin, who was *naib amir-i-majlis* of Sultan Firuz, died, he left behind 50 lakh tankas besides jewels, ornaments and costly robes. Imad-ul-Mulk Bashir-i-Sultani, who had been the Sultan's slave, left behind 13 crores tankas of which the Sultan confiscated 9 crores. However, these appear to be exceptions rather than the rule. Apart from being an insurance against uncertainty, the growth of such hoards was also an index of a slow growth of a money economy in the country. However, the growth of a money economy seems to have led to a change in the attitude towards trade and traders. Ibn Battutah alludes to the ships owned by the sultan of Delhi. On one occasion, the sultan, Muhammad bin Tughlaq, placed three ships at the disposal of Shihabuddin Kazruni, a friend and associate, who had a flourishing overseas trade, and was called a "king of merchants." Almost for the first time, traders began to be involved in the tasks of administration. Thus, Muhammad Tughlaq gave Shihabuddin the city of Khambayat in charge. If Battutah is to be believed, the Sultan had even promised him the post of the Wazir, but he was murdered at the instance of the Wazir, Khan-i-Jahan, while on his way to Delhi.

We are also told that Abul Hasan Ibadi of Iraq, who lived in Delhi, used to trade with the money of Sultan Muhammad bin Tughlaq, and to buy weapons and goods for him in Iraq and Khurasan. Other nobles may have followed the Sultan's example, though we have no evidence of it. On balance, it appears that the major investments of the nobles were not in trade but in orchards, the numbers of which grew sharply under Firuz with the growing prosperity of the nobles. However, further development in the direction of productive investments by the nobles had to await the re-centralization of the empire under Akbar.

We have little information about the education and cultural outlook and values of the Turkish nobles. Apparently, they were not illiterate: even slaves purchased by merchants in the slave market of Samarqand and Bokhara were educated before being resold. Although many of the slaves were newly converted, they had imbibed the Islamic religious and cultural norms prevalent in Central Asia, Khurasan etc. Nonetheless, they could hardly have imbibed the cultural graces of an old and well-established nobility. Nor could they be expected to be knowledgeable patrons of culture, though it was considered a mark of prestige to patronize poets and writers, sometimes even to give them extravagant rewards. This began to change with the rise of Amir Khusrau and his companion, Amir Hasan Sijzi, towards the end of the 13th century. Gradually, a new Indo-Muslim culture developed, and many nobles and sufis actively contributed to it. Thus, Zia Nakkshabi (d. 1350) wrote on many subjects including poetry, and had a number of Sanskrit works translated into Persian.

Thus, from being merely rude warriors, the nobles began slowly to emerge as patrons of culture as well.

(b) The Chiefs—Emergence of "Zamindars"

Although the Rajputs had lost state power almost all over north India, with the exception of Rajasthan and adjacent areas, and in the remoter hill regions of the Himalayas, Bundelkhand, etc., Rajput rajas continued to dominate large tracts of the countryside even in the centrally administered areas of Punjab, the doab, Bihar Gujarat, etc. They were called rai, rana, rawat, etc. However, the term 'chief' has been applied to them. They had their own armed forces, and generally lived in the countryside in their fortresses. We have little idea of their numbers or the strength of their forces, but they were important in the political, social and economic life of the countryside. Although the contemporary sources invariably portray them as enemies against whom constant *jihad* was not only legitimate but necessary, a relationship of permanent hostility was not feasible for the Turkish rulers, or for them. For the Turkish rulers, it was convenient to allow them to rule the areas under their control as long as they paid a stipulated sum of money regularly as tribute, and generally behaved in a loyal manner.

We have evidence of a growing political relationship between the Turkish rulers and the Hindu chiefs. Thus, we are told that Hindu *rais* from a hundred *kos* used to come and witness the splendour of Balban's court. After Balban's victory over Tughril in Bengal, he was welcomed in Awadh by many, including the *rais* of the area. Later, when Firuz Tughlaq invaded Bengal, he was joined by the *rais* of eastern U.P., the most important of them being Udai Singh, the Rai of Gorakhpur and Champaran, who paid 20 lakhs of tribute that was due from him.

In another instance, when Malik Chhajju, a nephew of Balban and governor of Kara rebelled against Jalaluddin Khalji, he was joined by the local *rais*, and *rawats* and *payaks* of the area who "swarmed around with their forces like ants and locusts." They stood by his side in his contest with Jalaluddin Khalji. Malik Chajju was defeated, but from this time onwards, Hindu chiefs seem to have been in attendance of the Sultan at his court. Thus, we hear that under Firuz Tughlaq, Aniratthu who was "lord of two royal canopies (*chatra*)," Rai Madar (or Ballar) Deva, Rai Sumer, Rawat Adhiram, etc. were not only allowed to attend, but were allowed to sit down in the court.

Despite these growing political linkages during the Sultanat rule, the position of the chiefs was one of considerable uncertainty. It was a part of the policy of the sultans of Delhi to overthrow the Hindu chiefs whenever they could, or at any rate, to try and reduce their powers and privileges by extending the imperial system of revenue administration to the territories dominated by the chiefs. While such a process did not, in all probability, reduce the actual burden on the cultivators, it meant a reduction of the perquisites of the chiefs, and possibly other intermediaries.

By the beginning of the 14th century, we find increasing references to the zamindars. This term, which does not exist outside India, was used increasingly to designate the hereditary intermediaries. Amir Khusrau was amongst the first to use it. In course of time, the term began to be applied to the *khuts* and *muqaddams* and *chaudhris*, and even to those former chiefs who had been forced or pressurized to pay not a fixed lump sum, but a sum fixed on the basis of land-revenue assessment. Under the Mughals, and word "zamindar" began to be used for all hereditary owners of land or those who had a hereditary share in the land revenue. Even chiefs were included in this category.

We have little idea of the life style of the privileged rural sections, but generally their affluence is contrasted to the poverty of the rest.

ii. Adjuncts to the Ruling Class: Judicial and Junior Administrative Officers, and the Ulema

The ruling classes, especially the nobility, could hardly have functioned without the help of a group of lower functionaries, in addition to the large number of servants, slaves and other retainers they employed. These functionaries can be broadly divided into two: judicial and religious functionaries, on the one hand, and revenue and administrative functionaries on the other. The former consisted of *qazis* and *muftis* who were appointed in every city where there was a sizable population of Muslims. They dispensed civil justice where Muslims were concerned, leaving the Hindus to deal their own cases on the basis of customary law, and the *Dharmashastras*. They also dealt with criminal justice. At their head was the Chief Qazi. In the capital and perhaps in other cities there was a *Dad Bak* who was responsible for checking arbitrary exaction of taxes, and supervising and controlling the *amirs* who were responsible for surveying and keeping a record of properties of Muslims for purposes of taxation. There was also the *muhtasib* who worked under the kotwal and was responsible for seeing that the Muslims did not openly violated the *sharia*, or disregard compulsory obligations such as observation of *roza*, *namaz* etc. He was also responsible for checking weights and measures.

All these posts were paid, and their numbers grew as the size of the Muslim population in the country increased. There were also Imams, *muazzins* etc. who were appointed in various mosques, and reciters of the Holy Quran who were appointed to mausoleums, or were called to various religious functions. In addition, there were religious divines who were appointed as teachers in various schools (*maqtab*), colleges (*madrasa*), etc. All these sections broadly constituted the theological class or *ulema*. The *ulema* were highly respected. As a general rule, they had undergone a course of training in Muslim Law, logic and theology, including some knowledge of Arabic. In addition to these official classes, there was a large group of Muslim scholars, pious men etc. who received support from the state through stipends, grant of revenue-free lands etc.

We have little idea of the social base of this large and amorphous group of people. In general, they formed what in modern times would be called the lower middle and middle classes, though some of the *ulema* rose to the position of chief qazis etc., and became more a part of the ruling class. Very often, poets, scholars, historians, doctors and lower functionaries in the government—the *amils* (revenue collectors), *muharrirs* (accountants) etc. came from the same social class. We can also call this class the literati, or the educated, literate class. As we know, in a country which was predominantly illiterate, people who were educated and could also speak in the name of religion, had enormous prestige. Nevertheless, the *ulema*, as a class, did not enjoy a high reputation among the discerning sections. Bughra Khan, the son of Balban, warned his son, Kaiqubad, against the latter day theologians whom he described as "greedy rogues whose highest duty was this world and not the next." Amir Khusrau considered the qazis who accepted judicial offices to be corrupt and ignorant, and unfit to occupy any responsible positions in the kingdom. They were arrogant and vain, and were generally considered time-servers who were prepared to sacrifice their principles and beliefs to please those in powers. In general, the Sultans did not allow them to have any say in political affairs, confining them to deciding judicial cases, religious matters and education. Nonetheless, the *ulema* did play a positive role in acting as a bridge between the ruling classes and the ordinary Muslims, and imbuing the Muslims with a sense of unity. Simultaneously, it must be noted that many of the *ulemas* were foreigners who had taken refuge in India on account of the Mongols, or were attracted to India by its prosperity. They had little understanding of India, and they and a section of theologians in India accentuated social tensions and bitterness between the ordinary Hindus and Muslims by constantly harping on elements of religious conflict, ignoring the sense of social amity that generally prevailed among the people.

A large number of clerks and officials were needed to man the growing machinery of administration at the centre, and in the various provincial and district towns following the new system of revenue administration introduced by Alauddin Khalji. The power of these officials, possibilities of corruption and oppression on their part, and the harsh corrective steps taken by Alauddin against them have been described graphically by Barani. We do not know the social background of these new recruits to government service. A large number of them may have been converted into Indian Muslims, or members of the *ulema* class. If we exclude the *muqaddams* and the *patwaris* who were Hindus, and who lived in the villages, most of these lower officials must have been Muslims. However, Hindus seem to have entered into this class under Muhammad bin Tughlaq. This would explain the selection by him of a small number among them to high positions. Thus, we have the emergence of a class of Persian knowing Hindus by this time.

iii. The Trading & Financial Classes

India had an old tradition of trade and a well developed class of traders and financers since ancient times. Thus, laws relating to contract, loans, sale and purchase are set out by the *Dharmashastras*. The emergence of the Vaishyas as a separate trading community, and their being included in the category of the *dvija* (lit. twice born or the privileged sections) is an index of their position in the social and economic life of the country. It is, however, necessary to make a distinction between the leading merchants or *nagar streshtins* from the ordinary shop-keepers (*banik*), and transporters (*banjaras*). The former, according to the *Panchantantra*, a 5th century fable, were considered socially close to the ruler, and mingled freely with his family members. The leading merchants not only dealt with wholesale and long distance trade, which included foreign trade, but also dealt with finance and money-changing. Long distance trade was financed, insured against risk, and money transported from place to place through the system of *hundis*.

The establishment of a strong centralized empire in north India; the establishment of a sound currency system, mainly based on the silver tanka; the growing security of roads; growth of towns, and opening up of India to the Islamic world were important factors which led to the growth and expansion of India's overland trade to West and Central Asia, as well as overseas trade, mainly from Gujarat. This is testified to by the frequent reference to the Multanis as traders and financers. As is well known, throughout the medieval times, Multan was a very important trading centre, being linked directly across the Bolan Pass to Qandhar, Herat and Bokhara which was the junction of the "silk road", extending eastward across Central Asia to China, and westward across Iran to Constantinople and Lebanon. Multan was also linked via the river Indus to the western sea ports. It would appear that the bulk of the Multanis were Hindus.

We have already referred to Barani's accounts how the Multanis and the Sahs of Delhi had become so rich by lending money to the nobles that gold and silver was to be found in their houses alone. Barani testifies to the wealth and prosperity of the Multanis and the Sahs in other ways also. He says that Jalaudin Khalji bluntly refused to take stern action against the Hindus who even at the capital, Delhi, had full religious freedom, and the wealthy ones among them, obviously the Multani traders and merchants, were leading a life of ease and pleasure, with no fear about the safety of their life and property.

Another section of traders to whom Barani refers to are the *dallals* or brokers. The brokers were commission agents who charged a fee for bringing buyers and sellers together. Their emergence is an index of the growth of trade at Delhi. We are told that buyers of different commodities, especially textiles, used to throng to Delhi following the control of the market by Alauddin. Barani refers to brokers especially in the context of Alauddin's effort to control the sale of horses. He uses strong words about these *dallals* many of whom, specially the horse traders, were Muslims. They formed a rich and powerful group which, on occasions, could even defy the Sultan, and disregard his orders.

The Muslim traders at Delhi were generally foreigners—Iraqis, Iranians, Khurasanis, etc. although we hear of a few Muslim Multanis. Thus, the father and grand-father of Hisamuddin, whom Alauddin had appointed a qazi, had been leading merchants of Multan. According to Ibn Battutah, in India all the foreign traders were called Khurasanis. The Afghans were another group of Muslim trader. They specialized in caravan trade, and trade in horses.

We have little idea about the trading communities in different parts of India. Gujarat had a well established tradition of trade, and of trading communities, both India and foreign. We have already referred to an Egyptian, Shihabuddin Kazruni, who owned many ships, and lived at Khambayat. The Jains, the Marwaris, the Gujarati banias and the Bohras were also active, according to traditional accounts. It was from one of these traders that Malik Kafur was procured for Alauddin.

iv. Standard of Living

Contemporary chroniclers give a lot of space in describing the extravagant life style of the Sultans—their palaces, their furnishings, the lavish expense on the upkeep of the large number of women and relatives in their harems, their costly cloths and jewellery, expenses on the royal stables, and their extravagant gifts to nobles, poets, the learned and the saintly etc. Such a life style had become customary, and was also supposed to impress the subjects and the courtiers.

We need not concern ourselves unduly with the life style of individual sultans, any more than we need bother about the life styles of the modern day play-boys, except that the Sultans, being centres of patronage and accepted as leaders of society, exercised a tremendous influence on the life-style and behaviour pattern of the elites.

We have already noticed the growing affluence of the nobles from the time of the rise of the Tughlaqs. However, even during the reign of Balban, we are told that his cousin, Malik Kishli Khan, on one occasion gave in gift all his horses and 10,000 tankas to poets and minstrels. Fakhruddin, the kotwal of Delhi under Balban, used to give financial grants to 12,000 readers of Quran, and give dowries to 1000 poor girls each year. He never wore the same dress twice, or slept in the same bed twice. Balban's *diwan-i-arz*, Imad-ul-Mulk, was famous for the lavish repast, consisting of fifty to sixty trays of food which were served to his officials and clerks every day. Mir Maqbul, a noble of Muhammad Tughlaq, used to spend three and a half lakh tankas on his personal expenses. Khan-i-Jahan, the wazir of Firuz, had 20,000 women in his harem. Such examples of extravagence on the part of the nobles can be multiplied.

The life style of nobles did lead to the setting up of specialized industries in different parts of the country, catering to the demand created by them. It is difficult to estimate the number of people employed in such industries, or those who provided them services. But their numbers must have been considerable, since most of the nobles did not hoard their riches. Nor did the nobles invest their wealth in productive enterprises, except in gardens during the reign of Muhammad Tughlaq, more specially under Firuz.

We have little idea of the standard of living of the junior bureaucrats, members of the judiciary and the ecclesiastical classes and professionals, such as hakims, poets, musicians, etc. Some of the famous hakims seem to have been financially well off. The position of the poets etc. depended upon the nature of the patronage they received. Thus, the father of Amir Khusrau had a stipend of 1200 tankas a year from Balban when he was a noble. Ahmad Chap, Balban's *ariz*, once gave 10,000 tankas, 100 horses and 320 dresses for the royal musicians to sing at his house. In general, these sections led a life of comfort, but not affluence.

As far as the general population in the towns is concerned, their standard of living was largely determined by prices and wages. We have little idea of prices before Alauddin Khalji. By his market control measures, Alauddin ensured the supply of cheap food stuffs. Thus, Barani tells us that wheat was sold at 7½ *jital* per *man*, barley at 4 *jitals*, and good quality rice at 5 *jitals*. However, while the cost of subsistence was low, wages were also low. Thus, we are told that in Alauddin's reign, the wages of an artisan amounted to 2 or 3 *jitals* per day or about 1½ to 2 tankas a month.[1] Barani tells us that six *jitals* worth of bread and meatstew, i.e. a bare subsistence would suffice for seven or eight persons. The salaries of servants, we are told, were 10 to 12 tankas, probably a year. The salary fixed for the cavalrymen by Alauddin, 234 tankas a year, or about 20 tankas a month for the soldier and his mount was thus one which allowed the trooper to live in some style. We are told that after the death of Alauddin, the price control system collapsed, and prices rose rapidly, with wages rising four times. These figures cannot be calculated exactly. By analyzing the prices mentioned by Ibn Battutah, it seems that prices rose a little over one-and-a-half times. Wages may have risen in the same proportion. Prices and wages were higher still during the early years of Firuz's reign. During his reign, according to Afif, without any effort on the Sultan's part, the prices declined almost to the level of Alauddin's reign. However, wages still remained high. The causes of the fluctuation of the prices of food grains—whether they were linked to good harvest and expansion of cultivation, or was part of a world-wide shortage of silver is still a matter of debate among historians.

v. Towns and Town Life: Artisans and Slaves

We have already seen that there was a revival of towns in north India from the 10th century. This process was considerably accelerated from the 13th century as a result of Turkish centralization, and the growth of a new city-based ruling class with a high standard of living. Apart from Delhi, which Ibn Battutah calls the largest city in the eastern part of the Islamic world, we are told that Daultabad (Deogiri) equalled Delhi in size. Other cities which rose to prominence in north India during the period were Multan, Lahore, Kara (near modern Allahabad), Lakhnauti and Khambayat.

---

1. In north India, 48 *jitals* made a tanka. Alauddin's *man* was equivalent to 16 kgs. of modern times.

The economic life of the town was dominated by the nobles and their retinues, traders and shop-keepers, as we have noted. The largest section in the cities consisted of the servants and slaves, artisans, soldiers, and a miscellaneous group consisting of peddlers, musicians, performers (*nat*), self-employed people and beggars. We hardly have a profile of these miscellaneous sections, i.e. their lifestyles, social background etc. It seems that the cities performed the function of a large social churner whereby people of diverse backgrounds and ethnic origins, slaves, artisans, and others came to live together. The entry to the city was carefully regulated by the kotwal, who was not only responsible for the maintenance of law and order, but regulated the markets, and houses of ill-fame (gambling, prostitution, etc.) According to tradition, people following a particular profession lived in a particular area (*mohalla*) which was locked at night for the sake of safety. There was a definite pattern in the lay-out of the towns: there was a separate quarter for the king and the nobles, while scavengers, leather-workers, beggars etc. were allotted quarters at the outskirts of the towns, but within the town-wall. Delhi had a large mass of beggars who thronged the houses of the nobles for charity, or resorted to mausoleums, shrines of sufi saints etc. Like the ordinary population, they carried arms, and could sometimes create problems of law and order.

The city was a centre of many crafts; weaving, painting on cloth, embroidery, etc. The royal *karkhanas* employed many artisans in preparing costly items, such as cloth embroidered with gold and silver thread, silk etc. But most of the artisans worked at home, and were organised in guilds along caste lines. However, not all the specialized crafts, such as weaving, were located in the towns. In south India and Gujarat, there were many villages and small towns which specialized in particular types of textile production. Thus, unlike medieval Europe, we should not divide crafts in India into water-tight compartments between towns and the countryside. The craft link between the towns and the countryside was also a factor which facilitated the movement of artisans from the countryside to the towns.

Slaves

Another large section in the town consisted of slaves and domestic servants. Slavery had existed in India as well as in West Asia and Europe for a long time. The position of different types of slaves—one born in the household, one purchased, one acquired and one inherited is discussed in the Hindu *Shastras*. Slavery had been adopted by the Arabs and later, by the Turks also. The most usual method of acquiring a slave was to capture in war. Even the *Mahabharata* considered it normal enslave a prisoner of war. The Turks practiced this on a large scale in their wars, in and outside India. Slave markets for men and women existed in West Asia as well as in India. The Turkish, Caucasian, Greek and Indian slaves were valued and were sought after. A small number of slaves were also imported from Africa, mainly Abyssinia. Slaves were generally bought for domestic service, for company, or for their special skills. Skilled slaves or comely boys, and handsome girls sometimes fetched a high price. Skilled slaves were valued and some of them rose to high offices as in the case of the slaves of Qutbuddin Aibak.

Slave raiding was widely practised in West and Central Asia, the *ghazis* being specially used to capture and then convert slaves from Central Asia. The early Turkish rulers, such as Qutbuddin Aibak, continued this practice in India. Thus, when he invaded Gujarat in 1195, he captured and enslaved 20,000 persons, and another 50,000 during his raid of Kalinjar. However, we do not hear of any such large scale enslavement during the campaigns of Balban and Alauddin Khalji, although slaves were still considered a part of the booty. More often captured prisoners of war were slaughtered, only a few chosen ones being brought back as slaves. But during campaigns of "pacification" in the country-side, large number of men, women and children were enslaved, and sold in the slave market at Delhi. The sale and purchase of slaves was such a routine matter that Barani mentions the price of slave-girls and handsome boys along with cattle! However, unlike Central Asia where captured Turkish slaves were used for military purposes, the slaves sold in the market in Delhi were used mainly for domestic service. This was so common than even clerks did not think it amiss to employ slaves. Generally, slaves were not used or trained for being craftsmen, though maid-servants were often used for spinning, and we hear of even sufi saints living on the earnings of their slaves.

A departure from this practice was made by Firuz Tughlaq. He instructed the bigger nobles to capture slaves whenever they were at war, and to pick out and send the best among them for the service of the Sultan. Even the various subordinate chiefs were asked to follow this practice. In this way, 180,000 slaves were collected. While some of them were trained for religious studies, 12,000 among them were trained as artisans, and dispersed into various paragans.

This suggests an acute shortage of trained artisans in the towns. The slaves also formed a corp of armed guards. However, the effort to create a corp of Janissaris on the Turkish model failed. The corp of slaves tried to act as king maker at the death of Firuz and was defeated and dispersed.

Although domestic slavery continued under the Mughals, the slaves did not play any important role in manufacturing, or in the military. However, there is little doubt that the practice of slavery was not only inhuman, it lowered the status of free labour, and depressed wages.

vi. Women, Caste, Social Manners and Customs

There were hardly any changes in the structure of the Hindu society during the period. The *Smriti* writers of the time continued to assign a high place to the brahmanas, while strongly denouncing the unworthy members of the order. According to one school of thinking, the brahmanas were permitted to engage in agriculture not only in times of distress, but also in normal times since officiating at sacrifices, etc. did not furnish means of subsistence in the Kali Age.

The *Smriti* texts continue to emphasize that punishing the wicked and cherishing the good was the duty of the kshatriyas, and that the right to wield weapons for the purpose of protecting the people likewise belonged to them alone. The duties and occupations of shudras and their disabilities were more or less repeated. While the highest duty of the shudra was the service of the other castes, he was allowed to engage in all occupation, except to deal in liquor and meat. The ban on the study and recitation of the Vedas by shudras was repeated, but not on hearing the recitation of the Puranas. Some writers go as far as to say that not only eating a shudra's food but also living in the same house with him, sitting in the same cot and receiving religious instructions from a learned shudra were to be avoided. This may be regarded as an extreme view. However, the severest restrictions were placed on mingling with the *chandalas* and other 'outcastes'.

There was little change in the position of women in the Hindu society. The old rules enjoining early marriage for girls, and the wife's obligation of service and devotion to the husband, continued. Annulment of the marriage was allowed in special circumstances, such as desertion, loathsome disease, etc. But not all writers agree with this. Widow remarriage continued to be regarded among the practices prohibited in the Kali Age. But this apparently applied to the three upper castes only. Regarding the practice of sati, some writers approve it emphatically, while others allow it with some conditions. A number of travellers mention its prevalence in different regions of the country. Ibn Battutah mentions with horror the scene of a woman burning herself in the funeral pyre of her husband with great beating of drums. According to him, permission from the Sultan had to be taken for the performance of sati.

Regarding property, the commentators uphold the widow's right to the property of a sonless husband, provided the property was not joint, i.e. had been divided. The widow was not merely the guardian of this property, but had the full right to dispose of it. Thus, it would appear that the property rights of women improved in the Hindu law.

During this period, the practice of keeping women in seclusion and asking them to veil their faces in the presence of outsiders, that is, the practice of purdah became widespread among the upper class women. The practice of secluding women from the vulgar gaze was practised among the upper class Hindus, and was also in vogue in ancient Iran, Greece, etc. The Arabs and the Turks adopted this custom and brought it to India with them. Due to their example, it became widespread in India, particularly in north India. The growth of purdah has been attributed to the fear of the Hindu women being captured by the invaders. In an age of violence, women were liable to be treated as prizes of war. Perhaps, the most important factor for the growth of purdah was social—it became a symbol of the higher classes in society, and all those who wanted to be considered respectable tried to copy it. Also, religious justification was found for it. Whatever the reason, it affected women adversely, and made them even more dependent on men.

During the Sultanat period, the Muslim society remained divided into ethnic and racial groups. We have already noticed the deep economic disparities within it. The Turks, Iranians, Afghans and Indian Muslims rarely married with each other. In fact, these sections developed some of the caste exclusiveness of the Hindus. Converts from lower sections of the Hindus were also discriminated against.

The Hindu and Muslim upper classes did not have much social intercourse between them during this period, partly due to the superiority complexes of the latter and partly due to the religious restrictions of inter-marriage and inter-dining between them. The Hindu upper castes applied to the Muslims the restrictions they applied to the shudras. But it should be borne in mind that caste restrictions did not close social intercourse between the Muslims and the upper caste Hindus and the shudras. At various times, Hindu soldiers were enrolled in Muslim armies. Most of the nobles had Hindus as their personal managers. The local machinery of administration remained almost entirely in the hand of the Hindus. Thus, occasions for mutual intercourse were manifold. The picture of the two communities being confined within themselves and having little to do with each other is, thus, neither real nor one which could be practised. Nor is it borne out by the evidence available to us. Conflict of interests as well as differences in social and cultural ideas, practices and beliefs did, however, create tensions, and slowed down the processes of mutual understanding and cultural assimilation.

10

POLITICS, STATE, SOCIETY AND THE ECONOMY IN SOUTH INDIA UNDER VIJAYANAGAR AND BAHMANID RULE (C. 1350-1565)

The decline of the Delhi Sultanat was accompanied by the rise of Vijayanagar and Bahmanid kingdoms which dominated India south of Vindhyas for more than 200 years. Although these kingdoms constantly fought with each other, they maintained law and order within their territories, and on the whole provided stable governments which enabled the growth of trade and commerce. Many of the rulers devoted themselves to the growth of agriculture, and built cities and capitals with magnificent buildings. Many of them were also patrons of art and culture.

Thus, in contrast to north India, two large territorial states emerged and functioned in south India from the middle of the 14th century onwards. A new situation arose with the break up of the Bahmanid kingdom towards the end of the 15th century, and the disintegration of the Vijayanagar empire later, following its defeat at the battle of Talikota in 1565. This was also the period when a European power, the Portuguese, entered the Asian scene, and tried on the basis of its naval strength to establish its domination over the seas and its bordering areas and to capture the overseas trade.

i. The Vijayanagar Empire—its Nature and Conflict with the Bahmani Kingdom

There is no agreement among scholars regarding the early origins of the Vijayanagar kingdom. While the role of Harihar and his brother, Bukka, in the foundation of the kingdom are generally accepted, the early origins of the family are far from clear. According to tradition, they belonged to a family of five brothers, and had been feudatories of the Kaktiyas of Warangal, and later joined the service of the ruler of Kampili in modern Karnataka, gradually rising to the position of ministers. When Kampili was over-run and conquered by Muhammad bin Tughlaq for giving refuge to a Muslim rebel, the two brother, it is said, were captured, and sent to Delhi as prisoners, and converted to Islam. Soon a rebellion broke out at Kampili against Turkish rule, and the brothers were sent to suppress the rebellion, but they forsook their new faith and joined the rebellion. A number of modern scholars reject this traditional account. According to them, there is little evidence of the brothers serving at Warangal, nor of their subsequent capture and conversion. According to them, Harihar and Bukka belonged to the group of 75 *nayaks* of Karnataka who had rebelled against Turkish rule, and that they belonged to a strong Shaivite family. They deny that the family had any earlier links with Andhra. Whatever the controversy, the point for us to note is that in building their system of administration, the Vijayanagar rulers not only used the Tamil traditions of Chola rule, but also Telugu and Kannada traditions of the Kakatiyas and the Hoysalas. Thus, they were not mere provincial leaders, but represented the entire south.

There was a complicated situation in south India following the collapse of Tughlaq rule. Some of the old surviving kingdoms, such as the Hoysalas of Mysore, lingered on and a number of new principalities arose. Of these the most important were the Sultans of Madurai, the Valema rulers of Warangal, and the Reddis of Telingana. Later, the Bahmani kingdom rose to the north of the Vijayanagar kingdom. These principalities constantly fought against each other, or allied themselves according to need. Thus, in the struggle against the Sultan of Madurai, the Hoysala ruler, Ballal III, was defeated and executed in 1342. Taking advantage of this situation, Harihar and his brothers launched upon a campaign of expansion, and soon the whole of the Hoysala kingdom passed into their hands. This was followed by a protracted struggle against the Sultanat of Madurai. The Madurai Sultanat was wiped out by 1377. Vijayanagar rule now extended in the south upto Rameshwaram, and included parts of Kerala which had been parts of the Madurai sultanat. Earlier, Harihar had established a new capital, Vijayanagar, on the river Tungbhadra. According to tradition, he did so on the advice of the sage, Vidyaranya. However, according to another tradition, the city was built by Bukka who succeeded his brother in around 1356, and ruled till 1377.

Vijayanagar had to meet the rising power of the Bahmani Sultans in the north who, from time to time, received the support of the Valema rulers of Warangal and the Raya of Telingana who were afraid of the rising power of Vijayanagar, and looked upon the Bahmani ruler as a kind of a balancing factor.

The Bahmani kingdom was founded in 1347 by an Afghan noble, Alauddin Hasan, whose family had risen in the services of Alauddin Khalji. According to a popular legend, mentioned by Ferishta who wrote in the 17th century, Hasan has risen in the service of a brahman, Gangu, and was, therefore, known as Hasan Gangu. We do not know how far this legend is correct. After his elevation to the throne, Alauddin Hasan, in order to raise the status of his family, tried to trace his descent from the Iranian heroes, Isfandar and Bahman, and added the words "Bahman Shah" to his name. It was from this title that the kingdom was called the Bahmani kingdom.

The interests of the Vijayanagar rulers and the Bahmani sultans clashed in three separate and distinct areas; in the Tungbhadra doab, in the Krishna-Godavari delta, and in the Marathwada country. The Tungbhadra doab was the region between the rivers Krishna and Tungbhadra. On account of its wealth and economic resources, it had been the bone of contention between the Western Chalukyas and the Cholas in the earlier period, and between the Yadavas and the Hoyalas later on. The struggle for the mastery of the Krishna-Godavari basin which was very fertile and which, on account of its numerous ports, controlled the foreign trade of the region, was often linked with the struggle for the Tungbhadra doab. Thus, the rulers of the area allied themselves sometimes to the Bahmani kingdom, or sometimes sided with Vijayanagar to save themselves. In the Maratha country, the main contention was for the control of the Konkan and the ares which gave access to it. The Konkan was a narrow strip of land between the Western Ghats and the sea. Its principal port Goa was, thus, of great importance to the southern states.

Military conflict between the Vijayanagar and the Bahmani kingdoms was a constant feature almost throughout the existence of these two kingdoms. This had several effects; it emphasised the military aspect of both the kingdoms; also, the conflict between the two was often portrayed in religious terms. However, the various kingdoms

and states allied themselves more on secular than religious considerations. Although claiming to be defender of Hindu interests,
Vijayanagar rulers did not hesitate from employing a contingent
of Muslims horsemen, armed with bows. As we have seen, their
early struggle was against the Hoysala rulers who were Hindus.
Later, the Gajpati rulers of Orissa invaded and occupied parts of
the Vijayanagar kingdom, leading to a Vijayanagar-Bahmani alliance against them. The rulers of Warangal also allied themselves
for a long time with the Bahmani rulers against Vijayanagar.

The religious dimension cannot, however, be ignored altogether.
It made the conflict between Vijayanagar and the Bahmani sultans
more bitter, leading to widespread devastation in the contested areas and the neighbouring territories, with considerable loss of life
and property. Both sides sacked and burnt towns and villages, imprisoned and sold into slavery men, women and children, and committed other barbarities, often in the name of religion.

The battle for the Tungbhadra doab had commenced as early as
1356 when the Bahmani forces had attacked and captured Raichur,
but which was recovered by Harihar the following year. Warfare
between the two sides continued in recurrent cycles. Thus, in 1367,
Bukka embarked upon a war in association with the ruler of
Warangal to recover the areas lost to the Bahmani ruler earlier. We
are told that when Bukka I assaulted the fortress of Mudkal in the
disputed Tungbhadra doab, he slaughtered the entire garrison, except one man. When this news reached the Bahmani sultan, he was
enraged and, on the march, vowed that he would not sheath his
sword till he had slaughtered one hundred thousand Hindus in revenge. In spite of the rainy season and the opposition of the
Vijayanagar forces, he crossed the Tungbhadra,the first time a
Bahmani sultan had in person entered the Vijayanagar territory. There
are different versions about the outcome of the battle. According
to Persian sources, the Vijayanagar ruler was defeated, and had to
retire into the jungles. We hear for the first time of the use of ar-
tillery by both the sides in the battle. However, the Bahmani sultan could not gain a decisive victory, and the war dragged on for
several months, during which a wholesale slaughter of men, wom-
en and children went on. Finally, a kind of a treaty was patched
up which restored the old position whereby the doab was shared
by the two sides. A vague promise was also made that in future
wars the two sides would not slaughter helpless, unarmed inhabitants. However, this hardly had an effect on future warfare.

The elimination of the Sultan of Madurai in the south enabled Vijayanagar under Harihar II (1377-1404) to successfully embark upon a forward policy in the north-east and west. As we have noted, there were a series of Hindu principalities in the north-east region. The rulers of Orissa to its north, as well as the Bahmani sultans were also interested in this area. Although the ruler of Warangal had helped Hasan Gangu in his struggle against Delhi, his successor had invaded Warangal and seized the strong-hold of Kaulas and the hill fort of Golconda. Vijayanagar had been too busy in the south to intervene. The Bahmani Sultan fixed Golconda as the boundary of his kingdom and promised that neither he nor his successor would encroach against Warangal any further. To seal this agreement, the ruler of Warangal presented to the Bahmani sultan a throne set with valuable jewels. It is said that it had been originally prepared as a present to Muhammed bin Tughlaq. The alliance of the Bahmani kingdom and Warangal lasted for over 50 years and was a major factor in the inability of Vijayanagar to overrun the Tungbhadra doab, or to stem the Bahmani offensive in the area.

The battles between Vijayanagar and the Bahmanis are described in great detail by medieval writers. However, they are not of much historical importance to us, the position of the two sides remaining more or less the same, with the fortune of war swinging sometimes to one side, and sometimes to the other. Harihara II was able to maintain his position in the face of the Bahmani-Warangal combine. His greatest success was in wresting Belgaum and Goa in the west from the Bahmani kingdom. He also sent an expedition to the north of Sri Lanka.

After a period of confusion, Harihar II was succeeded by Deva Raya I (1404-1422). Early during his reign, there was renewed fight for the Tungbhadra doab. He was defeated by the Bahmani ruler, Firuz Shah, and had to pay ten lakhs of huns, pearls and elephants as an indemnity. He also agreed to marry his daughter to the Sultan, ceding to him in dowry Bankapur in the doab in order to obviate all future disputes. The marriage was celebrated with great pomp and show. When Firuz Shah Bahmani arrived near Vijayanagar for the marriage, Deva Raya came out of the city and met him with great pomp. From the gate of the city to the palace, which was a distance of ten km, the road was spread with cloths of gold, velvet, satin and other rich stuffs. The two monarchs rode on horseback together from the centre of the city square. The relations of Deva Raya joined the cavalcade, marching on foot before the two kings. The festivities lasted three days.

This was not the first political marriage of this type in south India. Earlier, the ruler of Kherla in Gondwana had married his daughter to Firuz Shah Bahmani in order to effect peace. It is said that this princess was the favourite queen of Firuz. However, these marriages by themselves could not bring about peace. The question of the Krishna-Godavari basin led to a renewed conflict between Vijayanagar, the Bahmani kingdom and Orissa. Following a confusion in the Reddi kingdom, Deva Raya entered into an alliance with Warangal for partitioning the Reddikingdom between them. Warangal's defection from the side of the Bahmani kingdom changed the balance of power in the Deccan. In consequence, Deva Raya was able to inflict a shattering defeat on Firuz Shah Bahmani, and annexed the centre territory up to the mouth of the Krishna river.

Deva Raya I did not neglect the arts of peace. He constructed a dam over the Tungbhadra so that he could bring a canal into the city to relieve the shortage of water. It irrigated the neighbouring fields also, for we are told that the canal increased his revenues by 350,000 pardaos. He also build a dam on the river Haridra for irrigation purposes.

After some confusion, Deva Raya II (1425-1446), who is considered the greatest ruler of the dynasty, ascended the throne at Vijayanagar. In order to strengthen his army he inducted more Muslims into it. According to Ferishta, Deva Raya II felt that the superiority of the Bahmani army was due to their sturdier horses and their large body of good archers. He, therefore, enlisted 2000 Muslims, gave them jagirs, and commended to all his Hindu soldiers and officers to learn the art of archery from them. The employment of Muslims in the Vijayanagar army was not new, for Deva Raya I is said to have kept 10,000 Muslims in his army. Ferishta tells us that Deva Raya II assembled 60,000 Hindus well skilled in archery, besides 80,000 cavalry, and 2,00,000 infantry. These figures may be exaggerated. However, the collection of a large cavalry must have put a strain on the resources of the State since most of the good mounts had to be imported, and the Arabs, who controlled the trade, charged high prices for them.

With his new army, Deva Raya II crossed the Tungbhadra river in 1443 and tried to recover Mudkal, Bankapur, etc., which were south of the Krishna river and had been lost to the Bahmamani sultans earlier. Three hard battles were fought, but in the end the two sides had to agree to the existing frontiers.

Nuniz, a Portuguese writer of the sixteenth century, tells us that the kings of Quilon, Sri Lanka, Pulicat, Pegu, Tenasserim (in Burma) and Malaya paid tribute to Deva Raya II. It is doubtful whether the Vijayanagar rulers were powerful enough on the sea to extract regular tribute from Pegu and Tenasserim. Perhaps, what was meant was that the rulers of these countries were in contact with Vijayanagar, and had sent presents to secure its goodwill. Sri Lanka, however, had been invaded a number of times. This could have not been attained without a strong navy.

Under a series of capable rulers, Vijayanagar emerged as the most powerful and wealthy state in the south during the first half of the fifteenth century. A number of travellers who visited Vijayanagar during the period have left a graphic account of the city and the country. The Italian traveller, Nicolo Conti, who visited Vijayanagar in 1420, says of the city "The circumference of the city is sixty miles, its walls carried up to the mountains, and enclose the valley at their foot... . In this city there are estimated to be ninety thousand men fit to bear arms. Their king is more powerful than all the other kings in India." Ferishta also says: "The princes of the house of Bahmani maintained their superiority by valour only; for in power, wealth and extent of the country, the Rayas of Bijanagar (Vijayanagar) greatly exceeded them."

Abdur Razzaq who had travelled widely in and outside India, and was an ambassador at the court of Deva Raya II, says: "This latter prince has in his dominions three hundred ports, each of which is equal to Calicut, and on terra firma his territories comprise a space of three months journey." All travellers agree that the country was thickly populated with numerous towns and villages. Abdur Razzaq says: "The country is for the most part well cultivated, very fertile. The troops amount in number to eleven lakhs."

Abdur Razzaq considers Vijayanagar to be one of the most splendid cities anywhere in the world which he had seen or heard of. Describing the city, he says: "It is built in such a manner that seven citadels and the same number of walls enclose each other. The seventh fortress, which is placed in the centre of the others, occupies an area ten times larger than the market place of the city of Herat." Starting from the palace, there were four bazars "which were extremely long and broad." As was the Indian custom, people belonging to one caste or profession lived in one quarter of the town. The Muslims appear to have lived in separate quarters provided for them. In the bazars as well as the king's palace, "one sees numerous running streams and canals formed of chiselled stone, polished and smooth." Another later traveller says that the city was larger than Rome, one of the biggest towns in the western world at that time.

The kings of Vijayanagar were reputed to be very wealthy. Abdur Razzaq mentions the tradition that "in the king's palace are several cell-like basins filled with bullion, forming one mass." The hoarding of wealth by the ruler was an ancient tradition. However, such hoarded wealth remained out of circulation, and sometimes invited foreign attack.

There has been a good deal of debate among scholars about the nature of the Vijayanagar state. Nilkanth Shastri considered it the nearest to a war state. He traces this to the view put forward by a Vijayanagar ruler that the income of the state should be divided into four parts, one part for various works, two, i.e. half for warfare, and the remainder saved for an emergency. He also lays emphasis on the *amaram* system whereby its holder, the *nayak*, who was granted a piece of territory had, in return, to maintain a number of troops, horses and elephants for the service of the ruler, and swear loyalty to him.

Vijayanagar was a war state only in the sense that all medieval states had to be constantly ready for war. The success of the rulers of Vijayanagar in meeting their Muslim opponents was largely based on the fact that they not only copied their mode of cavalry warfare but also, as we have seen, inducted a large number of mounted Muslim archers in their army. The rulers of Vijayanagar also maintained a large standing army which, we are told, was paid in cash. Thus, while continuing traditional forms, the rulers of Vijayanagar also tried to adopt some new features.

There is a difference of opinion whether the Vijayanagar state was a loose association of semi-autonomous military and territorial leaders, the *nayaks*, or was a centralised state on the model of the Delhi sultanat. In this context it should be remembered that the *amaram* cannot be equated to the Turkish *iqta* system. The *nayaks* were *not* former slaves or subordinates of the ruler in whose service they rose, with the ruler having the power to transfer them at will or even to remove them. The *nayaks* were hereditary territorial lords in their own right. While they promised service and loyalty to the ruler whose grant legitimized their position, they ran their own administration, and paid a part of their income to the ruler. We are told that there were 200 *nayaks* in the Vijayanagar kingdom. The rulers tried to control them, but could not remove them. Also, in some of the outlying areas in the south and the west, local rulers who had accepted the Vijayanagar suzreignty continued to rule. Thus, the area administered directly by the Vijayanagar rulers must have been much smaller than the size of the empire.

Despite limitations, Vijayanagar was a centralized state. The nayaks were strictly controlled till the last quarter of the fifteenth and early sixteenth century. The land tax was heavy and was the basis on which the rulers were able to maintain a large standing army. According to Abdur Razzak, near the ruler's palace was the *diwan-khana* "which is extremely large and presents the appearance of a *chihal situn*, or a forty-pillared hall where the records are kept and the scribes seated."

The Vijayanagar state has been called " a citadel of (Hindu) orthodoxy and conservatism". Thus, it is argued, the rulers spent a lot of time and attention in building and repairing temples and *maths*, and prided themselves on bearing the titles of "protectors of the Vedas, and the Vedic path". They also gave great favours to the brahmans, who were not only given grants of revenue-free lands, but were appointed commanders of armies and forts. The military assignment given to the brahmans, and their important political role was, however, motivated not by religious sentiments but by a desire to use the brahmans as a balancing factor against the powerful Kannad *nayaks*. In matters of religion, the Vijayanagar rulers were not narrow. Although Saivities to begin with, they did not discriminate against the other sects among the Hindus. They also give patronage to Jainism. The Christian missionaries who had settled down in south India were allowed to do missionary work, and make conversions among the Hindus. The Muslim soldiers employed in the army were given freedom for offering *namaz*, and in general there were good relations among the Hindus and the Muslims. The only case of blatant intolerance that can be cited is when in 1469, the Vijayanagar ruler, Mallikarjuna Raya, in a fit of anger hearing that the Muslim traders of Bhatkhal had sold horses to the Bahmani ruler, ordered the extirpation of all Muslims in the city. We are told that 10,00 Muslims were massacred, and the survivors fled to Goa. This folly and crime led to retaliation from the Bahmani ruler, and the loss of Belgaum and the surrounding region to the Bahmani ruler.

ii. The Bahmani Kingdom—its Growth and Disintegration

We have already traced the rise of the Bahmani kingdom, and its conflict with the Vijayanagar empire till the death of Deva Raya II (1446). The most remarkable figure in the Bahmani kingdom during the period was Firuz Shah Bahmani (1397-1422). He was well-acquainted with the religious science, that is, commentaries on the Quran, jurisprudence, etc., and was particularly fond of logic, and of the natural sciences such as botany, geometry etc. He was a good calligraphist and a poet and often composed extempore verses. According to Ferishta, he was well versed not only in Persian, Arabic and Turkish, but also in Telugu, Kannada and Marathi. He had a large number of wives in his *haram* from various countries and regions, including many Hindu wives, and we are told that he used to converse with each of them in their own language.

Firuz Shah Bahmani was determined to make the Deccan the cultural centre of India. The decline of the Delhi Sultanat helped him, for many learned people migrated from Delhi to the Deccan. The king also encouraged learned men from Iran and Iraq. He generally spent his time till midnight in the company of divines, poets, reciters of history and the most learned and witty among his courtiers. He had read the Old and New Testaments, and he respected the tenets of all religions. Ferishta calls him an orthodox Muslim, his only weakness being his fondness for drinking wine and listening to music.

The most remarkable step taken by Firuz Shah Bahmani was the induction of Hindus in the administration on a large scale. It is said that from his time the Deccani brahmans became dominant in the administration. The Decanni Hindus also provided a balance against the influx of foreigners called *afaqis* or *gharibs*. Many of the foreigners from West Asia were Persians, under whose influence Persian culture and also Shia doctrines grew in the kingdom. The Bahmani rulers were tolerant in religious matters, and though most of them were Sunnis, they did not persecute Shiism. Nor was *jizyah* levied on the Hindus during the early phase of Bahmanid rule. We have no reference to *jizyah* in the subsequent period also. If collected later on, it was collected as a part of land-revenue *(kharaj)*. Firuz Shah Bahmani encouraged the pursuit of astronomy and built an observatory near Daulatabad. He paid much attention to the principal ports of his kingdom, Chaul and Dabhol, which attracted trading ships from the Persian Gulf and the Red Sea, and poured in luxury goods from all parts of the world.

Firuz Bahmani started the Bahmani expansion towards Berar by defeating the Gond Raja Narsingh Rai of Kherla. The Rai made a present of 40 elephants, 5 maunds of gold and 50 maunds of silver. A daughter of the Rai was also married to Firuz. Kherla was restored to Narsingh who was made an amir of the kingdom and given robes of state, including an embroidered cap.

Firuz Shah Bahmani's marriage with a daughter of Deva Raya I and his subsequent battles against Vijayanagar have been mentioned already. The struggle for the domination of the Krishna-Godavari basin, however, continued. In 1419, the Bahmani kingdom received a setback, Firuz Shah Bahmani being defeated by Deva Raya I. This defeat weakened the position of Firuz. He was compelled to abdicate in favour of his brother Ahmad Shah I, who is called a saint (*wali*) on account of his association with the famous sufi saint Gesu Daraz. However, Ahmad Shah was also considered a saint by the Hindus, so much so that his *urs* (death anniversary) continued to be celebrated jointly till recent times. Ahmad Shah continued the struggle for the domination of the eastern seaboard in south India. He could not forget that is the last two battles in which the Bahmani sultan had been defeated, the ruler of Warangal had sided with Vijayanagar. In order to wreck vengeance, he invaded Warangal, defeated and killed the ruler in the battle, and annexed most of its territories. In order to consolidate his rule over the newly acquired territories, he shifted the capital from Gulbarga to Bidar. After this, he turned his attention towards Malwa, Gondwana and the Konkan.

Age of Mahmud Gawan (1463-1482)

The second half of the fifteenth century saw the gradual rise of the Bahmani kingdom as the leading power in the south. This had been presaged by the conquest of Warangal by Ahmad Shah which showed that the balance of power was shifting in favour of the Bahmaids. Following the death of Deva Raya II, there was confusion in Vijayanagar which provided an opportunity to the Gajpati rulers of Orissa to expand their power and influence in the area. The Bahmanids used the opportunity to consolidate their position in the south, and to expand northwards towards Berar and Khandesh, and westwards towards the Konkan. This brought them into conflict with the rulers of Malwa and Gujarat.

During this period, struggle between the *Afaqis* (Newcomers), and the Deccanis (Oldcomers) created confusion in the internal affairs of the Bahmani kingdom till Mahmud Gawan rose to power and prominence. Not much is known about the early life of Mahmud Gawan. An Iranian by birth he comes first to our notice in 1456 when he was put at the head of a force to deal with a pretender who had risen against the reigning sultan. Mahmud Gawan was introduced to the ruler, and steadily gained in influence so that in 1461 when the sultan died, and a minor succeeded him, Mahmud Gawan was appointed a member of the council of regency, set up to look after the affairs of the state. Following a series of invasions by the ruler of Malwa, the council of regency was dissolved, and in 1463 a new prince was seated on the throne who appointed Mahmud Gawan as *wakil-i-sultanat* (prime minister), with the tile of Khwaja-i-Jahan and Malik-ut-Tajjar. Although Mahmud Gawan had never been a trader *(tujjar)*, this title had been awarded by some preceding rulers upon leading nobles.

Mahmud Gawan dominated the affairs of the state for twenty years. During the period, Mahmud Gawan tried to extend the frontiers of the kingdom towards the east and the west. In the east, he came into conflict with the Gajpati ruler of Orissa, and joined hands with Vijayanagar to oust him from the Caromondal coast. He also made further conquest at the cost of Orissa.

Mahmud Gawan's major military contribution, however, was the over-running of the western coastal areas, including Dabhol and Goa. The loss of these ports was a heavy blow to Vijayanagar. Control of Goa and Dabhol led to further expansion of the overseas trade with Iran, Iraq, etc. Internal trade and manufactures also grew.

Mahmud Gawan also tried to settle the northern frontiers of the kingdom. Since the time of Ahmad Shah I, the kingdom of Malwa ruled by the Khalji rulers had been contending for the mastery of Gondwana, Berar and the Konkan. In this struggle, the Bahmani sultans had sought and secured the help of the rulers of Gujarat. After a great deal of conflict, it had been agreed that Kherla in Gondwana would go to Malwa, and Berar to the Bahmani sultan. However, the rulers of Malwa were always on the lookout for seizing Berar. Mahmud Gawan had to wage a series of bitter battles against Mahmud Khalji of Malwa over Berar. He was able to prevail due to the active help given to him by the ruler of Gujarat.

It would thus, be seen that the pattern of struggle in the south did not allow divisions along religious lines, political and strategic considerations and control over trade and commerce being more important causes of the conflict. Secondly, the struggle between the various states of north India and in south India did not proceed completely in isolation from each other. In the west, Malwa and Gujarat were drawn into the affairs of the Deccan, and in the east, Orissa was involved in a struggle with Bengal and also cast covetous eyes on the Coromandel coast.

The expansion of the Bahmani kingdom towards the east and the west led to a resurgence of the conflict with Vijayanagar. But by this time Vijayanagar was no match for the Bahmani kingdom. Mahmud Gawan not only annexed the Tungabhadra doab, but made a deep raid into the Vijayanagar territories, reaching as for south as Kanchi.

Mahmud Gawan carried out a number of internal reforms. Some of these were aimed at limiting the power of the nobles. Thus, the old provinces (*tarafs*) were further sub-divided from four into eight, and the governor of each fort was to be appointed directly by the sultan. The salaries and obligations of each noble were fixed. For maintaining a contingent of 500 horses, a noble received a salary of 1,00,000 huns per year. The salary could be paid in cash or by assigning a jagir. Those who were paid by means of jagir wer allowed expenses for the collection of land revenue. In every province, a tract of land (*khalisa*) was set apart for the expenses of the Sultan. Efforts were made to measure the land and to fix the amount to be paid by each cultivator to the state.

Mahmud Gawan was a great patron of the arts. He built a magnificent *madrasa* or college in the capital, Bidar. This fine building, which was decorated with coloured tiles, was three storeys high, and had accommodation for one thousand teachers and students who were given clothes and food free. Some of the most famous scholars of the time belonging to Iran and Iraq came to the *madrasa* at the instance of Mahmud Gawan.

One of the most difficult problems which faced the Bahmani kingdom was strife among the nobles. The nobles were divided into old-comers and new-comers or Deccanis and *Afaqis*. As a newcomer, Mahmud Gawan was hard put to win the confidence of the Deccanis. Though he adopted a broad policy of conciliation, the party strife could not be stopped. His opponents managed to poison the ears of the young Sultan who had him executed in 1482. Mahmud Gawan was over 70 years old at the time. The party strife now became even more intense. The various governors became independent. Soon, the Bahmani kingdom was divided into five principalities; Golconda, Bijapur, Ahmadnagar, Berar and Bidar. Of these, the kingdoms of Ahmadnagar, Bijapur and Golconda played a leading role in the Deccan politics till their absorption in the Mughal empire during the seventeenth century.

The Bahmani kingdom acted as a cultural bridge between the north and the south. It also established close relations with some of the leading countries of West Asia, including Iran and Turkey. The culture which developed as a result had its own specific features which were distinct from north India. These cultural traditions were continued by the successor states and also influenced the development of Mughal culture during the period.

iii. Climax of the Vijayanagar Empire and its Disintegration

As mentioned earlier, there was confusion in the Vijayanagar empire after the death of Deva Raya II. Civil wars broke out among various contenders to the throne. Many feudatories assumed independence in the process. The authority of the Raya shrunk to Karnataka and to some portions of the western Andhra region. After some time, the throne was usurped by the king's minister, Saluva. The earlier dynasty, thus, came to an end. Saluva restored internal law and order, and founded a new dynasty. This dynasty also soon came to an end and a new dynasty (called the Tuluva dynasty) was founded by Krishna Deva Raya (1509-30) who was the greatest figure of this dynasty. Some historians consider him to be the greatest of all the Vijayanagar rulers. Krishna Deva had not only to re-establish internal law and order, but he had also to deal with the old rivals of Vijayanagar, viz., the successor states of the Bahmani kingdom and the state of Orissa which has upsurped many Vijayanagar territories. In addition, he had to contend with the Portuguese whose power was slowly growing. They were using their control over the seas to browbeat the smaller vassal states of Vijayanagar in the coastal areas in order to gain economic and political concessions. They had even offered to buy the neutrality of the Raya by promising him assistance in recovering Goa from Bijapur and giving him a monopoly in the supply of horses.

In the series of battles lasting seven years, Krishna Deva first compelled the ruler of Orissa to restore to Vijayanagar all the territories up to the river Krishna. Having thus strengthened himself, Krishna Deva renewed the old struggle for the control of Tungabhadra doab. This led to a hostile alliance between his two main opponents, Bijapur and Orissa. Krishna Deva made grand preparations for the conflict. He opened the hostilities by overrunning Raichur and Mudkal. In the battle which followed, the Bijapur ruler was completely defeated (1520). He was pushed across the river Krishna, barely escaping with his life. The Vijayanagar armies also reached Belgaum in the west, occupied and sacked Bijapur for a number of days and destroyed Gulbarga before a truce was made.

Thus, under Krishna Deva, Vijayanagar emerged as the strongest military power in the south. However, in their eagerness to renew the old feuds, the southern powers largely ignored the danger posed to them and to their commerce by the rise of the Portuguese. Unlike the Cholas and some of the early Vijayanagar rulers, Krishna Deva seems to have paid scant attention to the development of a navy.

The conditions in Vijayanagar during this period are described by a number of foreign travellers. Paes, an Italian who spent a number of years at Krishna Deva's court, has given a glowing account of his personality. He remarks: "He is a great ruler and a man of much justice, but subject to sudden fits of rage." He cherished his subjects, and his solicitude for their welfare became proverbial.

Krishna Deva was also a great builder. He built a new town near Vijayanagar and dug an enormous tank which was also used for irrigation purposes. He was a gifted scholar of Telugu and Sanskrit. Of his many works, only one in Telugu on polity, and a drama in Sanskrit are available today. His reign marked a new era in Telugu literature when imitation of Sanskrit works gave place to independent works. He extended his patronage to Telugu, Kannada and Tamil poets alike. Foreign travellers like Barbosa, Paes and Nuniz speak of his efficient administration and the prosperity of the empire under his sway. The greatest achievement of Krishna Deva lay in the broad toleration that prevailed in his empire. Barbosa says: "The king allows such freedom that every man may come and go and live according to his own creed, without suffering from annoyance, without enquiry whether he is a Christian, Jew, Moor or heathen." Barbosa also pays a tribute to Krishna Deva for the justice and equity prevailing in his empire.

After the death of Krishna Deva, there was a struggle for succession among his relations since his sons were all minors. Ultimately, in 1543, Sadashiva Raya ascended the throne and reigned till 1567. But the real power lay in the hands of a triumvitrate in which the leading person was Rama Raja. Rama Raja was able to play off the various Muslim powers against one another. He entered into a commercial treaty with the Portuguese whereby the supply of horses to the Bijapur ruler was stopped. In a series of wars he completely defeated the Bijapur ruler and also inflicted humiliating defeats on Golconda and Ahmadnagar. It seems that Rama Raja had no larger purpose than to maintain a balance of power favourable to Vijayanagar between these three powers. At length, they combined to inflict a crushing defeat on Vijayanagar at Bannihatti, near Talikota, in 1565. This is called the battle of Talikota or the battle of Rakshasa-Tangadi. Rama Raja was surrounded, taken prisoner and immediately executed. It is said that 1,00,000 Hindus were slain during the battle. Vijayanagar was thoroughly looted and left in ruins.

The battle of Bannihatti is generally considered to mark the end of the great age of Vijayanagar. Although the kingdom lingered on for almost a hundred years, its territories decreased continually

and the Raya no longer counted in the political affairs of south
India.

The concept of kingship among the Vijayanagar rulers was high.
In his book on polity, Krishna Deva Raya advises the king that "with
great care and according to your power you should attend to the
work of protecting (the good) and punishing (the wicked) without
neglecting anything that you can see or hear." He also enjoined
upon the king to "levy-taxes from his people moderately."

In the Vijayanagar kingdom the king was advised by a council
of ministers which consisted of the great nobles of the kingdom.
The kingdom was divided into *rajyas* or *mandalam* (provinces) below which were *nadu* (district), *sthala* (sub-district) and *grama* (village). However, the Chola traditions of village self-government were
considerably weakened under Vijayanagar rule. The growth of hereditary nayakships tended to curb their freedom and initiative.

Historians are not agreed about the condition of the peasantry
under the Vijayanagar rule, because most of the travellers had little knowledge about village life and, thus, spoke of it in very general terms. In general, it may be presumed that the economic life
of the people remained more or less the same; their houses were
mostly thatched with a small door; they generally went about bare-
footed and wore little above the waist. People of the upper classes
sometimes wore costly shoes and a silk turban on their heads, but
did not cover themselves above the waist. All classes of people were
fond of ornaments, and wore them "in their ears, on their necks,
on their arms, etc."

We have very little idea about the share of the produce the peasants were required to pay. According to an inscription, the rates
of taxes were as follows:

One-third of the produce of kuruvai (a type of rice) during
winter.

One-fourth of seasame, ragi, horsegram, etc.

One-sixth of millet and other crops cultivated on dry land.

Thus, the rate varied according to the type of crops, soil, method
of irrigation, etc.

In addition to the land-tax, there were various other taxes, such
as property tax, tax on sale of produce, profession taxes, military
contribution (in times of distress), tax on marriage, etc. The sixteenth century traveller, Nikitin, says: "The land is overstocked with
people, but those in the country are very miserable while the nobles are extremely affluent and delight in luxury."

Trade and agriculture grew under the Vijayanagar rule. As village self-rule declined, there was the growth of a class of locally powerful people who used their position for developing agriculture by providing additional irrigation facilities for which an extra charge was made. The state also built large irrigation reservoirs. Many temples, which enjoyed rent-free villages, also used their resources for this purpose.

Urban life grew under the Vijayanagar empire and trade flourished. Many of the towns grew around temples. The temples were very large and needed supply of food stuff and commodities for distribution of *prasadam* to the pilgrims, service of God, the priests, etc. The temples were rich and also took active part in trade, both internal and overseas. There was direct trade with China, and we hear of large Chinese junks loading pepper. Trade with the Arab countries and Iran was also active.

Thus, despite continuous wars, there was growth of trade and urbanisation in south India between 14th and 16th centuries. Agriculture also developed. This was reflected in the cultural growth during the period.

11

ESTABLISHMENT OF PORTUGUESE CONTROL IN THE INDIAN SEAS AND ITS ECONOMIC AND POLITICAL IMPACT

The landing of Vasco da Gama at Calicut in 1498 with three ships, guided by two Gujarati pilots[1] is generally regarded as the beginning of a new era in world history, especially in the relationship between Asia and Europe. Although Asia and Europe had been in commercial relations with each other since antiquity, the opening of direct sea-relations between the two was not only the fulfilment of an old dream—according to the Greek historian, Herodotus, the Phoenicians had rounded Africa in the 6th century BC, it presaged big increase of trade between the two. This, however, was only one of the objectives of the Portuguese. For the Portuguese, the opening of a sea-route to India would give a big blow to the Muslims—the Arabs and Turks, who were the traditional enemies of Christianity, and were posing a new threat to Europe by virtue of the growing military and naval power of the Turks. A direct sea-link with India would displace the virtual monopoly of the Arabs and Turks over the trade in eastern goods, especially spices. They also vaguely hoped that by their exploration of Africa they would be able to link up with the kingdom of the legendary prior John, and be in a position to attack the Muslims from two sides. Thus, the commercial and religious objectives supported and justified each other.

A search for a sea route to India had been attempted in post-Roman times by Genoa. In 1291, a Genoese, Ugolino di Vivaldo, had set out with two galleys to find his way to India by the ocean route, but was never heard of. Subsequently, the lead in this search was taken by Portugal. From 1418, Dom Henrique, the ruler of Por-

[1]Some historians name Abdul Majid as the pilot, but Abdul Majid was a well known Arab geographer, and the question of his being there or piloting the ship does not arise. Nor does Vasco da Gama mention his name.

tugal, called Henry the Navigator, sent two to three ships every year for the exploration of the West Coast of Africa. The occupation of Africa upto the mouth of the river Congo between 1443 and 1482 gained Portugal trade in ivory, slaves, and gold dust, and whetted their appetite. The rounding of the southern tip of Africa in 1487 by Megallan opened the sea-route to India. But it was another ten years before it was taken up by Vasco da Gama.

At the outset, it should be made clear that while the Europeans had their own objectives, their seeking a direct sea-route to India was not because the Arabs and Turks hindered in any way the trade of eastern good to Europe or were charging excessive taxes. In fact, with the rise of Islam, the Arabs had emerged as the principal traders of the world, especially in the field of long distance trade. Their merchants, sailors and geographers linked even more closely than before the sea-trade between the Mediterranean and Asia, and in Asia between West Asia, India, East Africa, South-East Asia and China.

Nor were the Turks allergic to trade. The trade from the Orient flowed from the Persian Gulf via Hormuz and Basra to the Levant, and from the Red Sea via Jeddah to Cairo and Alexandria in Egypt. There were also land-routes leading to Black Sea ports. The custom duties levied on these goods was a rich source of profit to the Arab and Turkish rulers, and they had every reason to protect and cherish this trade. Despite the Pope banning trade with the heathens, i.e. Muslims, Genoese and Venetian merchants were active in the trade in oriental goods. In fact, the Venetian merchants had a virtual monopoly of buying the oriental goods in Egypt and the Levant, and distributing them all over Europe. Though the Venetians and the Turks fought long and bitter naval battles, neither side pushed it to a level which might harm their mutual trade. They were hence considered "complementary enemies". The principal rivals of the Venetians in Europe were the Genoese. The Genoese were also active in distributing oriental goods in Europe, but had been side-lined by the Venetians. The capture of Constantinople by the Turks in 1453 was a big blow to the Genoese because the Black Sea ports, their principal mart for oriental goods, were gradually closed to them. This, and their old rivalry with Venice were the main factors which led Genoa to help Portugal and Spain with ships, money and nautical skills in searching for a sea-route to India. As is well known, Christopher Columbus who 'discovered' America (or re-discovered, because the Norsemen had reached there earlier, as also the Red Indians) in 1492 in his effort to find a sea-route to India was a Genoese.

Interest in the search for a sea-route to India was spurred also by the Renaissance which challenged rooted modes of thought, and created a new spirit of daring. At its background was the economic growth of Europe from the 11th century. Recent research shows that with growing prosperity and growth, the dietary habits of the Europeans had also changed, with more meat being consumed. Much of the cattle in Europe had to be killed during winter due to shortage of fodder, and the meat salted away. Oriental spices were even more in demand in order to make the salted meat more palatable.

Growing interest ir oriental trade was shown by the arrival of many Genoese traders in the Indian Ocean from the thirteenth century onwards. The names of the Venetians, Nicolo Conti and Barbosa, of the Russian Nikitin are only a few among the many others who travelled on the Indian Ocean, and reached India during this period. The Pope also showed his growing interest in the search for a sea-route to India when in 1453, he issued a Bull granting Portugal "in perpetuity" whichever lands it "discovered" beyond the Cape in Africa upto India, on condition of converting the "heathens" of those lands to Christianity. It will be seen that this also implied excluding the other Christian powers from participating in this noble enterprise!

i. The Asian Oceanic Trade Network before the Coming of the Portuguese

In order to understand the impact of the Portuguese on Indian and Asian trade and economy, a brief review of the nature, structure and working of the Asian oceanic trade net work before the coming of the Portuguese is necessary. This is specially so because during the hey-day of European colonial domination, many wrong and unfounded notions about Asian trade and economy, and the role of the European traders in the region were put forward. Many of these have had to be discarded or modified as a result of the researches carried out in recent years, both by European and Asian scholars. Their researches themselves have been shaped by the new outlook which emerged following the end of the era of colonialism, the economic growth of the countries of the region, and their efforts to re-explore their roots, and mutual linkages.

First and foremost, the new researches have tended to show that there was no basic difference in the internal structure of trade and commerce between Asia and Europe before the rise of industrial capitalism in the west. Thus, both European and Asian merchants sought exclusive information about the markets they operated in. The bigger traders in Asia were remarkably flexible in their approach. They were prepared to trade in any commodity which was anticipated to yield a good profit. There was, thus, much less specialisation than in the modern times. There was, however, a clear distinction between wholesale traders and retailers. The big merchants who were the most active in emporia or long distance trade, could be active both in domestic and foreign trade. They could also be bankers, money-lenders and insurance agents. Some of them had their own ships, although the carrying of goods, both over-land and over-seas, was also a specialised vocation. A definite pattern of trade between different regions and ports had developed, as a result of wind movements, ocean currents, and distances. Thus, journeys originating in the Red Sea, or the Persian Gulf ports did not generally go beyond Gujarat, or the Malabar ports. Goods for south-east Asian ports were shipped from Gujarat, Malabar or the Coromondal. Chinese traders, and Chinese junks, or ocean going ships had earlier come to Malabar. But following a ban on foreign trade by the Ming rulers in the fifteenth century, Chinese traders did not go beyond the south-east Asian states.

The captaincy of ships over these vast distances needed nautical skills and experience for which the Asian sailors—Arabs, Indians, Malays and Chinese were not wanting. The captains (*nakhudas*) of ships were highly esteemed. They commanded good wages, and also had a part interest in the goods they were carrying. The ships also contained many small traders, to whom the word peddler can be applied. The big traders, however, did not fall in this category. Apparently, they stayed at their base of operations. In their working, Asian merchants, like Europeans, drew upon family connections, as also on associations based on community of interest, region etc. Thus, we hear of the association of merchants called Karimi, located at Aden in the Yemen, whose activities extended upto China. Burmese merchants also had their own trade associations, as also the Indians. Thus, Maniraman was an association of South Indian merchants which remained active in domestic and foreign trade for a long time.

We do not have much information about the rich trading families of Asia during this period, because such records never found their way to national archives. However, we do hear of rich merchant, such as the Iranian, Ramist, who around 1100 AD organised commercial activity extending from Aden to India and to China; of Gamel-al-Din Ibrahim Tibe who in the thirteenth century organised a fleet of one hundred ships which travelled to South India and the Far East. The names of Vastupal and Tejpal in Gujarat are well-known. They were also very rich Chetti merchants in Tamilnadu, in Bengal and the Maraccars in Malabar. Considering that the Asian trade at the times was much bigger than the European trade—some modern historians assess it at ten times the volume of European trade, it is not surprising that some of the richest merchants were to be found in Asia at the time. Yet, for a long time, the Asian traders were indiscriminately called peddlers by some European scholars, and many of our own scholars accepted it. However, it is not these merchant-princes who mattered. What mattered or is significant, in fact, was the size and range of the trading communities in Asia, the multiplicity of their activities, their undoubted entrepreneurial skills, and the financial and shipping resources which they disposed of. Also, unlike many of the European traders, the Asian traders did not depend upon their states for political or military support.

A second misnomer was the concept that the oriental trade consisted only of "the great and the trifling," i.e. luxury goods. This may have been largely true for trade with Europe which imported in the main, silk and jade from China, spices from the Spice Islands and India, and some types of cloth from the Middle East. But in the Indian Ocean region, the items exchanged included the basic necessities of life, such as salt, sugar, grains and clothing, in addition to luxury items such as spices, horses, silk, Chinese porcelain, incense, ivory, glass, jewellery and finely cut precious stones, slaves etc. Trade in the necessities of life was necessary because in areas such as the south-east Asian Islands, rice production was very limited, as also clothing. Salt, sugar and food-grains were needed in the Middle East. Also, pre-modern merchant ships could not have operated without low value bulk cargo which could serve as ballast. Thus, goods brought to India or China included heavy cargoes, such as dates, sugar, building material, and timber. Climate and geography also dictated the movement of goods, and the direction of trade. Thus, ships from the Middle East reached the Indian sea ports before the arrival of the monsoon. The goods were transhipped there, and carried in different bottoms to the south-east Asian countries or China. Malacca was also another point of transhipment. While the Chinese did not go beyond Java-Sumatra, the Arabs and Indians traded right upto China. Thus, both the range of trade, and the bulk of the goods carried was impressive for the pre-modern world.

A third misnomer is that Asian ships could not make long distance voyages across open seas because their ships were frail, and Asians lacked the necessary nautical techniques. Modern research shows that these ideas lack a foundation. It were the Indians who had started the open sea voyage from Gujarat to Aden, and across the Indian Ocean to South-East Asia and to East Africa. Thus, when Vasco da Gama sailed for Calicut from Malindi in East Africa, he found four Indian ships there. The Portuguese, Covilhan, travelling on Arab ships, had covered the itinerary which was later followed by Vasco da Gama.

Much has been made of the Indian tradition of sewing ships instead of nailing them. According to the Arab geographers, the nailing of ships began in the region of the Persian Gulf region in the 10th century. However, sewn ships continued to be used because these had greater flexibility than nailed ships, and could be repaired more easily. This was an advantage in the shallow waters and swift currents of the Persian Gulf region. That both sewn and nailed ships were in operation in the Indian waters was noted by the Portuguese, Gaspar Correa, writing in the early part of the sixteenth century. He says that the sewn ships "remain as secure as if they were nailed. There are other ships which have the planks nailed with thin nails with broad heads."

Nor were these ships small in size. By the time the Portuguese came, the boats plying in the region were from 350 to 400 tonnes which was heavy tonnage for the time, and had several masts. Although the Chinese junks which were several storeyes high were the most advanced in ship construction at the time, the type of ship used in the Indian waters was the Arab *boom*. Since timber for ships was not available in Arabia or Persia, most of these ships were generally built in the Gujarat or the Malabar region Regarding nautical techniques, the Chinese had a mariner compass since the 10th century, According to a modern work on Arab navigation, they had a compass which was a floating needle and was of use on ships in the Indian seas, but, perhaps, was not widely used. Arab and Indian sailors fixed their position on the open sea with the help of stars, using the azimuthal sidereal-rose (compass card or *kamal*). With regard to navigational instruments, a modern scholar, John Villiers, points out that of the two Gujrati pilots given to Vasco da Gama at Malindi in East Africa by the local ruler, "the elderly one was familiar with the use of the quandrant and the kamal, and perhaps also with the astrolabe. Apparently, he was more familiar with these new fangled instruments than were Vasco and his men."

The traders who actively participated in the sea-borne sea-trade of Asia followed well established conventions which had developed in course of time. The traders were not only Arabs and Iranians but Jews, Armenians and even Genoese. Apart from Gujaratis and Tamil Chettis, the Javanese were also active in the sea trade. The life and property of these traders were protected by the rulers, and certain well defined commercial laws were observed. Custom duties were generally kept within limits. While the conventions were violated sometimes, such violation would harm the concerned state since trade was highly competitive, and in the situation, traders would move away to another port. According to convention, the rulers, while taxing trade, did not try to dominate the seas, or protect or expand their trade by armed intervention on land or sea.

In Asia, the only armaments the ships carried were soldiers and rockets as a safeguard against sea-pirates who were active on the coasts on Oman and Malabar, as also in South-East Asia and China. Notable exceptions to this had been the Chola naval expeditions against Java-Sumatra in the 14th century, and Chinese Admiral Cheng He's seven voyages between 1417 and 1433, carrying a large flotilla of ships armed with rockets and thousands of soldiers upto East Africa and Jedda. While these ships conducted some trade, their primary purpose was of showing the Chinese flag and making the governments of the region more receptive to Chinese trade, influence and culture, But due to domestic reasons, the Chinese discontinued such expeditions and even banned foreign trade. The Chinese expeditions made so little impact that they are not even mentioned by any of the native observes in the countries visited by the Chinese fleet.

Due to all these factors, the fourteenth and fifteenth centuries were unusually prosperous in the history of the Indian Ocean. Although by the second half of the 15th century, Chinese traders had withdrawn under the orders of the Chinese Court, and the Karimi merchants of Yemen, as well as the Jews had stopped their operations—perhaps in the face of Arab competition, there was no "comercial vacuum", as has been argued by some historians. Nor was there any Arab monopoly of trade in the western India Ocean, though the Arabs were certainly the richest and the most powerful group of long distance traders in the region.

These factors explain why the Portuguese, who came to Asia for capturing the trade in Asian goods to Europe, stayed behind to capture the trans-Asian trade through use of force.

ii. *The Portuguese Estado da India*

When Vasco da Gama landed in Calicut, he was cordially received by the Zamorin, and permitted to trade in spices, and to set up a factory (ware-house) on the coast. The spices carried back by Vasco da Gama were computed at sixty times the cost of the entire expedition. But this did not satisfy the Portuguese ruler. The Portuguese wanted to enforce a monopoly over the spice trade to Europe, and claimed the right of searching the ships of Arab traders. This led to a fight in which the Portuguese living in their factory were massacred. In retaliation, the Portuguese ships bombarded Calicut before they withdrew. In 1502, Vasco da Gama returned with a fleet of twenty-five vessels, and demanded that the Zamorin should expel all the Muslim merchants settled there, and not to allow any Muslim merchants to land at any of his ports, or to have any trade relations with them. The Zamorin rejected these demands on the ground that the port of Calicut was open to all, and that it would be impossible to prohibit anyone from trade, whether he was a Muslim or not. Gama's answer was a brutal assault on Calicut. This was followed by establishing a number of forts at Cochin, Quilon etc. to dominate the Malabar trade.

What was at issue here were two different philosophies of relationship between trade and the state. The Asian convention was of open trade, with the governments backing and supporting trade but not using their military or naval strength to promote or protect it. This was so even in China where the Court had always exercised close control over foreign trade, and treated items of import as "tribute". On the other hand, the Mediterranean tradition which the Portuguese brought with them was of a combination of trade with warfare on land and sea. This approach was profoundly upsetting to the Asian traders, as well as to many of the small states of the region, such as Calicut, Cochin, etc. which, like some of the city states of Europe, were heavily dependent on trade, but followed the convention of open trade without the use of military or naval force.

Alarmed at the growing power of the Portuguese, the Sultan of Egypt fitted a fleet and sent it towards India. The fleet was joined by a contingent of ships from the ruler of Gujarat. The Zamorin of

Calicut also lent his support, as also the rulers of Bijapur and Ahmednagar. After an initial victory in which the son of the Portuguese governor, Don Almaida, was killed, this combined fleet was routed by the Portuguese in 1509. This naval victory made the Portuguese navy supreme in the Indian Ocean for the time being, and enabled the Portuguese to extend their operations towards the Persian Gulf and the Red Sea.

Shortly afterwards, Albuquerque succeeded as the governor of the Portuguese possessions in the east. He advocated and embarked upon a policy of dominating the entire oriental commerce by setting up forts at various strategic places in Asia and Africa. This was to be supplemented by a strong navy. Defending his philosophy, he wrote "A dominion founded on a navy alone cannot last." Lacking forts, he argued, "neither will they (the rulers) trade or be on friendly terms with you."

Albuquerque initiated this new policy by capturing Goa from Bijapur in 1510. The island of Goa was an excellent natural harbour and fort. It was strategically located, and from it the Portuguese could command the Malabar trade and watch the policies of the rulers in the Deccan. It was also near enough to the Gujarat seaports for the Portuguese to make their presence felt there. Goa was, thus, suited to be the principal centre of Portuguese commercial and political activity in the east. The Portuguese were also able to extend their possession on the mainland opposite Goa, and to blockade and sack the Bijapuri ports of Danda-Rajouri and Dabhol, thus paralysing Bijapur's sea-trade on the mainland. They sacked and blockaded the Bijapuri ports of Danda-Rajouri and Dabhol till the Adil Shah came to terms by ceding Goa. From their base at Goa, the Portuguese further strengthened their position by establishing a fort at Colombo in Sri Lanka, and at Achin in Sumatra, and the Malacca port which controlled the exit and entry to the narrow gulf between the Malay peninsula and Sumatra. The Portuguese also established a station at the island of Socotra at the mouth of the Red Sea, and besieged Aden. Vasco da Gama failed to capture Aden—his only failure in the area. However, he forced the ruler of Ormuz which controlled entry into the Persian Gulf to permit them to establish a fort there.

During this period, a major concern of the Portuguese was to bring under control the forts of Diu and Cambay which were the centres of Gujarati trade to the Red Sea. The Portuguese made two attempts in 1520-21 to capture Diu but both were defeated by its governor, Ahmad Ayaz.

The Ottomon Turks, under Sulaiman, were passing through the most magnificent period of their history; they were poised to attack Europe, and also to complete their conquests in Asia. In 1529, the Turks besieged Vienna which was saved by the timely intervention of the Poles. Earlier, the Turks had defeated the ruler of Iran in 1514 and then conquered Syria, Egypt and Arabia. This implied an increasing role of the Ottoman Turks in the Indian Ocean.

The sultan of Gujarat sent an embassy to the Ottoman ruler congratulating him on his victories, and seeking his support. In return, the Ottoman ruler expressed a desire to combat the infidels, that is the Portuguese, who had disturbed the shores of Arabia. From this time onwards, there was a continuous exchange of embassies and letters between the two countries. After ousting the Portuguese from the Red Sea in 1529, a strong fleet under Sulaiman Rais was despatched to aid Bahadur Shah, the ruler of Gujarat. Bahadur Shah received it well, and two of the Turkish officials, who were given Indian names, were appointed governors of Surat and Diu respectively. Of these two, Rumi Khan was later to earn a great name for himself as a master-gunner.

In 1531, after intriguing with local officials, the Portuguese attacked Daman and Diu, but the Ottoman commander, Rumi Khan, repulsed the attack. However, the Portuguese built a fort at Chaul lower down the coast.

Before the Gujarat-Turkish alliance could be consolidated, a bigger threat to Gujarat appeared from the side of the Mughals. Humayun attacked Gujarat. In order to meet this threat, Bahadur Shah granted the island of Bassein to the Portuguese. Following the expulsion of the Mughals from Gujarat, he once again appealed to the Ottoman sultan for help and tried to limit the Portuguese encroachments at Diu. However, Bahadur Shah was killed in 1536 in a fracas with the Portuguese. Subsequent efforts to recapture Diu failed.

The Turks made their biggest naval demonstration against the Portuguese in Indian waters in 1536. Their fleet consisted of 45 galleons carrying 20,000 men, including 7000 land soldiers or janissaries. Many of the sailors had been pressed into service from the Venetian galleys at Alexandria. The fleet, commanded by Sulaiman Pasha, an old man of 82, who was the most trusted man of the Sultan and had been appointed the governor of Cairo, appeared before Diu in 1538 and besieged it. Unfortunately, the Turkish admiral behaved in an arrogant manner so that the Sultan of Gujarat withdrew his support. After a siege of two month, the Turkish fleet retired, following news of the arrival of a formidable Portuguese armada to relieve Diu.

The Turkish threat to the Portuguese persisted for another two decades. In 1531, Peri Rais, who was assisted by the Zamorin of Calicut, attacked the Portuguese forts at Muscat and Ormuz. Meanwhile, the Portuguese strengthened their position by securing Daman from its ruler. A final Ottoman expedition was sent under Ali Rais in 1554. The failure of these expeditions resulted in a change in the Turkish attitude. In 1566, the Portuguese and the Ottomans came to an agreement to share the oriental trade, including spices, and not to clash in the Arab Sea. Following this, the Ottomans shifted their interest once again to Europe. This precluded a future alliance with the rising Mughal power and the Turks against the Portuguese.

iii. The Portuguese Impact on the Indian Ocean Trade Network

The Portuguese ended the era of unarmed open sea- trade in the Indian waters, and gave a big blow to the virtual Muslim monopoly of the trade in the western part of the Indian Ocean, and their trade of eastern goods to Europe.

However, the Portuguese effort to push out the Muslims from the trade in oriental goods, and to establish a Portuguese monopoly over the trade in West Asia had only limited success. Thus, by the middle of the sixteenth century, inspite of the large volume of spices brought to Lisbon and marketed in Europe, mainly through Antwerp, the Black Sea ports and the markets of the Levant and Egypt were as well supplied with eastern goods—spices, dyes, and cotton and silk textiles as before. It may be noted that right from the beginning, the Portuguese king had declared trade in spices, drugs, dyes including indigo, copper, silver and gold, and arms and ammunition to be royal monopolies. Traders of no other country, whether in Asia or Europe, including Portuguese private traders and royal officials, were permitted to trade in these commodities. Even ships engaged in trade in other commodities had to take a permit or *cartaze* from Portuguese officials. The Portuguese attempted to force all ships going to Malacca or to East Africa to pass through Goa, and to pay tolls there. Any ship which was suspected of carrying "contraband" or banned goods, or which refused to be searched could be treated as a prize of war, and sunk or captured, and the men and women aboard treated as slaves.

The Portuguese soon found that they stood to lose more on land than gain on sea by continuing such practices, because traders who lost on sea put pressure on their governments to retaliate against Portuguese trade in their areas. Also, it was impossible to police the trade along all the lagoons on the coasts in Asia. Sea-pirates preying on Portuguese ships were active in areas such as Oman, Malabar, and South-East Asia, and Portuguese policies brought them greater encouragement and support from traders and small rulers.

Hence, the rules regarding giving *cartazes* to local traders had to be liberalised. This included Muslims traders. Trade in horses which was exclusively in the hands of Muslims, was a highly profitable trade. It was also of great strategic importance to various rulers. The Muslims were also active in trade in many other commodities, such as textile products, glass, aromatics and coffee in which the Portuguese had neither the money nor the ships to engage themselves. Hence, the dictates of trade and profit soon overcame religious prejudices.

The Portuguese were unable to monopolise even the trade in pepper and spices. This was so because, in the first place, the Portuguese private traders were unhappy with the royal attempt to monopolise the trade in these commodities. Royal officials, who received small salaries, were often in league with private traders, Portuguese as well as Arabs, Gujaratis etc. to line their own pockets. In consequence, the *cartaze* system proved to be both corrupt and leaking like a sieve.

The Arab and Gujarati traders in these commodities also found ways and means the get round the Portuguese trade embargo. The Portuguese control over the Indian Ocean waters remained incomplete because of their failure to capture Aden and thereby control entry to the Red Sea. The Turkish conquest of Syria, Egypt and Arabia, and the expansion of their naval power, both in the eastern Mediterranean and the Red Sea, made it difficult for the Portuguese to effectively carry out their blockade of *Bab-el-Mendel*, the entrance to the Persian Gulf. At the other end of the Indian Ocean, the Portuguese control even on the Spice Islands weakened. The Portuguese had to contend with a naval power there willing to take on their warships. This was the north Sumatra ruler, Sultan Ali Mughayat Shah. Using the traditional Javanese naval skills, he was able to defeat the Portuguese in many naval skirmishes, and to capture large number of guns from the Portuguese to fortify Acheh. He also approached the Ottoman Sultan for military equipment. The Ottomans had a high reputation in the field of casting guns. They supplied bronze guns of a calibre to enable Acheh in north Sumatra to withstand a siege. This enabled Acheh to emerge as a major centre of the export of spices, in competition to Malacca which was under Portuguese control. Arabs and Gujaratis who were well entrenched at Malacca, used Acheh as a centre for export of spices to the Red Sea via the Laccadives, thereby by-passing the Portuguese controlled Malabar waters.

Thus, the structure of the Asian trade net-work; the strength and resourcefulness of the Asian merchants, Arabs, Gujaratis, Tamils and others, who had long experience of operating the system; the naval and military strength of Turkey and of the ruler of north Sumatra, and the internal limitations of the Portuguese and of the working of the *cartaz* system in the Portuguese Empire of India—or the *Estado da India*—were important factors in limiting the success of the Portuguese. It should be kept in mind that Portugal itself was a small country, and though it had developed rapidly in the field of commerce, its financial resources were limited. Thus, German and Italian merchants and merchant-houses became the principal agents for distributing all over Europe the eastern goods brought to Lisbon by the Portuguese. Demand in Asia for European goods which could be exchanged for purchase of pepper and other eastern goods was limited. Hence, precious metals, especially silver had to be exported. But unlike Spain, Portugal did not have the silver mines in America to fall back on, and had to depend heavily on Italian and German financiers. The expectation of the Portuguese king that Portuguese control of the coastal trade of India would pay for the export of pepper and other eastern goods to Europe also remained a misnomer. Hence, the Portuguese trade to Europe remained confined to only twelve to thirteen ships being sent each year from Lisbon to India. However, this picture changed by the end of the 16th century. The share of the private Portuguese traders— mainly New Christians—in the Portuguese trade to Europe rose sharply, amounting to over 90 per cent of the total. The additional cargo consisted mainly of textiles and precious stones. The Portuguese private traders financed this trade by large scale involvement in Asian trade. However, for the Portuguese government the Portuguese enterprise in the western part of the Indian Ocean remained, what Steensgaard calls, largely a "redistributive enterprise", i.e. its main source of income was taxing the trade of others rather than expanding trade, or opening up new lines of trade. A real expansion of trade between Europe and the East had to await the coming of the Dutch and the English in the 17th century.

However, it was in the Far East that the Portuguese had some limited success in expanding trade and opening up new avenues. They took over the export of textiles from the Coromondal Coast to the Indonesian Archipelago where, in exchange, they could purchase spices. There was never any question of monopolising the trade in spices there, the Javanese and the Malays being active in the field. The Portuguese carried spices to China, buying Chinese silk in exchange, and taking it to Japan in exchange for silver. This exchange was very profitable because the Peking court had banned the Chinese from foreign trade for fear of piracy. Hence, the Portuguese could step in. But the Portuguese could take only one great ship every year from Macau to Japan.

Apart from this trade, another avenue of trade which the Portuguese opened up was trade to south America via the Philippines. There was a consistent demand for Indian cotton goods in the Philippines. Since the Spanish rulers had banned Muslims and Protestants from trading with the Philippines, it gave a good opening to the Portuguese. They also accommodated some Armenians and Gujaratis in the trade. From the Philippines, Spanish galleons took the Indian textiles to South America where they were exchanged for silver. The profits of the Far Eastern trade was so profitable that Portugal could afford to take a more relaxed stand on its pepper trade in the Indian Ocean.

Thus, the second half of the sixteenth century emerges as an era of growing partnership between the Portuguese and Asian merchants. Many Arabs and Gujarati merchants found it more profitable to load their goods on Portuguese ships, while Portuguese private traders or officials used Asian ships to evade the royal monopolies.

It has been argued that the Portuguese established transparency in the eastern trade by setting up a network of factories or warehouses in widely separated areas whereby markets and prices became more stabilised, hence transparent. Modern research does not support this argument. Wide fluctuation in prices was a characteristic of pre-modern trade. Also, Indian and Arab merchants knew the distinction between spot and future markets. For spot markets, they had ware-houses which were necessary in order to get the best prices, buying when there was a glut, and selling when there was a shortage. Coffee was an example of such a commodity. But for fine textiles, and goods such as spices, the goods and prices had to be fixed in advance. The Asians managed this through their own trade associations and family network. The Portuguese tried to fix the prices of black pepper in advance by pressurising or giving inducements to local rulers in Malabar to supply pepper to them at fixed prices, leaving it to the ruler to procure the supplies through

local traders, or to deal directly with the cultivators. The Portuguese policy was unpopular because they tried to use political pressure to depress the prices paid to the cultivators, and of trying to
prevent their competitors from bidding. Hence, any expansion of
the production of spices was of little benefit to the cultivators.

Despite claiming to be lords of the territories of the East, the
Portuguese impact on the political system in Asia was small. They
were too few in numbers to try to capture and keep hold of any
large territories on the mainland in India or elsewhere. Hence, they
wisely decided to keep their control confined to islands, and to forts
on the coast which could be defended and supplied by sea. The
island of Goa, which became their seat of government, was a prime
example of this. Apart from this, they could, by threats and per-
suasions, induce rulers of small states, such as Calicut, Cochin,
Craganore etc. to act as their agents or brokers in the spice trade.

The Portuguese set-up at Goa was controlled by a Governor-Gen-
eral, assisted by a Council which included the Ecclesiastical Head.
On account of their small numbers, the Portuguese encouraged mixed
marriages and, in course of time, a new Indo-Portuguese or Goanese
society came into being. But the society and government itself was
organised on rigid racial lines, people of pure Portuguese origin
being at the head of the society, and people of mixed origins at
the bottom. Nor were the latter given any share in political power. The Church exercised on occasions the dreaded *"auto da fe"* or
burning at the stake to root out heresy among Christians.

Thus, the contribution of the Portuguese in the field of politics
or expansion of world trade remained negligible. However, the significance of the Portuguese opening the direct sea-route to India
cannot be dismissed as inconsequential. It opened the way for India's closer integration with the growing world economy, and contributed to the further growth of a market economy in India. It
was also a blow (though not a breach) to what a modern historian, Kirti Chaudhuri, calls India's "introspectiveness". As a result
of the Portuguese contact, many products of the Latin American
world—potato, corn, pineapple entered the Indian rural economy,
just as new breeds of fruits had come in the wake of the Turks.
Thus, the Indian peasant was not allergic to accepting new products if it meant a profit for him. Under Portuguese supervision,
ship-building, using western techniques, was started at Cochin.
However, for reasons which are not yet fully understood, some other
technologies which had made an impact or had far-reaching effects,
such as printing, clocks etc. though introduced in Goa, did not find
acceptance on the mainland.

The crucial question remains: why did Indian powers permit the domination of the Indian Ocean by a small, and economically backward state such as Portugal for more than a century? As is well known, the Portuguese domination of the Indian Ocean was ended in the seventeenth century, not by Asian powers but by the Dutch and the British. We shall take this question up in the context of the rise of the Dutch and the British.

The basis of Portugal's success in establishing its naval domination of the Asian seas has been much debated. It is now accepted that technologically, the Indo-Arab *boom* and the Chinese *junk* could match the Portuguese galleons and caravelles in their strength, holding capacity for goods in view of its tonnage, and capacity to sail even in the face of the wind with their lateen (triangular) sail. They had sufficient nautical skills to travel on open seas. Where the Portuguese were superior was the maneuvering capacity of their ships, the Indo-Arab ships being slow and clumsy on account of their heavy sails. Also, the hulls of the Portuguese ships were stronger to withstand the shock of firing cannons. But, it has been argued, it was above all the determination of the Portuguese sailors which decided the issue. The Indians, more used to fighting pirates, had no stomach for fighting on sea, unbacked by their own rulers.

Thus, it was not military and naval technology alone, but a number of other factors which enabled the Portuguese to establish a naval domination over the Indian seas for more than a century. The Indian powers reconciled themselves to this dominations because it did not threaten their own political positions on the mainland. Nor did it adversely effect their income from overseas trade. Hence, the task of undertaking a naval conflict with the Portuguese appeared difficult, uncertain of success, and likely to yield little financial returns.

The Asian oceanic trade extended from the Mediterranean in the West to Japan in the east. Within this huge area, there were three natural geographic zones—the Arabian Sea, the Bay of Bengal, and South China Sea. Within each of these zones there were important ports which catered to a large volume of trade.

In the earlier period, Persian and Arab merchants used to sail from the Persian Gulf to Canton with stops at Gujarat, Malabar and the Malacca Straits. We have evidence of Chinese jumks coming upto Malabar. Indian merchants also travelled to Canton where there was a sizeable colony of Indian merchants. However, gradually a kind of a regional specialization had come about. Arab merchants who had largely replaced the Persian merchants came up only to Cambay in Gujarat or Calicut in Malabar. Chinese merchants came up only to Malacca. Indian merchants travelled both in the Arab Sea in the west and the Bay of Bengal trade in the East. Regional specialisation implied that the ports in Gujarat, Malabar and Malacca had facilities such as anchorage, ware housing and banking as well as providing a merchant an outlet for goods brought in, and supplying goods sought by visiting ships. Thus, they became centres of what are called entrepot trade.

India played a crucial role in this Asian trade network not only because of its central geographic position, but also because India was able to provide, at competitive prices, a wide range of goods, from food items such as rice, sugar and oil to raw materials, such as cotton and indigo. Even more important, it was able to provide in large quantity and at competitive prices a wide range of manufactional goods, mainly textiles. There was demand for Indian textiles both in South-east Asia, on the east coast of Africa and in the Middle East. This, as a modern historian, Om Prakash, puts it made India "the industrial hub of the region surrounded by west Asia on one side and Southeast Asia on the other."

However, it should be noted that during the period, the size of the ships plying the trade rose gradually from 400 to 1000 tons so that the total tonnage of the ships reaching Lisbon from India rose from about 26,000 tons in 1501-10 to 48,000 tons in 1581-90. It declined thereafter, although the Portuguese trade remained substantial till the first quarter of the 17th century. The amount of pepper carried by the Portuguese remained more or less steady at 20,000 light quintals (of 51.4 kilograms each). The increased tonnage to Lisbon may be accounted for by private traders who were Jews forcibly converted to Christianity. Recent research shows that during the second half of the 16th century, private trade to Lisbon consisted of about 90 percent of the imports. These consisted of gems and indigo, but predominantly of textiles. The Indian textiles brought in by these traders were to be introduced to European markets.

It has been pointed out by Om Prakash in his book *European Commercial Enterprise in Pre-Colonial India* that by establishing a direct sea link with India the Portuguese overcame "the transport technology barrier" to the growth of trade between Asia and Europe. "The volume of this trade was no longer subject to the capacity constraint imposed by the availability of pack-animals and river boats in the Middle East." But an actual transformation of this trade network came into operation only by the seventeenth century.

12

RISE OF REGIONAL KINGDOMS IN NORTH INDIA AND A SYSTEM OF BALANCE OF POWER

Timur's invasion of Delhi in 1398 hastened the downfall of the Tughlaq dynasty, and the end of the Sultanat of Delhi. Even before Timur's invasion, the weakness of the Sultanat of Delhi had become manifest to all, with the emergence of two kings, one at Firuzabad and another at Delhi and the breaking away of many provincial kingdoms. The Deccani states, and Bengal in the east, and Sindh and Multan in the west had broken away towards the end of Muhammad bin Tughlaq's rule, and after some feeble efforts, Firuz had reconciled himself to their loss. Following the Timurid invasion, the governors of Gujarat, Malwa, and Jaunpur (in the east Uttar Pradesh) declared themselves independent, while Khizr Khan assumed full powers in the Punjab. With the expulsion of the Muslim governor from Ajmer, the various states of Rajputana also asserted their independence. Even within the Delhi region, the rulers were hard put to assert their control

While these various provincial kingdoms and Rajput states fought against each other, it would be wrong to consider the 15th century a period of decadence and decline in north India. Politically, warfare between the various states rarely extended beyond the border regions, with a definite pattern of balance of power emerging between the states located in the various regions—east, west and north. In the west, Gujarat, Malwa and Mewar balanced and checked the growth of each other's power. In the east, Bengal was checked by the Gajpati rulers of Orissa, as also by the Sharqi rulers of Jaunpur. In the north, while Kashmir remained aloof, the rise of the Lodis at Delhi towards the middle of 15th century led to a long drawn-out struggle between them and the rulers of Jaunpur for the mastery of the Ganga-Jamuna doab.

The balance of power began to break down by the end of the 15th century. With the final defeat of Jaunpur by the Lodis, and the extension of their rule from Punjab upto the borders of Bengal, the Sultanat of Delhi had been virtually re-established, and the heat was on eastern Rajasthan and Malwa. Meanwhile, Malwa itself had started disintegrating due to internal factors, leading to a sharpened rivalry between Gujarat and Mewar. The Lodis, too, were keen to use the situation in order to extend their rule over the region. Thus, Malwa once again became the cock-pit of the struggle for mastery of north India.

Culturally, the new kingdoms which arose tried to utilise local cultural forms and traditions for their own-purposes. This was mostly manifested in the field of architecture where efforts were made to adopt and adapt the new architectural forms developed by the Turks by utilising local forms and traditions. In many cases, encouragement was given to local languages, while political necessity compelled many of them to establish a closer association with Hindu ruling elites. This, in turn, had an effect on the processes of cultural rapprochement between the Hindus and the Muslims which had been working apace.

i. Eastern India—Bengal, Assam and Orissa

As we have noted earlier, Bengal had frequently asserted its independence from Delhi, taking advantage of its distance, difficulty of communications by land or water, and the fact that its hot and humid climate often did not suit soldiers and others used to the drier climate of north-western India.

Due to the preoccupation of Muhammad Tughlaq with rebellions in various quarters, Bengal again broke away from Delhi in 1338. Four years later, one of the nobles, Ilyas Khan, captured Lakhnauti and Sonargaon, and ascended the throne under the title Sultan Shamsuddin Ilyas Khan. Ilyas Khan extended his dominions in the west from Tirhut to Champaran and Gorakhpur, and finally upto Banaras. This forced Firuz Tughlaq to undertake a campaign against him. Marching through Champaran and Gorakhpur, the territories newly acquired by Ilyas, Firuz Tughlaq occupied the Bengali capital Pandua, and forced Ilyas to seek shelter in the strong fort of Ekdala. After a siege of two months, Firuz tempted Ilyas out of the fort by feigning flight. In a hard fought battle, the Bengali forces were defeated. But Ilyas Khan once again retreated into Ekdala.

Finally, a treaty of friendship was concluded by which the river
Kosi in Bihar was fixed as the boundary between the two kingdoms. Though Ilyas exchanged regular gifts with Firuz, he was in
no way subordinate to him. Friendly relations with Delhi enabled
Ilyas to extend his control over the kingdom of Kamrup (in modern Assam). He also made plundering raids upto Kathmandu in
Nepal, and in Orissa.

Ilyas Shah was a popular ruler and had many achievements to his
credit. When Firuz was at Pandua, he tried to win over the inhabitants of the city to his side by giving liberal grants of land to the
nobles, the clergy and other deserving people. His attempt failed. The
popularity of Ilyas enabled him to set up a dynasty which, in one
form or another, ruled for more than a hundred years.

Firuz Tughlaq invaded Bengal a second time when Ilyas died
and his son, Sikandar, succeeded to the throne. Sikandar followed
the tactics of his father, and retreated to Ekdala. Firuz failed, once
again, to capture it, and had to beat a retreat. After this, Bengal
was left alone for about 200 years and was not invaded again till
1538 after the Mughals had established their power at Delhi. It was
overrun by Sher Shah in 1538, but Akbar had to reconquer it after
the end of the Sur dynasty.

The most famous sultan in the dynasty of Ilyas Shah was
Ghiyasuddin Azam Shah (1389-1409). He was known for his love
of justice. It is said that once he accidentally killed the son of a
widow who complained to the qazi. The Sultan, when summoned
to the court, humbly appeared and paid the fine imposed by the
qazi. At the end of the trial, the Sultan told the qazi that if he had
failed in his duty, the would have had him beheaded. The qazi
told him that he would have had him scourged if he had not obeyed
his orders.

Azam Shah had close relations with the famous learned men of
his times, including the celebrated Persian poet, Hafiz of Shiraz.
He re-established friendly relations with the Chinese. The Chinese
emperor received his envoy cordially and, in 1409, sent his own
envoy with presents to the sultan and his wife, and a request to
send Buddhist monks to China. This was accordingly done. Inci-
dentally, this shows that Buddhism had not died completely in Bengal
till then. Six years later, his successor, Sultan Saifuddin, again sent
a letter written on a gold plate, and a giraffe to the Chinese emperor.

The revival of contact with China helped in the growth of the
overseas trade of Bengal. Chittagong became a flourishing port for

trade with China. Ocean going ships were built in Bengal, and its exports included fine quality textiles. Bengal also became a centre for the re-export of Chinese goods. Mahuan, the Chinese interpreter to the Chinese envoy, has left an account, and mentions mulberry trees, and the production of silk in Bengal, and paper which was as glossy as deer's skin.

During this period, many sufis came to Bengal. They were welcomed by the Sultan, and encouraged with grant of rent-free lands. These saints impressed the people by their simple style of living, and their deep devotion and saintliness. These saints are credited with effecting conversions to Islam on a large scale, particularly in the eastern part of Bengal where Buddhism was widely prevalent, and poverty was wide-spread. Perhaps, the conversions were due in large measure to social, cultural and other factors, but credit for conversion was given to the blessing (*barkat*) of the saints.

Powerful Hindu rajas continued to live under the Muslim rulers of Bengal, and to be associated with the affairs of the state. Thus, Raja Ganesh of Dinajpur, who had a large estate and his own army, first became a king-maker to the successors of Sultan Saifuddin, and later assumed the throne himself. The basis of Ganesh's support is not clear. Some of the Turkish nobles and theologians sent an invitation to the ruler of Jaunpur to deliver the land of Islam from *kufr*. A Jaunpur army was sent to Gaur for the purpose, and won a victory. But it could not stay on because of the active struggle between the rulers of Jaunpur and Delhi. Raja Ganesh, who was an old man, died soon after, and was succeeded by his son who preferred to rule as a Muslim. However, the affairs in the kingdom remained unsettled till Alauddin Husain succeeded to the throne in 1493, and set up a new dynasty which continued to rule till the rise of Sher Shah.

Freed from threat of military invasion from Delhi as a result of agreement with Firuz, and the subsequent weakness of the Delhi Sultanat, the Sultans of Bengal adorned their capitals, Gaur (old Lakhnauti) and Pandua 25 kms to the north, with magnificent buildings. However, only a few of them have survived, though the ruins over a large area indicate the extensive scale of the building activities. The largest building which has survived is the Adina mosque. This mosque was large enough to accommodate several thousand people. Although the stones used in the mosque were mostly those pillaged from temples and other buildings from Lakhnauti, the use of broad sloping arches (called 'drop' arches), pillars of a special type, and curvilinear roofs indicate that a new

style of architecture, independent of Delhi, and using local traditions had developed. This mature style of architecture is to be seen
in the *Dakhil Darwaza* (second half of 15th century). The buildings
were mostly of brick and mortar, stone being used sparingly. The
adoption of the lotus, swan etc., as decorative motifs showed the
influence of Hindu traditions.

The Sultans also patronised the Bengali language. The celebrated
poet, Maladhar Basu, compiler of *Sri-Krishna-Vijaya*, was patronised
by the sultans and was granted the title of Gunaraja Khan. His son
was honoured with the title of Satyaraja Khan. But the most significant period for the growth of the Bengali language was the rule of
Alauddin Hussain (1493-1519). Some of the famous Bengali writers
of the time flourished under his rule.

A brilliant period began under the enlightened rule of Alauddin
Hussain. The Sultan restored law and order, and adopted a liberal
policy by offering high offices to Hindus. Thus, his wazir was a
talented Hindu. The chief physician, the chief of the bodyguard,
the master of the mint were all Hindus. The two famous brothers
who were celebrated as pious Vaishnavas, Rupa and Sanatan, held
high posts, one of them being the sultan's private secretary. Krittibas,
the translator of *Ramanayana* into Bengali, was said to have been
closely associated with Sanatan. Some of the nobles of Alauddin
Hussain gave patronage to Bengali poets. The sultan is also said
to have shown great respect to the famous Vaishnavite saint,
Chaitanya, and no obstacles were placed in his path of giving a
new spiritual ethos to Bengali life.

Hussain Shah tried to extend his territories in the north into
Assam, in the south-west towards Orissa, and south-east towards
Chittagaon and Arakan. Of these, he was most successful in extending his empire towards Chittagaon and Arakan. Although details of the conquest are lacking, control over the port of Chittagaon
was an important link with the overseas trade with south-east Asia,
extending upto China, on the one hand, and with Africa on the
other. In a series of hard fought battles, Tipperah in the east was
also captured and annexed.

Assam

The rulers of Bengal had always tried to bring the rich and fertile valley of Brahmaputra in modern Assam under their control.
With the decline of the Palas by the middle of the 12th century,
the Brahmaputra valley was divided into a number of warring principalities. Gradually, the rulers of Kamrup and Kamta in the west

(Persian historians use them interchangeably) brought under their control the area between the Kartoya and the Barnadi rivers. To their east were the Ahoms. The Ahoms belonged to the great Tai group of tribes which dominated south China and many south-east Asian countries. They came to the Brahmaputra valley from Yunan in the first half of the 13th century and, under their ruler Sukapha, established their control over the modern districts of Dibrugarh and Sibsagar. In course of time, the entire valley began to be called Assam after their name.

We have already seen how Muhammed bin Baktiyar Khalji had led an expedition in Kumrup, aimed at Tibet, but had to suffer a disastrous defeat in an area which was little known to him. The subsequent efforts of Turkish governors and rebel rulers of Bengal to bring the area under their subservience and to establish themselves in Gauhati also failed due to climate, geography and the stout resistance of the local people. However, for some time the rulers of Kamrup/Kamta was forced to pay an annual tribute in gold and elephants to Bengal, and this became a basis of its future claims.

The independent sultans of Bengal took up where their predecessors have failed. Ilyas Shah invaded Kamrup, and occupied its capital. However, the Ahoms were not happy at the presence of Turks so near their frontier, and shortly, with their help, the ruler of Kamrup threw the Turks across the river Kartoya which was now accepted as the north-eastern boundary of Bengal.

However, the rulers of Bengal were determined to bring Kamrup under their control at the first suitable opportunity. This they found an account of the hostility between the ruler of Kamrup and the Ahoms. Alauddin Hussain Shah invaded, occupied and annexed the western part, consisting of modern Cooch-Bihar upto Hajo.

Despite the internal political situation, and recurrent fights, both within the valley and with the governors and the sultans of Bengal, Kamrup and Kamta maintained their ancient traditions of scholarship, and of Sanskrit learning. Simultaneously, a new language, Assamese, based on the intermingling of the various people and tribes, emerged. The first literary work in Assamese is supposed to be Hem Saraswati's *Prahlad Charit*. A new incentive was given with the rise of neo-Vaishnavite movement under Shankardeva (b. 1449). Like the bhakti saints of north-western India, Shankardeva and his followers emphasised prayers and devotion in preference to ritual. In order to reach the people, these saints spoke and wrote in Assamese. Their centres, called *namghoras*, became active centres for the dissemination of the new faith, and its literature.

Thus, the 15th century can be called a period of literary and cul-/ tural renaissance in Assam. Another development of the period was the steady Hinduization of the Ahoms, by incorporating their gods into the Hindu pantheon, marriage with Hindu noble families etc. The Ahom rulers were aware that accepting Hinduism implied giving the ruler a divine status which strengthened his position vis-a-vis the nobles. Also, by incorporating the cognate clans and bordering tribes, Hinduism strengthened the new polity.

Orissa

In those days, the boundaries of Orissa were not clearly demarcated from Bengal. The Ganga rulers, who came to power in middle of the 11th century and ruled till the middle of the 15th century, unified the three areas—Utkal, Kalinga, and Kosala which constitute present Orissa. The Ganga rulers were great warriors and temple builders. Narsinghdeo, (d. 1264) considered one of the greatest rulers, built the famous sun temple at Konark. He invaded and occupied Radha in south Bengal, and even invested Lakhnauti more than once which was saved by the timely intervention of a Delhi army. At the time, the Orissa frontier with Bengal was the Saraswati river which then carried much of the waters of the Ganga. Thus, a large part of the modern Midnapore district and parts of the Hugli district were included in Orissa. The Orissa rulers, it seemed, tried to extend their frontiers upto the Bhagirathi, but could not do so in the face of opposition from the rulers of Bengal.

At the beginning of his reign, Ilyas Shah raided Jajnagar (Orissa). It is said that overcoming all opposition, he advanced up to the Chilka Lake and returned with a rich booty, including a number of elephants. A couple of years later, in 1360, while returning from his Bengal campaign, Firuz Tughlaq also raided Orissa. He occupied the capital city, massacred a large number of people, and desecrated the famous Jagannath temple. These two raids destroyed the prestige of the royal dynasty but it lingered on till the middle of 15th century when a new dynasty, called the Gajpati dynasty, came to the fore. The Gajapati rule marks a brilliant phase in Orissa history. The Gajapati rulers were mainly instrumental in extending their ruler in the south toward Karnataka. As we have seen, this brought them into conflict with Vijayanagar, the Reddis and the Bahmani sultans. Perhaps, one reason why the Gajapati rulers preferred aggarandizement in the south was their feeling that the sultans of Bengal were too strong to be easily dislodged from the Bengal-Orissa border. While this brought them glory and booty, the Orissa rulers could not hold on to their southern conquests for any length of time, due to the power and capabilities of the Vijayanagar and Bahmani rulers. That the Orissa rulers were able to engage successfully in battles at the same time in such far-flung areas in Bengal and Karnataka testifies to their strength and prowess. The Orissa language also developed during the period, with many works being produced in poetry and prose.

Thus, the various regions of the east prospered during the period. Although Bengal was the most powerful among the various kingdoms of the regions, it was not, despite plundering them, able to bring the states of Assam and Orissa under its control. A threat to the freedom of Bengal developed when the Lodi rulers over-ran Jaunpur with whom the rulers of Bengal had friendly relations. The defeated ruler of Jaunpur took shelter in the Bengal kingdom and was accorded a warm welcome. A threatened collision was averted, although the armies of Bengal and Delhi stood face to face for some time. As a result of the agreement, Bihar was silently partitioned between the two.

ii. Western India: Gujarat, Malwa and Rajasthan

On account of their size, rich and fertile lands and salubrious climate, Gujarat and Malwa were always regarded as rich prizes. Gujarat was famous for its excellent handicrafts and its flourishing sea-ports from which much of north India's sea-trade was conducted. Malwa and Rajasthan were important transit centres, linking the products of the Ganga valley with the sea-ports of Gujarat. Hence, control over Malwa and Gujarat and the road link across Rajasthan had always been the concern of any imperial power in the north or south.

During the 15th century, Malwa and Gujarat balanced each other. While both tried to bring the border states of Rajasthan under their domination, they were unable to make deep in-roads into Rajasthan, mainly on account of the rise of Mewar under Rana Kumbha. But this balance began to break down during the early decades of the 16th century, leading to a new, emerging situation.

Gujarat

Under Firuz Tughlaq, Gujarat had a benign governor who, according to Ferishta, "encouraged the Hindu religion and thus promoted rather than suppressed the worship of idols." He was suc-

ceeded by Zafar Khan whose father, Sadharan, was a Rajput who
was converted to Islam, and had given his sister in marriage to
Firuz Tughlaq. After Timur's invasion of Delhi, both Gujarat and
Malwa became independent in all but name. However, it was not
till 1407 that Zafar Khan formally proclaimed himself the ruler in
Gujarat, with the title Muzaffar Shah. Dilawar Khan Ghuri, the governor of Malwa, had declared himself independent at Mandu a few
years earlier.

The real founder of the kingdom of Gujarat was, however, Ahmad
Shah I (1411-42), the grandson of Muzaffar Shah. During his long
reign, he brought the nobility under control, settled the administration, and expanded and consolidated the kingdom. He shifted
the capital from Patan to the new city of Ahmedabad, the foundation of which he laid in 1413. He was a great builder, and beautified the town with many magnificent palaces and bazars, mosques
and *madrasas*. He drew on the rich architectural tradition of the Jains
of Gujarat to devise a style of building which was markedly different from Delhi. Some of its features are: slender turrets, exquisite stone-carving, and highly ornate brackets. The Jama Masjid in
Ahmedabad and the Tin Darwaza are fine examples of the style
of architecture during the time. Ahmad Shah tried to extend his
control over the Rajput states in the Saurashtra region, as well as
those located on the Gujarat-Rajasthan border. In Saurashtra, he
defeated and captured the strong fort of Girnar, but restored it to
the Raja on his promise to pay tribute. He then attacked Sidhpur,
the famous Hindu pilgrim centre, and levelled to the ground many
of the beautiful temples there. In addition to *peshkash* or annual
tribute, he imposed *jizyah* on the Hindu rulers in Gujarat which
had never been imposed on them earlier. However, just as *jizyah*
was collected as a part of the land-revenue (*kharaj*) from individuals in the Sultanat of Delhi, *jizyah* and *peshkash* must have been
collected together from the rajas. All these measures led many medieval historians to hail Ahmad Shah as a great enemy of the in-
fields, while many modern historians have called him a bigot. The
truth, however, appears to be more complex. While Ahmad Shah
acted as a bigot in ordering the destruction of Hindu temples, he
did not hesitate to induct Hindus in government. Manik Chand and
Motichand, belonging to the bania or commercial community, were
ministers under him. He was so strict in his justice that he had his
own son-in-law executed in the market-place for a murder he had
committed. Although he fought the Hindu rulers he fought no less
the Muslim rulers of the time, i.e. the Muslim rulers of Malwa,

Khandesh and the Deccan. He subordinated the powerful fort of Idar, and brought the Rajput states of Jhalawar, Bundi, Dungarpur, etc., under his control.

From the beginning, the kingdoms of Gujarat and Malwa were bitter rivals and were generally found in opposite camps on almost every occasion. The warfare between them, like the warfare between the rulers of Vijayanagar and the Bahmanis, did not, however, lead to any lasting change in their frontiers.

Muzaffar Shah had defeated and imprisoned Hushang Shah who succeeded Dilawar Khan as the ruler of Malwa. Finding it difficult to control Malwa, he had, however, released Hushang Shah after a few years and reinstated him. Far from healing the breach, it had made the rulers of Malwa even more apprehensive of Gujarat's power. They were always on the lookout for weakening Gujarat by giving help and encouragement to disaffected elements there, be they the rebel nobles, or Hindu rajas at war with the Gujarat ruler. The rulers of Gujarat tried to counter this by trying to install their own nominee on the throne of Malwa. This bitter rivalry weakened the two kingdoms, and made it impossible for them to play a larger role in the politics of north India.

Mahmud Begarha

The successors of Ahmad Shah continued his policy of expansion and consolidation. The most famous sultan of Gujarat was Mahmud Begarha. Mahmud Begarha ruled over Gujarat for more than 50 years (from 1459 to 1511). He was called Begarha because he captured two of the most powerful forts (*garhs*), Girnar in Saurashtra (now called Junagarh) and Champaner in south Gujarat.[1] The ruler of Girnar had paid tribute regularly, but Mahmud Begarha decided to annex his kingdom as a part of his policy of bringing Saurashtra under full control. Saurashtra was a rich and prosperous region and had many fertile tracts and flourishing ports. Unfortunately, the Saurashtra region was also infested by robbers and sea-pirates who preyed on trade and shipping. The powerful fort of Girnar was considered suitable not only for administering Saurashtra, but also as a base of operations against Sindh.

Mahmud Begarha besieged Girnar with a large force. Though the raja had only a few guns in the fort, he resisted gallantly, but

---

1. According to another version, he was called Begarha because his mustaches resembled the horns of a cow (*begarha*).

to no avail. It is said that the conquest of this inaccessible fort was
due to treason. The ruler of Girnar had forcibly taken the wife of
his *kamdar* (minister/agent) who schemed in secret the downfall of
his master. After the fall of the fort, the raja embraced Islam and
was entrolled in the service of the sultan. The sultan founded at
the foot of the hill a new town called Mustafabad. He built many
lofty buildings there and asked all his nobles to do the same. Thus,
it became the second capital of Gujarat.

Later in his region, Mahmud Begarha sacked Dwarka, largely
because it harboured pirates who ravaged the traders. Thus, the
immediate occasion for Mahmud's attack was the plaint of Maulana
Mahmud Samarquandi that while returning to Hormuz, he was
driven ashore and all his property looted by the pirates who were
sheltered by the local ruler. The campaign was, however, also used
to raze the famous Hindu temples there.

The fort of Champaner was strategically located for the Sultan's
plans of bringing Khandesh and Malwa under his control. The ruler,
though a feudatory of Gujarat, had close relations with the sultan
of Malwa. Champaner fell in 1454 after the gallant raja and his
followers, despairing of help from any quarter, performed the *jauhar*
ceremony and fought to the last man. Mahmud constructed a new
town called Muhammadabad near Champner. He laid out many
fine gardens there and made it his principal place of residence.

Champner is now in ruins. But the building that still attracts attention is the Jama Masjid. It has a covered courtyard, and many
Jain principles of architecture have been used in it. The stone work
in the other buildings constructed during this period is so fine that
it can only be compared to the work of goldsmiths.

Mahmud Begarha also had to deal with the Portuguese who were
interfering with Gujarat's trade with the countries of West Asia.
He joined hands with the ruler of Egypt to check the Portuguese
naval power, but he was not successful.

During the long and peaceful reign of Mahmud Begarha, trade
and commerce prospered. He constructed many caravan-sarais amd
inns for the comfort of the travellers. The merchants were happy
because roads were safe for traffic.

Though Mahmud Begarha had never received a systematic education, he had gained considerable knowledge by his constant association with the learned men. Many works were translated from
Arabic into Persian during his reign. His court poet was Udayaraja
who composed in Sanskrit.

Mahmud Begarha had a striking appearance. He had a flowing beard which reached up to his waist, and his moustache was so long that he tied it over his head. According to a traveller, Barbosa, Mahmud, from his childhood, had been nourished on some poison so that if a fly settled on his hand, it swelled and immediately lay dead.

Mahmud was also famous for his voracious appetite. It is said that for breakfast he ate a cup of honey, a cup of butter and one hundred to one hundred-fifty plantains. He ate 10 to 15 kilos of food a day and we are told that plates of meat patties (*samosas*) were placed on both the side of his pillow at night in case he felt hungry!

From the beginning, the rulers of Gujarat adopted a policy of entering into matrimonial relations with some of their subordinate Rajput rulers. Thus, in 1446, the daughter of the raja of Idar married the Gujarati ruler. The mother of Muzaffar Shah II was also a Rajput, and he himself married a number of Rajput princesses. Although many Hindus rose in the service of the Gujarati rulers, such as Rajya Rayan who was the chief Hindu noble of Mahmud Begarha, and Malik Gopi who was the chief minister, the policy of matrimonial alliances neither brought any changes in the overall policies of the sultans, nor brought the concerned families into a closer political union.

The Gujarat kingdom remained a powerful, well-administered and prosperous state of the country, and was powerful enough not to allow any serious encroachments on its territories and ports by the Portuguese. However, its efforts under Bahadur Shah to dominate Malwa and Rajasthan led to a clash with the Mughals and proved its undoing.

Malwa and Mewar

The state of Malwa was situated on the high plateau between Narmada and Tapti rivers. It commanded the trunk routes between Gujarat and northern India, as also between north and south India. As long as Malwa continued to be strong, it acted as a barrier to the ambitions of Gujarat, Mewar, the Bahmanis and the Lodi sultans of Delhi. The geographical situation in northern India was such that if any of the powerful states of the region could extend its control over Malwa, it would be well on its way to make a bid for the domination of the entire northern India.

During the fifteenth century, the kingdom of Malwa remained at the height of its power. The capital was shifted from Dhar to

Mandu, a place which was highly defensive and which had a great deal of natural beauty. Here the ruler of Malwa constructed a large number of buildings, the ruins of which are still impressive. Unlike the Gujarat style of architecture, the Mandu architecture was massive, and was made to look even more so by using a very lofty plinth for the buildings. The large-scale use of coloured and glazed tiles provided variety to the buildings. The best known among them are the Jama Masjid, the Hindola Mahal and the Jahaz Mahal.

From the beginning, the kingdom of Malwa was torn by internal dissensions. The struggle for succession between different contenders to the throne was accompanied by fighting between different groups of nobles for power and profit. The neighbouring states of Gujarat and Mewar were always ready to take advantage of this factionalism for their own purpose.

One of the early rulers of Malwa, Hushang Shah, adopted a broad policy of religious toleration. Many Rajputs, some of them from modern east UP, were encouraged to settle in Malwa and given rich grants. Rai Silhadi was one of these. Two of the elder brothers of Rana Mokal of Mewar were also granted jagirs in Malwa. From the inscription of the Lalitpur temple which was built during this period, it appears that no restrictions were placed on the construction of temples. Hushang Shah extended his patronage to the Jains who were the principal commercial merchants and bankers of the area. Thus, Nardeva Soni, a successful merchant, was the treasurer of Hushang Shah, and one of his adviser.

Unfortunately, all the rulers of Malwa were not equally tolerant. Mahmud Khalji (1436-69), who is considered the most powerful of the Malwa rulers, destroyed many temples during his struggle with Rana Kumbha of Mewar, and with the neighbouring Hindu rajas. Though his actions cannot be justified, most of them were carried out during periods of war, and cannot be considered part of any policy of general destruction of Hindu temples.

Mahmud Khalji was a restless and ambitious monarch. He fought with almost all his neighbours—the ruler of Gujarat, the rajas of Gondwana and Orissa, the Bahmani sultans, and even with the sultans of Delhi. However, his energies were principally devoted to overrunning south Rajputana and trying to subdue Mewar.

The steady rise of Mewar during the 15th century was an important factor in the political life of north India. With the conquest of Ranthambhor by Alauddin Khalji, the power of the Chauhans in Rajputana had finally come to an end. From its ruins a number of new states arose. Taking advantage of the decline of the Tughlaqs,

Rao Chunda of Marwar occupied Sambhar, Nagaur and Ajmer, and made Marwar the most powerful state of Rajasthan. However, Marwar received a set back due to the rising power of Mewar, and the hostility of the Bhatis, and the ruler of Multan. Later, Rao Jodha (1438-89) who had to lead a wandering life for some time, founded the new city and capital of Jodhpur (1459), and re-established the state.

Another state of consequence in the area was the Muslim principality of Nagaur. Ajmer which had been the seat of power of the Muslim governors changed hands several times and was a bone of contention among the rising Rajput states. The mastery of eastern Rajputana was also in dispute, the rulers of Delhi being deeply interested in this area.

The early history of the state of Mewar is obscure. Though it dated back to the eighth century, the ruler who raised it to the status of a power to be reckoned with was Rana Kumbha (1433-68). After cautiously consolidating his position by defeating his internal rivals, Kumbha annexed Sambhar, Nagaur, Ajmer, Ranthambhor etc., and brought the border states of Bundi, Kotah, Dungarpur etc., under his control. Since Kotah had earlier been paying allegiance to Malwa, and Dungarpur to Gujarat, this brought Kumbha into conflict with both these kingdoms. There were other reasons for the conflict, too. The Khan of Nagaur who had been attacked by Rana Kumbha had appealed for help to the ruler of Gujarat. The Rana had also give shelter at his court to a rival of Mahmud Khalji and even attempted to install him on the Malwa throne. In retaliation, Mahmud Khalji had given shelter and active encouragement to some of the rivals of the Rana, such as his brother, Mokal.

The conflict with Gujarat and Malwa occupied Kumbha throughout his reign. During most of the time, the Rana also had to contend with the Rathors of Marwar. Although sorely pressed from all sides, the Rana was largely able to maintain his position in Mewar. Kumbhalgarh was besieged a couple of times by Gujarat forces, while Mahmud Khalji was able to raid as far inland as Ajmer and install his own governor there. The Rana was able to repulse these attacks and retain possession of most of his conquests, with the exception of some of the outlying areas such as Ranthambhor. Rana Kumbha's facing two such powerful states against all odds was no small achievement.

Kumbha was a patron of learned men, and was himself a learned man. He composed a number of books, some of which can still be read. The ruins of his palace and the Victory Tower (Kirti Stambha) which he built at Chittor show that he was an enthusiastic builder as well. He dug several lakes and reservoirs for irrigation purposes. Some of the temples built during his period show that the art of stone-cutting, sculpture, etc., was still at a high level.

Kumbha was murdered by his son, Uda, in order to gain the throne. Though Uda was soon outsted, he left a bitter trail. After some time, in 1508, Rana Sanga, a grandson of Kumbha, ascended the *gaddi* of Mewar, after a long and bitter struggle with his brothers. The most important development between the death of Kumbha and the rise of Sanga was the rapid internal disintegration of Malwa. The ruler, Mahmud II, had fallen out with Medini Rai, the powerful Rajput leader of eastern Malwa who had helped him to gain the throne. The Malwa ruler appealed for help to Gujarat, while Medini Rai repaired to the court of Rana Sanga. In a battle in 1519, the Rana defeated Mahmud II and carried him a prisoner to Chittor but, it is claimed, he released him after six months, keeping one of his son as a hostage. Eastern Malwa, including Chanderi, passed under the over lordship of Rana Sanga.

The developments in Malwa alarmed the Lodi rulers of Delhi who had been trying to establish their hold on Malwa, Chanderi having tendered allegiance to the Lodi sultan earlier. This led to a series of clashes between the Lodi sultans and Sanga. In a battle in 1518 at Ghatoli, on the border of Harauti in south Rajasthan, Ibrahim Lodi suffered a serious reverse, but Sanga was wounded and lamed for life. It seems that there were a series of skirmishes between the Lodis and Sanga whose influence gradually extended to Pilia Khar, a river near Fatehpur Sikri in the region of Agra.

Meanwhile, Babur was knocking at the gates of India. It seems that a conflict for supremacy in north India was inescapable.

iii. North-West and North India—The Sharqis, the Lodi Sultans and Kashmir

After his invasion and attack on Delhi, since the Tughlaq sultan had run away, Timur had given Delhi to Khizr Khan, who had earlier been the governor of Multan. Before his departure, Timur had also assigned Multan and Dipalpur to Khizr Khan. However, the Tughlaq sultan had returned. Hence, Khizr Khan kept away from Delhi, keeping his control over Multan and the Punjab. After the death of the Tughlaq ruler in 1412, he entered Delhi, and set up a new dynasty which he called the Saiyid dynasty. The Saiyids were not subordinates of the Timurid rulers, although their names were included in the *khutba* for some time. However, the Saiyids were not able to establish themselves firmly, being threatened all the time by the Khokhars of the Punjab, the Mewatis, and the Sharqi rulers of Jaunpur.

The Jaunpur kingdom had been set up by Malik Sarwar, a prominent noble of the time of Firuz Tughlaq. Malik Sarwar had been the wazir for some time, and then had been nominated to the eastern areas with the title Malik-us-Sharq (Lord of the east). His successors came to be called the Sharqis after the title. The Sharqi sultans fixed their capital at Jaunpur (in eastern Uttar Pradesh) which they beautified with magnificent palaces, mosques and mausoleums. Only a few of these mosques and mausoleum survive now. They show that the Sharqi sultan did not just copy the Delhi style of architecture. They created a magnificent style of their own, marked by lofty gates and huge arches.

The Sharqi sultans were great patrons of learning and culture. Poets and men of letters, scholars and saints assembled at Jaunpur and shed lustre on it. In course of time, Jaunpur came to be known as the "Shiraz of the East". Malik Muhammad Jaisi, the author of a well-known Hindi work, *Padmavat*, lived at Jaunpur. The Sharqi sultanat lasted for less than a century. At its height, it extended from Aligarh in western Uttar Pradesh to Darbhanga in north Bihar, and from the boundary of Nepal in the north to Bundelkhand in the south. The Sharqi rulers were eager to conquer Delhi but they were not successful in doing so. With the establishment of the Lodis in Delhi towards the middle of the fifteenth century, the Sharqi rulers were gradually put on the defensive. They lost most of the areas in western Uttar Pradesh, and exhausted themselves in a series of bitter but futile assaults on Delhi. At length, in 1484, Bahlul Lodi, the ruler of Delhi, occupied Jaunpur and annexed the Sharqi kingdom. The Sharqi king lived on as an exile at Chunar for some time, and died broken hearted after repeated failures in regaining his kingdom.

The Sharqi rulers maintained law and order over a large tract following the collapse of the government in Delhi. They successfully prevented the rulers of Bengal in extending their control over eastern Uttar Pradesh. Above all, they established a cultural tradition which continued long after the downfall of the Sharqis.

We have mentioned the rise of the Saiyid dynasty after the end of the Tughlaqs. Threatened by the rulers of Jaunpur, the Saiyids had sought the help of the Afghan leader, Bahlul Lodi, who had established himself in Punjab along with a number of Afghan sardars. Bahlul Lodi checked the growing power of the Khokhars, a fierce warlike tribe which lived in the Salt Ranges. Soon, he dominated the entire Punjab. Called in to help the ruler of Delhi against an impending attack by the ruler of Malwa, Bahlul stayed on. Before long, his men took over the control of Delhi. Bahlul formally crowned himself in 1451.

The Lodis dominated the upper Ganga Valley and the Punjab from the middle of the fifteenth century. As distinct from the earlier Delhi rulers who were Turks, the Lodis were Afghans. Although the Afghans formed a large group in the army of the Delhi Sultanat, very few Afghan nobles had been accorded important positions. That is why Bakhtiyar Khalji who was part-Afghan had to seek his fortune in Bihar and Bengal. The growing importance of the Afghans in north India was shown by the rise of the Afghan rule in Malwa. In the south, they held important positions in the Bahmani kingdom.

Bahlul Lodi's energies were occupied mainly in his contest with the Sharqi rulers. Finding himself in a weak position, Bahlul invited the Afghans of Roh to come to India so that "they will get rid of the ignominy of poverty and I shall gain ascendancy." The Afghan historian, Abbas Sarwani, adds: "On receipt of these *farmans*, the Afghans of Roh came like locusts to join the service of Sultan Bahlul." This may be an exaggeration. But the incursion of the Afghans not only enabled Bahlul to defeat the Sharqis, it changed the complexion of the Muslim society in India, making the Afghans a very numerous and important element in it, both in south and north India.

The most important Lodi sultan was Sikandar Lodi (1489-1517). A contemporary of Mahmud Begarha of Gujarat and Rana Sanga of Mewar, Sikandar Lodi geared the kingdom of Delhi for the coming struggle for power with these states. He tried to subdue the Afghan sardars who had a sturdy sense of tribal independence, and were not accustomed to look upon the sultan as more than a first among equals. Sikandar made the nobles stand before him in order to impress them with his superior status. When a royal order (*farman*) was sent, all the nobles had to come out of the town to receive it with due honour. Thus Sikandar re-affirmed the supremacy of the sultan over his nobles. All those who held jagirs had to submit accounts regularly. Drastic punishments were given to those who embezzled money or were corrupt. Sikandar Lodi had only limited success in his efforts to control the nobles. At his death, Bahlul Lodi had divided the kingdom among his sons and relations. Though Sikandar had been able to undo this after a hard struggle, the idea of a partition of the empire among sons of the ruler persisted among Afghans.

Sikandar Lodi was able to establish an efficient administration in his kingdom. He laid great emphasis on justice, and all the highways of the empire were made safe from robbers and bandits. The prices of all essential commodities were remarkably cheap. The Sultan took keen interest in agriculture. He abolished the octroi duty on grains, and established a new measurement of a yard, called the *gazz-i-sikandari*, which continued to prevail till the Mughal times. The rent-rolls (*jama*) prepared in his time formed the basis of the rent-rolls prepared in the time of Sher Shah later on.

Sikandar Lodi is regarded as an orthodox, even a bigoted king. He sternly forbade the Muslims from following practices which were against the *shara* (Islami law), such as women visiting the graves of saints or processions being taken out in their memory. He reimposed the *jizyah* on the Hindus, and executed a brahmans for holding that the Hindu and Muslim scriptures were equally sacred. He also demolished a few well- known Hindu temples during his campaigns, such as the temples at Nagarkot.

Sikandar Lodi gave magnificent grants to scholars, philosophers and men of letters so that cultured people of all climes and countries, including Arabia and Iran, flocked to his court. Due to the Sultan's efforts, a number of Sanskrit works were translated into Persian. He was also interested in music and had a number of rare Sanskrit works on music translated into Persian. During the time, a large number of Hindus took to learning Persian and were recruited to various administrative posts.

Thus, the process of cultural rapprochement between the Hindus and the Muslims continued apace during his reign. Sikandar Lodi also extended his dominion by conquering Dholpur and Gwaliyar. It was during these operations that after careful survey and deliberations, Sikandar Lodi selected the site for the city of Agra (1506). The town was meant to command the area of eastern Rajasthan and the route to Malwa and Gujarat. It was also meant to control the rebellious nobles and rulers of the doab. In course of time, Agra became a large town and the second capital of the Lodis.

The growing interest of Sikandar Lodi in eastern Rajasthan and Malwa was shown by his taking the Khan of Nagaur under his protection, and by trying to make Ranthambhor transfer its allegiance from Malwa to Delhi. His successor, Ibrahim Lodi, even led a campaign against Mewar which, as has been noted earlier, was repulsed. The growing power of the Rana in Malwa, and the extension of his powers towards Agra and Bayana, presaged a conflict between Mewar and the Lodis. It is difficult to say what the outcome of this conflict would have been if Babur had not intervened.

Kashmir

An account of north India in the fifteenth century would be incomplete without mentioning the Kingdom of Kashmir. The beautiful valley of Kashmir was for long a forbidden land to all outsiders. According to Albiruni, entry into Kashmir was not allowed even to the Hindus who were not known personally to the nobles there. During this period, Kashmir was known to be a centre of Saivism. However, the situation changed with the ending of the Hindu rule around the middle of the fourteenth century. The devastating attack on Kashmir in 1320 by the Mongol leader, Dulucha, was a prelude to it. It is said that Dulucha ordered a wholesale massacre of men, while women and children were enslaved and sold to the merchants of Central Asia. The towns and villages were ravaged and plundered and set on fire. The hapless Kashmir government could offer no opposition to these doings, thereby losing all public sympathy and support.

One hundred years after the Mongol invasion, Zainul Abidin, considered the greatest of the Muslim monarchs of Kashmir, ascended the throne. Kashmir society had profoundly changed during this period. There had been a continuous incursion of Muslim saints and refugees from Central Asia into Kashmir, the Baramula route providing an easy access. Another development was the rise of a series of remarkable sufi saints called Rishis, who combined some features of Hinduism and Islam. Partly by the preaching of the saints and partly by force, the lower class population had converted to Islam. To complete the process, a vehement persecution of the brahmans began in the reign of Sikandar Shah (1389-1413). The sultan ordered that all brahmans and learned Hindus should become Musalmans or leave the valley. Their temples were to be destroyed and the idols of gold and silver were to be melted in order to be used for currency. It is said that these orders were issued at the instance of the king's minister, Suha Bhatt, who had converted to Islam, and was bent on harassing his former co-religionists.

The situation changed with the accession of Zainul Abidin (1420-70) who had all these orders cancelled. He conciliated and brought back to Kashmir all the non-Muslims who had fled. Those who wanted to revert to Hinduism, or had pretended to be Muslims in order to save their lives, were given freedom to do as they pleased. He even restored their libraries and the grants which the Hindus had enjoyed. The temples were also restored. More than one hundred years later, Abul Fazl noted that Kashmir had one hundred and fifty majestic temples. It is likely that most of them had been restored by Zainul Abidin. Zainul Abidin continued the policy of broad toleration in other spheres as well. He abolished *jizyah* and cow-slaughter, and to respect the wishes of the Hindus, withdrew the ban on *sati*. The Hindus occupied many high ranks in his governments. Thus, Sriya Bhatt was minister of justice and court physician. His first two queens were Hindus, being the daughters of the Raja of Jammu. They were the mothers of all of his four sons. He married a third wife after their death.

The Sultan was himself a learned man, and composed poetry. He was well versed in Persian, Kashmiri, Sanskrit and Tibetan languages. He gave patronage to Persian and Sanskrit scholars and, at his instance, many Sanskrit works such as the *Mahabharata* and Kalhana's history of Kashmir, *Rajatarangini,* were translated into Persian, and brought up-to-date. He was fond of music, and hearing of this, the Raja of Gwaliyar sent him two rare Sanksrit works on music.

The Sultan also looked after the economic development of Kashmir. He sent two persons to Samarqand to learn the art of paper-making and book-binding. He fostered many crafts in Kashmir, such as stone-cutting and polishing, bottle-making, gold-beating etc. He also encouraged the art of shawl-making, for which Kashmir is so famous. Musket-making and the art of manufacturing fireworks had also developed in Kashmir. The Sultan developed agriculture by making large number of dams, canals and bridges. He was an enthusiastic builder, his greatest achievement being Zaina Lanka—the artificial island in the Woolur lake on which he built his palace and a mosque.

Zainul Abidin is still called Bud Shah (the Great Sultan) by the Kashmiris. Though a great warrior, he defeated the Mongol invasion of Lakakh, conquered the Baltistan area (called Tibbat-i-khurd), and kept control over Jammu, Rajauri, etc. He, thus, unified the Kashmir kingdom.

The fame of Zainul Abidin had spread far and wide. He was in touch with the leading rulers in the other parts of India, as also the other leading rulers of Asia.

13

RELIGIOUS AND CULTURAL LIFE UNDER THE DELHI SULTANAT

The coming of the Turks into India and the establishment of the Delhi sultanat during the 13th century was a period of both turmoil and development. As we have seen, the initial phase was one of death and destruction on a large scale, with many beautiful temples being destroyed and palaces and cities ravaged. This process continued in phases as the empire expanded. But once a territory had been conquered, or had submitted, a process of peace and development started. This process began slowly in northern India where large areas remained under direct sultanat rule for 200 years.

The Turkish rulers were by no stretch of imagination rude barbarians. Coming from Central Asia during the 8th century, the Turks had, in course of time, accepted Islam. Thus, they inherited the Islamic culture of the area, which had reached a high level of development. Although the Abbasid Caliphate which had dominated the Islamic world for more than a century and a half was in a state of decline, and various competing states had risen, these states shared the cultural and administrative norms and standards set up by the Abbasids, with minor adjustments. The Turks who came into India not only considered themselves to be champions of Islam, but were proud of being inheritors of its rich tradition, whether it was in the field of architecture, literature, forms of government or science and technology. They had also adopted Persian which had emerged as the language of government and culture in Central Asia, Khurasan and Iran by the 10th century.

The Hindus, too, were the inheritors of a religious and cultural tradition which had evolved during thousands of years. The 4th and 5th centuries have often been considered the period of cultural and scientific climax in north India. In the subsequent period, though India began to lag behind in the field of science, and creative thinking had gradually dried up, the cultural traditions were still alive. Recent studies show that the period from the 8th century to the 12th century was by no means one of cultural decline, but one in which considerable building activity, specially in the field of temple architecture took place. Thus, magnificent temples were built at Khajuraho in Bundelkhand, in Orissa, and in various other places such as Mathura, Kashi, Dilwara, etc. These temples show a high level of skill in architectural forms and sculpture. There were also important developments in the field of religion and philosophy. Thus, Sankara set a seal on the philosophy of Vedanta, and a movement based on love and devotion to a personal God began in South India.

Contact between Hinduism, Buddhism and Islam had started much before Islam came to India. The interaction quickened after Islam's coming into India. However, it is necessary to separate the political aspect from the religio-philosophical aspects, even though they over-lapped. Some of the bigoted *ulemas*, such as Nuruddin Mubarak Ghazanavi at the court of Iltutmish, advocated a policy of inveterate hostility to the Hindus, especially the Brahmans, whom they considered the biggest enemies of the "true" faith—a policy, which we have seen, the rulers found inexpedient or unimplementable. Among a section of the Hindus, too, there was loathing and revulsion against the Muslims, and they adopted a policy of maintaining minimum contact with them.

However, despite these handicaps, and the seemingly irreconcilable nature of Islam and Hinduism, with Islam emphasizing strict monotheism, rejecting all Gods other than Allah whose last messenger was the Prophet, while Hinduism accepted unity in diversity with multifarious Gods, and image worship which the Muslims rejected, a slow process of mutual adjustment and rapproachement began. This process can be said to be seen at work in the fields of architecture, literature, music etc. It was also at work in the field of religion with the entry of sufism into the country, and the gradual development of a popular movement of bhakti in north India. The process continued apace during the fifteenth century and gathered force in the 16th and 17th centuries under the Mughals. But it would be wrong to assume that the elements of conflict had disappeared. Both conflict and the process of rapproachement continued side by side, with set backs under some rulers and in some regions, and faster development under some other rulers.

Thus, the elements of conflict and rapproachement have to be seen in perspective.

i. Architecture

One of the first requirement of the new rulers was houses to live in, and places of worship for their followers. For places of worship, they at first converted temples and other existing buildings into mosques. Examples of this are the Quwwat-ul-Islam mosque near the Qutb Minar in Delhi and the building at Ajmer called Arhai Din ka Jhonpara. The former had been a Jain temple at first, which had then been converted into a temple dedicated to Vishnu. The latter had been a monastery. The only new construction at Delhi was a facade of three elaborately carved arches in front of the deity room (*garbha griha*) which was demolished. The arcaded courtyard in front consisted entirely of pillars from thirty-seven temples of the area which had been looted. The style of decoration used on these arches is very interesting: no human or animal figures were used since it was considered to be un-Islamic to do so. Instead, they used scrolls of flowers and verses of the Quran which were intertwined in a very artistic manner. Soon, the Turks started constructing their own buildings. For the purpose they mostly used the indigenous craftsmen, such as stone-cutters, masons, etc., who were famous for their skill. Later, some master architects came to India from West Asia. In their buildings, the Turks used the arch and the dome on a wide scale. Neither the arch nor the dome was a Turkish or Muslim invention. The Arabs borrowed them from Rome through the Byzantine empire, developed them and made them their own.

The use of the arch and the dome had a number of advantages. The dome provided a pleasing skyline and as the architects gained more experience and confidence, the dome rose higher. Many experiments were made in putting a round dome on a square building, and in raising the dome higher and higher. In this way, many lofty and impressive buildings were constructed. The arch and the dome dispensed with the need for a large number of pillars to support the roof and enabled the construction of large halls with a clear view. Such places of assembly were useful in mosques as well as in palaces. However, the arch and the dome needed a strong cement, otherwise the stones could not be held in place. The Turks used fine quality lime mortar in their buildings. Thus, new architectural forms and mortar of a superior kind became widespread in north India with the arrival of the Turks.

The arch and the dome were known to the Indians earlier, but they were not used on a large scale. Moreover, the correct scientific method of constructing the arch was rarely employed. The architectural device generally used by the Indians consisted of putting one stone over another, narrowing the gap till it could be covered by a coping-stone or by putting a beam over a slab of stones. The Turkish rulers used both the dome and arch method as well as slab and beam method in their buildings.

In the sphere of decoration, the Turks eschewed representation of human and animal figures in the buildings. Instead, they used geometrical and floral designs, combining them with panels of inscriptions containing verses from the Quran. Thus, the Arabic script itself became a work of art. The combination of these decorative devices was called Arabesque. They also freely borrowed Hindu motifs such as the *bel* motif, the bell motif, swastika, lotus, etc. Like the Indians, the Turks were intensely fond of decoration. The skill of the Indian stone-cutters was fully used for the purpose. The Turks also added colour to their buildings by using red sandstone. Yellow sandstone or marble was used in these buildings for decoration and to show off the colour of the red sandstone.

The most famous and the most magnificent building built by the Turks during the 13th century was the tower or minar adjacent to the Quwwat-ul-Islam mosque. It was called the *mazana* or place from where the call for prayer (*azan*) was called. It was much later that this minar began to be called the Qutb Minar, possibly because it was started by Qutbuddin Aibak, or because, where completed by Iltutmish, Quibuddin Bakhtiyar Kaki, the famous sufi saint, was living at Delhi, and the minar began to be considered a token of his spiritual attainments. There is, however, no reason to believe that the minar was based on an earlier Rajput tower. This idea has arisen because some of the stones used at the base of the minar appear to be those belonging to some of the destroyed temples of the area. In an epigraph on the minar, the name of Fazl ibn Abul Maali is mentioned, but it is not clear from the damaged inscription whether he was the architect or merely or.e who supervised the work.

Although the tradition of building towers are to be found in India, West Asia and elsewhere, the Qutb Minar is unique in many ways. Its tremendous height of 71.4 metres (238 ft) becomes more effective by its tapering character. Originally, it was only four stories high, but the top of the minar was hit by lightening, and Firuz Tughlaq repaired it, and added a fifth storey. The main beauty of the minar lies in the skilful manner in which balconies have been projected, yet linked with the tower by a devise called "stalectite honey-con.bing". The skilful use of ribbed and angular projections in the body of the tower, the use of red and white sandstones in the panels and in the top stages add further to the effect.

The growth of the building activities of the Turks after the consolidation of the Delhi sultanat under Iltutmish is shown by the wide range of buildings belonging to this period. Thus, the mosque and group of buildings at Badaun (U.P), the lofty gate at Nagaur, and at Hansi and Palwal in Haryana are an index of the determination of the Turks to build their own buildings. Iltutmish's own tomb, built near the end of his reign, is an indication of the mixing of the Hindu and Muslim traditions of architecture. The tomb was a square building, but by putting pendantives and squinch arches in the corners, it was made octagonal on which a dome was built. This devise was used in many quare buildings later on. Even more remarkable was the intricate carving on the walls, where calligraphy was combined with Indian floral motives.

The second half of the 13th century saw the flocking into India of many scholars, including mathematicians and architects from West Asia, following the devastation caused there by the Mongols. Thus, we see the first true arch in the plain and simple tomb of Balban. That is to say, it was based on radiating voussoirs and a coping stone, not putting one stone over the other to cover the gap, and then put a stone or slab on top.

The Khalji period saw a lot of building activity. Alauddin built his capital at Siri, a few kilometres away from the site around the Qutb. Unfortunately, hardly anything of this city survives now. Alauddin planned a tower twice the height of the Qutb Minar but did not live to complete it. However, he added an entrance door to the Quwwat-ul-Islam mosque. This door, which is called the Alai Darwaza, had a number of novel features. It was the first building in which the dome was built not on the principle of overlapping courses of masonary, gradually decreasing in size as they rose upwards, but on the basis of radiating voussoirs. The horse-shoe arch used for the first time in the building, is pleasing in appearance. The decorative devices—merlons in the inside of the arch, use of lotus on the spandrel of the arch, and use of white marble in the trellis work and the marble decorative bands to set off the red sandstone give to the building an appearance of grace and strength which is considered a special feature of Indian architectural tradition.

Mosque architecture was also developed during this period as shown by the Jamaat Khana mosque at the mausoleum of the sufi saint, Nizamuddin Auliya.

There was great building activity in the Tughlaq period which marked the climax of the Delhi sultanat as well as the beginning of its decline. Ghiyasuddin and Muhammad Tughlaq built the huge palace-fortress complex called Tughlaqabad. By blocking the passage of the Jamuna, a huge artificial lake was created around it. The tomb of Ghiyasuddin marks a new trend in architecture. To have a good skyline, the building was put up on a high platform. Its beauty was heightened by a marble dome.

A striking feature of the Tughlaq architecture was the sloping walls. This is called "batter", and gives the effect of strength and solidity to the building. However, the batter is used sparingly in the buildings of Firuz Tughlaq. A second feature of the Tughlaq architecture was the deliberate attempt to combine the principles of the arch, and the lintel and beam. In the buildings of Firuz Tughlaq in the Hauz Khas, which was a pleasure resort and had a huge lake around it, alternate stories have arches and the lintel and beam. The same is to be found in some buildings of Firuz Shah's new fort which is now called the Kotla. The Tughlaqs did not generally use the costly red sandstone in their buildings but the cheaper and more easily available greystone. In the buildings of Firuz, rubble is finished by a thick coat of lime plaster which was colour washed in white—a method used in buildings till recent times. Since it was not easy to carve this type of stone or lime paster, the Tughlaq buildings have a minimum of decoration. But the decorative device found in all the buildings of Firuz is the lotus. A devise used in the tomb of Firuz Tughlaq is a stone-railing in front which was emphatically of Hindu design.

Many mosques were also built during this period, such as the Kalan mosque, the Khirki mosque. They were of undressed stone and lime plaster, and hence not very elegant. The pillars were thick and heavy. Also, the Indian builder had not yet developed the confidence of raising the dome high enough. Hence, the buildings appear squat.

The Lodis continued the Tughlaq tradition of using rubble or undressed stone and lime plaster in their buildings. But by this time, the Indian architects and masons had gained full confidence in the new forms. Hence, their domes rose higher in the sky. A new devise which appeared in India for the first time was the double dome. Tried experimentally at first, it appears in a developed form in the tomb of Sikandar Lodi. It became necessary as the dome rose higher and higher. By putting an inner cover inside the dome, the height remained proportionate to the room inside. This devise was later on used in all buildings.

Another architectural devise which was used for the first time in the tomb of Firuz's wazir, Khan-i-Jahan Telangani, was the octagonal tomb. Many features were added to it: a verandah was built around it with long, sloping *chajja* or eaves as a protection against sun and rain. As each corner of the roof, *chhatris* or kiosks were built. Both these features were of Gujarati or Rajasthani origin. Both the arch and the lintel and beam are used in their buildings.

Another device used by the Lodis was placing their buildings, especially tombs, on a high platform, thus giving the building a feeling of size as well as a better skyline. Some of the tombs were placed in the midst of gardens. The Lodi Garden in Delhi is a fine example of this. Many of these features were adopted by the Mughals later on, and their culmination is to be found in the Taj Mahal built by Shah Jahan.

By the time of the break-up of the Delhi Sultanat, individual styles of architecture had also developed in the various kingdoms in different parts of India. Many of these, again, were powerfully influenced by the local traditions of architecture. This, as we have seen, happened in Bengal, Gujarat, Malwa, the Deccan, etc.

Thus, we not only see an outburst of architectural activity but a coming together of the Muslim and Hindu traditions and forms of architecture. In the various regional kingdoms which arose during the fifteenth century, attempts were made to combine the style of architecture which had developed at Delhi with regional architectural traditions.

ii. Religious Ideas and Beliefs

Religion is both a complex phenomenon, and a sensitive subject, with the votaries of each religion claiming it to be unique and uninfluenced by any other faith. However, such rigid demarcations are difficult to maintain, especially when the followers of different religions live in the same geographical space, or when people convert from one faith to another, bringing with them some of their previous ideas, beliefs and practices. Travellers, including saints who moved from one place to another, wittingly or unwittingly became agents of transmitting "alien" ideas in the countries they visited.

Islam was the last of the great organised and structured religions which rose in the modern world. In its early formative phase, which is broadly considered to be the first three centuries of its existence, i.e. to the end of the 9th century, it came into contact with the older civilisations of the area—Iranian, Greeco-Byzantine, and Indian. The extent to which each of these influenced the evolution of the Arab-Islamic culture is a matter of debate among scholars. Greek thinking strongly influenced Islamic philosophy. The influence of Iran and Byzantine was strong in the fields of government, architecture etc. The influence of India in the fields of religion, philosophy and science is still a matter of controversy. However, we can hardly doubt that there was continuous interaction in these fields between India, and its neghbouring areas because of geographical, commercial and political reasons. Recent research shows that Nestorian Christianity, Manichism and Buddhism survived in the remote relgions of Khurasan and Central Asia till the tenth century, and that their temples, and Sanskrit and Buddhist books and scholars were still to be found in the area by that time. In the 9th century, works on Buddhism and Indian works dealing with astronomy and medicine, ethical books such as *Hitopadesh*, and treatise on logic and military science etc. were translated into Arabic. The Arabs were exceedingly keen to learn about the customs, manners, sciences and religions of the peoples they came into contact with, including Indians. Thus, Al-Kindi wrote a book on Indian religions. Al-Nadim, Al-Ashari, Shahrastani and many others devoted chapters in their books to describe and discuss Indian religion and philosophical systems. Al-Biruni who came from this area in the 10th century, notes sufi parallels in the *Yoga Sutra* of Patanjali which he translated into Arabic. According to some mordern thinkers, Indian atomic theory of Nyaya-Vaisheshik also influenced Islamic philosophy.

This shows that during the first three centuries of Islam, the Arabs were open-minded in accepting foreign ideas. However, despite this, the fundamental tenets and philosophy of Islam remained rooted in the Quran, and in the words and practice (*hadis*) of the Prophet.

(a) The Sufi Movement: Early Origins

The 10th century marked a new phase in the history of Islam. It saw the rise of Turks on the ruins of the Abbasid Caliphate, as well as important changes in the realm of ideas and beliefs. In the realm of ideas, it marks the end of the domination of the Mutazila or rationalist philosophy, the formation of orthodox schools based on the Quran and *hadis*, and the rise to prominence of the Sufi mystic orders.

The Mutazalites or Rationalists who were favoured by the Abbasid Caliphs, and used political power to persecute their opponents, tried to systematize theology by applying reasons (*aql*) to it. They were concerned with the nature of God, creation, relationship of man with God, nature of the soul etc. They argued that man was the author of his own actions, good or evil, and that the *Quran* was created, disagreeing with the orthodox view that it was the word of God and hence eternal and infallible.

The orthodox elements accused the Mutazalilites of spreading scepticism and atheism. They equated their philosophy of monism which held that God and the created world were fundamentally one, as being heretical on the ground that it abolished the difference between the Creator and the Created.

Sustained persecution and orthodox opposition led to the collapse of the Mutuzalites. This strengthened the hands of the "traditionalists" and led to the crystallization of the four schools of Islamic Law. Of these, the Hanafi school, which was the most liberal, was adopted by the eastern Turks who later came to India. The collapse of the Mulazalites also strengthened the hands of the sufi mystics.

Mystics, who later came to be called sufis, had risen in Islam at a very early stage. Most of them were persons of deep devotion who were disgusted by the vulgar display of wealth, and degeneration of morals following the establishment of the Islamic empire. Some of the early sufis, such as Hasan Basri, and his follower, the woman mystic Rabia (d. eighth century) laid great emphasis on prayer, continual fasting and disinterested love of God. Rabia lived the life of a hermit and her reputation travelled far and wide. By this time the mystics had started wearing a patched garment of wool (*suf*) which, according to them, was a legacy of the prophets, and Christian apostles and ascetics. Zunnu Misri of Egypt (died ninth century), who travelled widely in Arabia and Syria, worked out the concept of mystic union with God by a process of contemplation. Zunnu was accused of heresy, but was acquitted. The sufi concept of *fana* or spiritual merger of the devoted with God led to constant conflict with the orthodox *ulema*. Thus, Bayazid Bayat, whose grand-father was a Zorastrian, shocked the *ulema* by his statements uttered in a state of ecstacy, "Glory to me! How great is My Majesty"; "I saw the Kaba walking around me". His successor, Mansur bin Hallaj of Baghdad, was not so lucky and was imprisoned and executed on a charge of heresy (10th century). Mansur had travelled widely and visited Sindh also where, it is now established, he met some Hindu Vedantists. But, as has now became evident, Vedantist and yogic ideas were wide-spread in Iran, and it was hardly necessary to go to Sindh to learn about them. Mystic experience in various religions often led in the same direction. Mansur's proclamation of the doctrine "*Anal-Haq* (I am Truth/God)" was merely an expression of the sufi belief that unification with God was the highest stage of enlightenment. However, Mansur's refusal to recant, and his willingness to sacrifice his life for his beliefs conferred on the sufis not only the mantle of martyrdom, but the reputation of being men who were pure of heart, sincere and unconcerned with worldly gains.

In this way, a quietist movement based on love, devotion and contemplation gradually became transformed into a movement based on ecstatic love in which social norms, and religious beliefs and practices could be disregarded.

Sufism had spread far and wide in the Islamic world by the 10th century. Between the 10th and 12th centuries, the philosophical ideas, beliefs, practices such as holding the breath, or doing penance and fastings, the rise of various schools or *silsilahs*, and the organisation of *khanqahs* or hospices, established by many of the sufis had been worked out. In working out of the practices and organisation of the *khanqahs*, the organisation of Buddhist and Christian monastic systems played a definite role. Wandering Nath Panthi Yogis, with their headquarters at Peshawar, known in the Islamic world as Jogis, familiarized the sufis with the practices of *hath-yoga*. In fact, *Amrit Kund*, the Sanskrit book on *hath-yoga* was translated into Arabic at this time, and later into Persian.

A series of Persian poets spread the sufi message of mystic union and love far and wide. The four most famous of these poets were Sanai (d.c. 1131), Attar (d. 1230), Iraqi (d. 1289) and Rumi (d. 1273). Their poetry was considered the highest stage of mystical fervour and love, and made its way to all parts, including India. These poets were humane in their outlook, and were tolerant to people of all faiths. The lines from Sinai bring out this spirit:

"Faith and Infidelity, both are galloping on the
  way towards Him,
And are exclaiming (together);
He is one and none shares His kingdom."

Some of the sufis also supported musical gatherings (*sama*) in which a state of ecstacy was created. This again was frowned upon by the orthodox *ulema*.

Al-Ghazali (d. 1112), who is venerated both by the orthodox elements and the Sufis, tried to reconcile mysticism with Islamic orthodoxy. This he was able to do in a large measure. He gave a further blow to the "rationalist" philosophy by arguing that positive knowledge of God and His qualities cannot be gained by reason, but by revelation. Thus, the revealed book, Quran, was as vital for a mystic as for other Muslims.

Around this time, the Sufis were organised in 12 orders or *silsilahs*. However, these numbers kept varying, with new orders added, and some of the old ones dying out. In the early phase, the *silsilahs* provided stability, and enabled the sufis to withstand the hostility of the orthodox *ulema* and to pass on spiritual knowledge. The *silsilahs* were generally led by a prominent mystic who lived in a *khanqah* or a hospice along with his disciples. The link between the teacher or *pir* and his disciples or *murids* was a vital part of the sufi system. Every *pir* nominated a successor or *khalifa* to carry on his work. They also appointed *walis* or deputies for spiritual work in particular regions.

The Sufi orders are broadly divided into two : *ba-shara*, that is, those which followed the Islamic Law (*shara*) and *be-shara*, that is, those which were not bound by it. Both types of orders prevailed in India, the latter being followed more by wandering saints, the *qalandars*. Although these saints did not establish an order, or *silsilah*, some of them became figures of popular veneration, sometimes for the Muslims and Hindus alike.

The Chishti and the Suhrawardi Silsilahs

The Chishtis

The two most famous sufi orders, or *silsilahs* which flourished in India during the Sultanat period were the Chishti and the Suhrawardi. The Suhrawardis were active mainly in Punjab and Sindh, whereas the Chishtis were active at Delhi, and in the areas around it, including Rajasthan, parts of Punjab and modern U.P. These orders also spread to Bengal and Bihar, Malwa, Gujarat etc. and, later, to the Deccan. A different order, the Kubrawiya, operated in Kashmir. In general, sufis belonging to different orders were cordial to each other. Thus, Suhrawardi saints visited Delhi and were made welcome there, and Chishti saint visited Multan and were received cordially. This is because of the sufi tradition of dividing territories between different saints. Thus, when a musician who was going from Ajodhan in the Punjab to Multan and asked Baba Farid to pray for his blessing, the Baba replied that the limit of his spiritual influence was at a certain water tank and beyond it began the influence of the Suhrawardi saint, Shaikh Bahauddin Zakariya, whose prayer he should obtain.

The Chishti *sisilah* established in India by Muinuddin Chishti was essentially Indian, the order in Chisht (Afghanistan) having more or less died out there. We know little about the early life and activities of Muinuddin Chishti because he did not leave behind any book or a collection of his sayings or preaching. The accounts we have were written a hundred and fifty years after his death, and later writers added many fanciful stories, such as his persecution by Prithviraj Chauhan, and his miracles, which have become popular. Modern research shows that Muinuddin came to India not *before*, but *after* Muizzuddin Muhammad Ghuri's victory over Prithviraj, and moved to Ajmer only around 1206 by which time Turkish rule over it had been firmly established, and a sizeable Muslim population of Tukrish *ghazis* and forcibly converted prisoners-of-war had come into being. The Khwaja settled at Ajmer because like Chisht, it was a small town and away from the centre of political activity, Delhi. The Khwaja believed that for a spiritual life of seclusion, a small town was better than a large, bustling town. Thus, his disciple, Hamiduddin, settled down at Nagaur—another small town in Rajasthan which also had a sizeable Muslim population. Khwaja Muinuddin was married, but lived a simple, ascetic life based on piety and devotion to God. His main object was to help the Muslims to lead a life of devotion to God, not to effect conversions, since he believed faith was an individual's concern.

Muinuddin's fame as a saintly man grew gradully after his death (1235). Muhammad Tughlaq visited his grave, and a dome on his tomb and a mosque was built later by Mahmud Khalji of Malwa during the 15th century. Muinuddin's stature as a saint reached its peak under Akbar who was greatly devoted to him. Ajmer was politically important for Akbar, and Muinuddin's prestige as a saint, and as a man whose benevolence extended to all, irrespective of religious beliefs, was considered by him to be a positive element in a volatile situation.

The Chishti influence at Delhi was firmly established by Qutbuddin Bakhtiyar Kaki who moved from his birth place, Transoxiana, to Delhi in 1221. He was warmly welcomed by Sultan Iltutmish because his fame as a sufi saint had reached Delhi even before his arrival. Delhi had, by this time, acquired the reputation of being a leading centre of Islam (*qubbat-ul-Islam*), on account of the many eminent scholars, religious divines and fugitive princes seeking shelter there following the Mongol devastations of Central and West Asia. Bakhtiyar Kaki fulfilled the difficult task of establishing the Chishtis at Delhi as the principal sufi order, meeting the challenge both of clerical elements and the Suhrawardis. The former wanted to oust him from Delhi, and brought a charge of heresy against him for his resort to musical gatherings (*sama*). However, this charge was dismissed by Iltutmish who wanted to use sufi influence to counter the *ulema*. By this time, Bakhtiyar Kaki had become so popular that when he planned to leave Delhi for Ajmer, droves of people accompanied him outside the city for miles, and he had to cancel his departure. The Suhrawardi's orthodox approach failed to endear themselves to the people of Delhi.

The most famous disciple and successor of Bakhtiyar Kaki was Baba Fariduddin Ganj-i-Shakhar who lived at Hansi in modern Haryana, then shifted to Ajodhan which was on the Sutlej on the main route from Multan to Lahore. Baba Farid laid great emphasis on poverty, renunciation of worldly goods and attachments, control of the senses by fasting and other austerities, and adopting an attitude of humbleness and service to others. His outlook was so broad that some of the verses, ascribed to him were included in the *Guru Granth Sahib* of Nanak. (On linguistic grounds, some modern scholars think that though the ideas may have been his, the verses included in the *Guru Granth Sahib* were the work of his successors who also adopted the name Farid).

Nizamuddin Auliya (d. 1325) a chief successor of Baba Farid was undoubtedly the most famous Chishti saint at Delhi under whom the Chishtis reached their high water mark. He lived and worked at Delhi for fifty years during a period of great political upheaval—end of Balban's dynasty and the rise to power of Alauddin Khalji, the troubled period following the death of Alauddin, and the rise of the Tughlaqs. He survived through these repeated changes of dynasties and rulers because of the Chishti philosophy of staying away from politics, and not associating with rulers and nobles. Thus, when Khusrau, the Baradu, offered him a large sum of money, he accepted it but distributed it immediately among the needy. When subsequently asked by Ghiyasuddin Tughlaq to return the money, he replied that it was the money belonging to the Muslims, and had been distributed among them. It is not clear whether the Sultan was satisfied. Rumor had it that the Sultan wanted to take action against him, after his return from the Bengal campaign, and when asked, Nizamuddin said casually, "As yet, Delhi is far away (*hinoz Dehli durast*)." As is well-known, the Sultan died before reaching Delhi in the pavilion built by Muhammad bin Tughlaq to welcome him. Whether the story was true or not, it made Nizamuddin a living legend.

Nasiruddin Chiragh Delhi (d. 1356) was the last of the great Chishti saints at Delhi. Nasiruddin had been with Muhammad Tughlaq's army in Sindh when he died, and he helped in the elevation of Firuz to the throne. Firuz held him in great respect, and even called on him several times while at Delhi. But the saint reverted to the policy of keeping aloof from politics. Finding no one who would come up to his expectations, Nasiruddin Chiragh did not nominate any successor (*khalifa*), and ordered his relics—his patched cloak, his prayer-carpet, his wooden bowl, rosary, wooden sandals etc. to be buried with him. One result of Nasiruddin Chiragh's refusal to nominate a successor was that it led to a dispersal of the Chishti saints to different parts of the country, and led to the dissemination of the Chishti sufi ideas even more widely.

The Chishti saints laid great emphasis on a life of simplicity, poverty, humility and selfless devotion to God. They carried the concept of poverty to such an extreme that they did not live in pucca houses but mud covered and thatched houses, and wore patched clothes. They and their families sometiems remained without food for days. They considered that control of the senses was necessary for a spiritual life. For the purpose, they resorted to ascetic practices, such as fasting, holding of the breath etc. and self-mortification through penances. They advocated renunciation of the world, by which they meant renouncing wealth, government service, and association with (loose) women. This did not mean withdrawal from society. For Muinuddin Chishti, the highest form of devotion to God was nothing but to redress the misery of those in distress, to fulfil the needs of the helpless, and to feed the hungry. According to Nizamuddin Auliya, altruistic service was more important than obligatory prayers. Except Nizamuddin Auliya, all the leading Chishti saints were married, and had a family. Thus, married life for the saint was accepted, as long as it did not come in the way of his leading a spiritual life.

The Chishtis generally divided people into four categories. Of these, the mystics who preached to the others came in the highesst category, their disciples next. The rulers and the scholarly elements came in the third category, and the common people who had neither learning nor desire for spiritual elevation came in the fourth. For the disciples, the Chishtis advocated earning their livelihood from a profession. Agriculture and business was also accepted, but they were advised not to accumulate money beyond their daily needs. Honesty and fair dealing in business was emphasised. Family responsibility was accepted, but again it was not to be a barrier in spiritual progress. The values of forbearance, avoiding anger, or causing hurt to others, and a policy of love and tolerance or avoiding violence was emphasised, though it cannot be called a policy of non-violence because that was concerned with the attitude of the state.

The Chishtis made no discrimination between people on the basis of their wealth, religious beliefs, family status etc. At a time when the Turks had largely forgotten the Islamic concept of brotherhood, and looked down on the ordinary people, including the converts, the sufi attitude of non-discrimiation not only made them popular, but helped to relieve social tensions. Thus, the doors of Niamuddin Auliya's *Jamaat-khana* were always open to people for sympathy, support and advice. Although the main concern of the sufi saints was the amelioration of the condition of Muslims, their care and concern did not exclude the Hindus. Muinuddin Chishti's pupil, Hamiduddin Nagauri, was so careful of Hindu sentiments that he had become a vegetarian, and constantly urged his disciples to give up meat-eating.

The Chishti saints freely associated with Hindu and Jain yogis, and discussed with them various matters, especially yogic exercises. While welcoming voluntary conversions, they considered that preaching contributed little to the change of faith, only example. However, the Chishti saints were fully conscious of the strength of the Hindu faith. As a mystic exhorted:

"Oh you who sneer at the idolatry of the Hindus, learn also from him how worship is done." On one occasion, while strolling on his terrace with his friend, the poet Amir Khusrau, Nizamuddin Auliya saw a group of Hindus at worship. Greatly impressed at their devotion, he said to him, "Every community has its own path and faith, and its own way of worship."

It was this broad tolerance which went a long way in making the Chishtis a success in the predominantly non-Muslim Ganga Valley.

However, sufi orders differed in their attitude towards poverty, and the extent of tolerance to non-Muslims. The Qubrawiya order in Kashmir encouraged their supporters to demolish and desecrate Hindu temples. At the same time, they kept good relations with the Hindus.

The Suhrawardis

The Suhrawardis, while treading the same mystic path, differed from the Chishtis in important aspects. Thus, Bahauddin Zakariya, the founder of the order in India, did not believe in starvation or self-mortification but favoured an ordinary life in food and dress. Nor did he consider poverty to be a necessary means for a spiritual life. Unlike the Chishtis who refused to accept grant of villages as *iqta*, or grants for the maintenance of the saints and their *khanqahs*, but only accepted unsolicited gifts *(futuh)*, or uncultivated land *(ihya)* where the sufis could labour themselves, the Suhrawardis acceptd royal grants. Thus, Bahaduddin Zakariya was rich, and even led a life of affluence. He justified his riches by arguing that money enabled him to serve better the poor who thronged around him. Regarding the orthodox *ulema*, Bahauddin Zakariya laid emphasis on observing all the external forms of religion, i.e. *namaz, roza*, etc. He advocated a combination of scholarship *(ilm)* with mysticism. He did not reject *sama* or musical gathering, but indulged in it only occasionally. Despite this, the hostility of the orthodox *ulema* towards Bahauddin Zakariya did not abate. The successors of Bahauddin Zakariya continued to play a leading role in Punjab and Sindh for a century and a half after his death. In course of time, the Suharwardis extended their influence in Gujarat, Bengal and Kashmir. The Suhrawardis were opposed to some of the Hindu practices adopted by the Chishtis, such as bowing before the shaikh, presenting water to visitors, tonsuring the head of a new entrant to the mystic order etc. They were also more keen on conversions. Thus, the Subrawardi saint, Shaikh Jamaluddin, who had settled in Bengal, did not hesitate in making forcible conversions, and pulling down a Hindu temple at Devatalla near Pandua in order to create his *khanqah* there.

There was a major difference, also, in the attitude of the Chishtis and Suhrawardis towards the State. We are told that the Chishtis believed in cutting themselves off from kings, politics and government service because government service "distracted" a mystic from the single minded pursuit of the ideal of "living for the Lord alone". We are further told that medieval thinkers, such as Imam Ghazali, considered all the income of the State to come from prohibited sources so that service paid from these sources was illegal; and that the entire pattern of life at the court and the government was alien to the true spirit of Islam. Therefore, Imam Ghazali adds: "One should neither desire their continuation, nor praise them, nor enquire about their affairs, nor keep contact with their associates."

However, Islamic tradition was not uniform on this matter. While some of the orthodox *ulema* also pointed out the essentially un-Islamic aspects of the state as it evolved after the rule of the first four Caliphs, they and some sufis themselves underlined that the rulers of the world were the chosen of God the Almighty, and that under no condition showing disrespect to them or disobeying their orders was proper or permitted in *sharia*. They also quoted the Tradition that the Prophet had said 'Whoever obeys the sultan, obeys God and whoever obeys God obtains salvation.'

The Suhrawardi sufis, therefore, did not reject government service, The founder of the *silsilah*, Shihabuddin Suhrawardi, had close contact with the Caliph, preached in Baghdad under court patronage, and continued in government service. Bahauddin Zakariya, the founder of the Suhrawardi *silsilah* in India, accepted this tradition, and argued that visits to royal courts provided the saints opportunities to help the poor people by getting their grievances redressed by the sultan. He also felt that there was no reason why the sultan and his associates should be deprived of the spiritual ministrations of the saints.

The Suhrawardi saints also took active part in politics. Thus, Bahauddin Zakariya openly sided with Iltutmish, and invited Iltutmish when the Sultan wanted to add Sindh to his dominions by ousting Qubacha, although the Shaikh had received full backing and support from Qubacha.

The attitude of the Suhrawardi saints towards state and politics cannot be explained away by saying that the early Turkish sultans stood in need of the support of the religious classes in order to consolidate their power and build up an integrated and compact polity, because this argument would apply equally for the Chishtis. As we have shown, both the orthodox clerical elements and many sufis were ambivalent in their attitude towards the state. To most of them it was a necessary evil. Even then, they expected justice from the Sultans, and protection of the poor. A Chishti saint quoted the Prophet as saying: "If any woman goes to bed hungry in any town of a kingdom, she would hold the collar of the ruler on the Day of Judgement which is sure to come."

Thus, even the Chishtis expected the ruler to be benevolent. In such a situation, they could hardly adopt an attitude of hostility towards the state. The attempt of some modern historians to present the Chishtis as the representative of the masses, whereas the governing class by its very nature was an exploiting class, and an association with them would mean association with the exploiters, appears to be a grossly mistaken view of the situation. The Chishti saints tried to associate closely with the masses, but they can hardly be called representatives of the masses any more than the official clergy. Unlike Central Asia where many of the sufis were drawn from various professions—such as *attar* (dealer in perfumes or drugs), *hallaj* (cotton dresser), *qassab* (butcher), *haddad* (blacksmith) etc. in India most of the sufis came from the class of clergymen. Perhaps, Nasiruddin Chiragh, whose father was a dealer in *pashmina* shawls, was the only exception. While rejecting grant of villages, the Chishtis largely depended on *futuh* or unsolicited grants. The main source of this was undoubtedly the nobility supplemented by grants from merchants. The latter was an important source and most *khanqahs* were significantly located at or near important trade routes. But neither of these sections would have been provided *futuh* if the attitude of the ruler was one of hostility or opposition. Broadly, rulers welcomed the sufi because they considered that their blessings, and their goodwill with the people would not only enhance their own prestige but legitimize their position. Also, the sufis were a force of social harmony, and acted as a kind of a device for letting off steam to offset social tensions and mass discontent.

The Chishti saints, it would seem, were not as much opposed to government service and the state as has sometimes been made out. The full restrictions about government service and association with the rulers applied only to those disciples who were given patents of spiritual authority, and were asked to lead others on the mystic path. The ordinary disciples were not so strictly barred from government service. Shaikh Nasiruddin Chiragh Dehli said that government service was not necessarily an obstacle to contemplation and meditation. What the Chishti saints advocated, above all, was labour in which, as we have seen, crafts and agriculture were given primacy.

Thus, what the Chishtis advocated was maintaining a certain distance from the state and the ruling classes, while trying to create conditions in which the state could function in a more humanitarian way. There was no fundamental clash of interests between the two, though there were differences of approach. The proper functioning of the state was necessary for the sufis to tread the path of mysticism in peace, and the sufi attempt to create harmony helped in the process of the consolidation of the state and the Muslim society.

The Chishti advocacy of toleration between peoples of different faiths, their opening the doors of their *khanqahs* to all irrespective of their religious beliefs, their attitude of benevolence to all, their association with Hindu and Jain Yogis, and using Hindavi in their conversation and in their musical assemblies, created an atmosphere of greater interaction between the two major communities, the Hindus and the Muslims. It also helped, to some extent, to mitigate the harsher aspects of Turkish rule, and the manner in which Islam was interpreted by some of the Turkish warriors and some orthodox clergymen. However, it would be an exaggeration to believe that they were the means of a social and cultural revolution, as some modern scholars have argued. For such a revolution, a structural change in society was necessary which was hardly feasible and which, in any case, was beyond the capacity of the saints. Sufi saints in different parts of the country, including the wandering saints, followed their own courses, sometimes liberal, sometimes orthodox, sometimes a combination of the two. These need to be studied, without making broad generalisations, though we would not be too far wrong in saying that, on balance, and with some exceptions, the sufis followed a liberal rather than an illiberal course.

Some of the negative aspects of the sufi ideology should, not be lost sight of. The tradition of exaggerated reverence to the saint brought many devotees to the door of image worship, particularly when after the death of a saint, his tomb became an object almost of worship. Implicit obedience to the wishes of the saint sometimes created an atmosphere of sycophancy. That is why some of the wandering minstrels, the *qalandars*, were strongly opposed to the *khanqahs*.

Along with excessive book learning, the sufis denounced philosophy which they equated to rationalism. The orthodox *ulema* and the sufis included among the philosophers natural scientists. According to the biographer of Nizamuddin Auliya, the saint told the story how a philosopher, carrying books, had approached a Caliph, and told him that the motion of the heavens was of three kinds—natural, voluntary and involuntary. If a stone was thrown into the air it must fall to the ground, so such a motion was natural. Movement of human beings was voluntary motion. An involuntary motion was beyond the control of human beings. Based on such an argument, the motion of the heavens was involuntary, said the philosopher. Shaikh Shihabuddin Suhrawardi rushed to the Caliph to contradict this. He stressed that the involuntary nature of the heavenly motions was due to the miraculous activity of angels acting under divine command. He then proceeded to show the supernatural sight of angles moving the heavens.

Thus, under the influence of the sufis, miracle mongering and suspicion about science and scientists increased. It was in these adverse circumstances that philosophy and natural sciences grew in Central and West Asia, and in India during the subsequent centuries.

(b) The Bhakti Movement: Early Origins

The bhakti movement which stressed mystic realization of God within oneself, and the ultimate union of the individual with God, based on loving devotion on the part of the devotee and God's grace (*prasad*), had been at work in India long before the growth of sufism in Islam, and its arrival in India. The seed of bhakti can be traced to the *Vedas* in which some hymns are full of the sense of wonder before divinity which is sought to be perceived in a mystic manner. Such sentiments are also found in the *Upanishads*.

As the worship of personal Gods—Brahma, Vishnu, Mahesh grew in the post-Vedic age, the concept of bhakti or personal devotion to them also grew. Thus, we find elements of bhakti in the *Bhagawata* movement aimed at Vasudeva (later associated with Krishna) in the post-Maurya period, as also the rise of the *Pashupat* school devoted to the worship of Siva. The worship of a gracious (*avakokita*) Buddha who had refused *nirvana* in order to deal with the sufferings of humanity also arose at this time. In the final shape given to the *Ramayana* and *Mahabharata*, of which the *Bhagawat Gita* formed a significant part, bhakti was considered, along with *jnana* and *karma*, a path to salvation.

Two aspects of bhakti may be distinguished here. One was the path of devotion based on service to God with the devotee (*bhakta*) throwing himself completely at the mercy of God. This was the path of *prapatti* or surrender. It has been argued that the word *bhakta*, derived from the root *bhai*, meaning 'to apportion' literally means one who enjoys a share. Since the word *bhakta* was originally employed to denote a servant or retainer who shared the wealth of his master, in course of time the word was used for a devotee in view of his *dasabhava* or attitude of service. In any case, the path of *prapatti* was an easy one, and could be followed even by slaves, retainers and the lowly people because it did not need any book-learning or preparation.

The second aspect of bhakti was that of a bond based on pure love. This was based on equality rather than service, with the ideal changing from emancipation to that of participation in the life divine. This was exemplified in the legend of Prahald set out in the *Vishnu Purana* in which Prahald prays that he may be blessed with unwavering devotion to God wherever he is born. But gradually this bond was sought to be explained in terms of carnal love between a lover and his beloved, and the example chosen was the relationship of Krishna with Radha and the gopis. This, apparently, was first expounded in the *Bhagawata Puran* which is generally dated to the 9th century.

It was the latter aspect of bhakti, of loving devotion to Siva and Vishnu, which was emphasized by a remarkable series of saints who flourished in south India between the latter part of the 6th and the 10th centuries. Starting from the Tamil lands under the Pallava rulers, bhakti spread to different parts of south India, including the Pandya kingdom in southern Tamil lands, and to the Chera kingdom in Kerala. There were several new features in this movement. It was preached and spread by a large number of popular saints, called Adiyars or Nayanars who were Saivites, and the Alvars who were worshipers of Vishnu. Among them we find not only brahmans but many from low castes. There was among them a woman, Andal, who said that the relation of a devotee with God was like that of a loving wife towards her husband. The broad-based character of the saints made it clear that their message of loving devotion was not meant for any one section, but could be followed by all, irrespective of caste, family or sex. To that extent, the movement had an egalitarian approach which disregarded caste.

The main attack of the Nayanars and Alvars was against Buddhism and Jainism which were dominant in south India at the time. These saints were able to wean over people to their side because Buddhism and Jainism had, in course of time, become hide-bound, and enmeshed in meaningless ritualism with an emphasis on austerities to inflict pain on the body. Thus, they no longer catered to the emotional needs of the people. The Nayanars and the Alvars preached a simple faith in the language of the people, Tamil, using or incorporating local myths and legends. Thus, they were able to make a strong emotional appeal.

The movement was pushed forward by the support of many local rulers, the Pallava rulers to begin with. The change in the attitude of the rulers is generally ascribed to the influence of some eminent saint whose aura of saintliness combined with his capacity to make miracles, to the discomfiture of their Buddhist or Jain opponents, led to the change in the attitude of the ruler. Sometimes, the leading minister or the queen is also brought into the picture. While all these must have undoubtedly played a role, the rulers may have had their own political considerations. They could hope for greater legitimacy by allying themselves to a popular movement. This was reinforced by the rise of temples which played a role in stabilizing society, expanding agriculture and even taking part in trade. The temples were rewarded with royal gifts, including grant of lands, and the rulers were strengthened by the brahmans legitimizing their powers and position. In the immediate context, royal support was used, on occasions, to persecute the Jains and Buddhists. Thus, the Pallava king, Mahendra Varman, destroyed a Jain monastery after ousting the Jains from his court. Another rulers, Neduraman, is reputed to have impaled several thousands of Jains.

At the intellectual level, the Buddhist ideas and beliefs were given a death blow by Sankara who is placed at the end of the 8th and the beginning of the 9th century. Sankara systematized the Vedanta system, and was the great exponent of the phiosophy of *advaita* or non-dualism. According to him, the separation of God and the phenomenal world was due to ignorance, and the way to salvation was through the realization, by means of knowledge (*jnan*), that God and the created world was one. He used dialectics to demolish Buddhist ideas, and to establish that the Vedas were the fountainhead of knowledge.

With its trimph over Buddhism and Jainism, the bhakti movement in south India slowly began to lose its open, egalitarian character. While the saints often disregarded the caste taboos, they did not challenge the caste system as such, or the primacy of the brahmans. In the temples which proliferated, the deity was treated as a living king, and an elaborate ritual and ceremonial was developed to emphasize his position. These ceremonials were presided over by the brahmans who continued to use the traditional caste restrictions. This situation was sought to be modified by Ramanuja who is placed in the eleventh century. Ramanuja argued that for salvation, the grace of God was more important than knowledge about him. He further argued that the path of bhakti was open to all, irrespective of caste, and enrolled disciples from all castes. Unlike the Nayanars and Alvars who distrusted book learning, Ramanuja tried to link bhakti with the tradition of the Vedas.

Thus, Ramanuja was a bridge between the popular movement based on bhakti, and total surrender to God (*prapatti*), and the upper caste movement based on the Vedas. In this way, it was Ramanuja rather than Sankar who stood forth as the guiding spirit of a movement which brought important changes in popular religion, attitude to God, and His relationship with man. He, thus, prepared the ground for meeting the challenges of a new age.

It may be mentioned in passing that a more radical movement, represented by the Vir Shaiva or Lingayats, rose to prominence in the 12th century in parts of modern Karnataka. An old sect which was revised and reformed by Basava, the brahman prime minister of the Chalukyan rulers, the Lingayats were worshippers of Siva, and laid emphasis on love towards God, and bhakti as the means of attaining the goals of human life. They attached great importance to the guru, and rejected fasts, feasts or pilgrimages. They were strongly opposed to Buddhism and Jainism, as also to the Brahmans, and the values and social institutions associated with them. They upheld human equality, and denounced the caste system. All those who joined the sect were to eat together, intermarry, and to live in unity. They disapproved of child marriage. Divorce was allowed. Widows were treated with respect and they were allowed to marry again.

Popular Bhakti Movement in North India

Although the sentiment of bhakti had grown in the early phase in north India, its development as a mass phenomenon took place in the south, as we have seen. The popular bhakti movement which began in north India from the 14th-15th centuries onwards has often been considered an off-shoot of the southern movement. Interaction in the cultural field between north and south India was a continuous process, both among the Hindus and among the Buddhist and Jain scholars. During the 9th century, Sankara is supposed to have undertaken a journey to north India to engage in scholarly discussions because, according to tradition, such discussions in north and south were necessary to establish a system of thought. What is notable, however, is that despite this strong tradition, and the early origins of bhakti in north India, bhakti did not become a mass phenomenon in north India till the fifteenth century. This gap of five hundred years or more can only be explained in terms of the social, political and cultural conditions obtaining in the two regions. In south India, the bhakti movement began as a reaction against the rigidities of the Buddhists and the Jains. In north India, the Buddhists and the Jains had been ousted from their pre-eminent position much earlier, the Gupta rulers being strong champions of Hinduism Harsh, though a votary of Siva, had not discriminated against the Buddhists, but Buddhism had continued to decline. In the period following Harsh, a number of states called Rajput states came into being. There has been controversy regarding the origin of the Rajputs, but it is generally agreed that they were drawn from different sections—some from brahman or other castes, some from local tribes which were ruling over some tracts, some were even foreigners. The word Rajput itself originally meant a horse-trader. But as the various sections acquired control over land, and political authority, and their followers emerged as warriors, the brahmans accorded them the status of kshatriyas. In return, the brahmans received generous grants of land, and money for the building and maintenance of temples. They were also accorded positions in government as *raj-purohits*, or advisors of government on religion and polity. On occasions, they were sent on diplomatic missions. They were also assessed land-revenue at concessional rates—a tradition which continued in some of the Rajput states till their merger in the Indian Union. It was this local Rajput-Brahman alliance which dominated society and the cultural scene till the arrival of the Turks. The proliferation of temples and their wealth was an index of the prosperity of the brahmans, and their high status in the Rajput polity.

One result of this Rajput—Brahman alliance was that the Rajput rulers stood forth as the protectors of the four-fold *varna* system, which legitimized the privileges of the brahmans and a highly stratified, hierarchical society. Any sect or philosophical school which challenged this social order and the privileges of the brahmans had, thus, to face not only the hostility of the powerfully entrenched brahmans, but also invited repression at the hands of political authority. This may explain why the early stirrings of bhakti in north India did not lead to a broadening of the movement, though works on bhakti continued to be written in Sanskrit. At the grass-root level, it is possible to discern the rise of a number of dissident or heterodox movements during the period. These included the Tantrik and the Nathpanthi movements. The Tantrik *siddhas* were often drawn from the lower castes, and anyone, irrespective of caste or sex could, join them. They believed in the worship of female godesses, and believed that magical powers could be gained by following a set course which included asceticism. They were strongly opposed to the existing, unequal social order, and the brahmanical code of conduct and religious rites. To demonstrate their opposition to existing social norms, some of them partook forbidden food and drink, while some even advocated free love as a stage to the attainment of higher knowledge. Due to the hostility of the brahmans, and fear of political repression, some of them used elliptical language which only the initiates could understand. Although the Nathpanthis adopt-ed a high moral tone, the brahmans attacked all of them as being immoral and even enemies of state and society. Nevertheless, the Nathpanthis had spread all over India and, from their headquar-ters at Peshawar, even travelled all over West and Central Asia.

The coming of the Turks, the defeat of many Rajput rajas, the destruction of temples and trampling under-foot of images which were often represented not as symbols of God, but Gods themselves who were ministered to by the brahmans, not only dealt a heavy blow to the Rajput-Brahman alliance, but undermined the prestige of the brahmans. It was in this new situation that the movement of popular bhakti developed in many parts of north India.

A well-known sociologist, Max Weber, has argued that an apoc-alyptic movement such as bhakti was often the ideology of a de-feated ruling class, with aspects of quietism and suffering being emphasized. It is hardly possible to agree with this view because it would hardly explain the rise of the mass movement of bhakti in the south.

It has also been argued that bhakti grew in the north as a kind of a defence mechanism, to save Hindu society from the threat of subversion posed to it by the Turkish rulers, and the challenge faced from the Islamic ideology which was simple, and emphasized the ideas of brotherhood and equality. However, this does not to take into account the totality of the situation. As we have seen earlier, after an initial phase of warfare, the Hindus did not face any im-mediate threat of conversion, though prisoner of war, and even women and children captured in the course of operations were en-slaved and converted to Islam. Both rulers and saints, such as Nizamuddin Auliya, admitted that the Hindu faith was too strong to be affected either by threats of force, or the concept of brother-hood and equality held out by Islam. In any case, social equality had long disappeared in Islam, and the Turkish rulers looked down upon Hindu converts, especially those from the artisan and low castes.

It has also been argued that the only purpose of the bhakti saints was to carry out those reforms which would enable them to meet the Islamic ideological challenge. This appears rather lop-sided. As we have seen, Hindu and Buddhist ideas had influenced sufism in its formative phase. In India, the sufi emphasis on monotheism, on the role of the *pir* or *guru*, on mystical union with the 'beloved', etc. coincided with the ideas of many earlier sects and elements in Hinduism. With the entry of Islam, these common elements received renewed emphasis in Hinduism.

Thus, the bhakti movement marks a phase of symbiosis where common elements were emphasized. This aspect is more important than claims of mutual borrowing which are always a matter of dispute. Perhaps the first region in north India where the early stirrings of this movement can be seen is Maharashtra. Sant Jnaneshwar (c. 12th cent) wrote a commentary on *Gita* in which equal stress was laid on *jnan, karma* and *bhakti*. In a significant step, he wrote not in Sanskrit but in the language of the people, Marathi. Jnaneshwar's successor was Namdeva (14th century) whose poetry breathes a spirit of intense love and devotion to God. Namadeva is said to have travelled far and wide, and engaged in discussions with the sufi saints at Delhi. Another saint, Ramanada, who was a follower of Ramanuja, was born at Prayag (Allahabad) and lived there and at Banaras. He popularised the worship of Rama as an *avtar* of Vishnu. What is more, he taught his doctrine of bhakti to all the four varnas, and disregarded the ban on people of different castes cooking or eating their meals together. He is said to have enrolled disciples from all castes, including the low castes. Thus, his disciples included Ravidas, who was a cobbler by caste; Kabir, who was a weaver; Sena, who was a barber; and Sadhana, who was a butcher. Namadeva was equally broad-minded in enrolling his disciples.

Among those saints who carried the message of bhakti to the people, who were strongly critical of the religion of works, and of image worship and of the caste system, and made a strong plea for Hindu-Muslim unity the names of Kabir and Nanak stand pre-eminent.

There is a good deal of uncertainty about the dates and early life of Kabir. Legend has it that he was the son of a brahman widow who abandoned him, and that he was brought up in the house of a Muslim weaver. He learned the profession of his adopted father, but while living at Kashi, he came in touch with both the Hindu saints and sufis. He was also strongly influenced by the Nath-panthis. Kabir emphasised the unity of God whom he calls by several names, such as Rama, Hari, Govind, Allah, Sain, Sahib, etc. He strongly denounced idol-worship, pilgrimages, bathing in holy rivers or taking part in formal worship, such as *namaz*. Nor did he consider it necessary to abandon the life of a normal householder for the sake of a saintly life. Though familiar with yogic practices expounded by the Nath-panthis, he did not consider asceticism, or book-learning important for true knowledge.

Kabir's sharpest barbs were directed against the religious leaders of the two communities, Hinduism and Islam, who misused the credulity of the people for their purposes, and tried to parade their book-learning without understanding the essence of religion. Kabir derived from his belief in the unity of God, his concept of human equality. This led him to attack the existing hierarchical order of society, and those who prided themselves on their wealth, control over land, family, race etc. Since the State upheld the unjust social order, Kabir advised the saint to stay away from royal courts.

Belief in the oneness of God also led Kabir to the conclusion that all religions were different roads to the same goal. Hence, he considered the differences among the Hindus and the Muslims to be meaningless.

Since Kabir was illiterate and his message was carried by word of mouth and was written down much later, there have been much additions and alterations to his message, so much so that it is difficult to distinguish between the two. Kabir was not a social reformer but hoped that human conduct would shape society.

Different ideas have been expressed on the influence of Kabir on the large mass of the Hindus and the Muslims. Despite Kabir, the two religions continued in their set ways. Nor was there any breach in the caste system. In course of time, the followers of Kabir, the Kabir-panthis, shrank into a small sect. But Kabir's mission needs to be seen in a broader context. He created a climate of opinion which continued to work through the ages, so that Kabir became a symbol of human equality, Hindu-Muslim unity, and opposition to cant and hypocrisy in all forms.

Guru Nanak, from whose teachings the Sikh religion was derived, was born in a Khatri household in the village of Talwandi (now called Nanakana) on the bank of river Ravi in 1469. Although married early, and trained in Persian to take his father's profession of accountancy, Nanak showed a mystic, contemplative bent of mind, and preferred the company of saints and sadhus. Sometimes later, he had a mystic vision and forsook the world. He composed hymns and sang them to the accompaniment of the *rabab*, a stringed instrument played by his faithful attendant, Mardana. It is said that Nanak undertook wide tours all over India and even beyond it, to Sri Lanka in the south, and Mecca and Madina in the west. He attracted a large number of people towards him, and his name and fame spread far and wide before his death in 1538.

Like Kabir, Nanak laid emphasis on the one God, by repeating whose name and dwelling on it with love and devotion, one could get salvation without distinction of caste, creed or sect. However, Nanak laid great emphasis on the purity of character and conduct as the first condition of approaching God, and the need of a guru for guidance. Like Kabir, he strongly denounced idol-worship, pilgrimages and other formal observances of the various faiths. He advocated a middle path in which spiritual life could be combined with the duties of the householder.

Nanak had no intention of founding a new religion. His catholic approach aimed at bridging distinctions between the Hindus and the Muslims, in order to create an atmosphere of peace, goodwill and mutual interaction. Like Kabir, Nanak also believed in human equality and brotherhood, and strongly denounced the caste system. He also considered the rulers of his time to be irreligious tyrants. However, unlike Kabir, he postulated an ideal state which would be presided over by a philosopher-king who would base his conduct on morality, justice and equality.

The liberal sufis, and the nirguna bhakti saints posed a challenge to the orthodox elements in Islam and Hinduism. The response of the orthdox sections was varied—from open hostility to finding common meeting points with them, and redefining the old faith in a manner to meet their challenge. The struggle between these two trends, one liberal and non-sectarian, and the other orthodox and traditional, was at the heart of many intellectual movements and religious controversies during the sixteenth, seventeenth and subsequent centuries. In this continuing struggle, the impact of Kabir, Nanak and many others of the same way of thinking was by no means insignificant.

The Vaishnavite Movement

Apart from the non-sectarian movements led by Kabir and Nanak, the bhakti movement in north India developed around the worship of Rama and Krishna, two of the incarnations of the god Vishnu. The childhood escapades of Krishna and his dalliance with the milkmaids of Gokul, especially with Radha, became the theme of a remarkable series of saint-poets who used them in an allegoric manner to depict the relationship, in its various aspects, of the individual soul with the supreme soul. Born and educated in Nadia which was the centre of Vedantic rationalism, Chaitanya's tenor of life was changed when he visited Gaya at the age of 22 and was initiated into the Krishna cult by a recluse. He became a god-intoxicated devotee who incessantly uttered the name of Krishna.

Like the early sufis, Chaitanya popularised musical gathering or kirtan as a special form of mystic experience in which the outside world disappeared by dwelling on God's name. Chaitanya is said to have travelled all over India, including Vrindavana where he revived the Krishna cult. But most of his time was spent at Gaya. He exerted an extraordinary influence, particularly in the eastern parts of India, and attracted a large following, including some Muslims and people from the low castes. He did not reject the scriptures or idol-worship, though he cannot be classified as a traditionalist.

The writings of Narsinha Mehta in Gujarat, of Meera in Rajasthan, of Surdas in west Uttar Pradesh, and of Chaitanya in Bengal and Orissa reached extraordinary heights of lyrical fervour and of love which transcended all boundaries, including those of caste and creed. These saints were prepared to welcome into their fold everyone, irrespective of caste or creed. All the saint poets mentioned above remained within the broad framework of Hinduism. Their philosophic beliefs were a brand of Vedantic monism which emphasised the fundamental unity of God and the Created world. The Vedantist philosophy had been propounded by a number of thinkers, but the one who probably influenced the saint poets most was Vallabha, a Tailang brahman, who lived in the last part of the fifteenth and the early part of the sixteenth century.

The approach of these saint-poets was broadly humanistic. They emphasised the broadest human sentiments—the sentiments of love and beauty in all their forms. Like the non-sectarian, *nirguna* saints, their criticism of the caste system did little to weaken it. They did, however, provide an escape route for select ones, especially those who were suffering from the inequities of the caste system by promising them not only the prospect of release (*moksha*), but as *bhaktas,* gave them a high status even in the phenomenal world. Thus Ravidas says:

My caste is low, my deeds are low,
And lowly is my profession,
From this low position,
God has raised me high,
Says Ravidas the *chamar.*

The basic concepts of the saint-poets were reciprocated in a remarkable degree by the sufi poets and saints of the period. During the fifteenth century, the monistic ideas of the great Arab philosopher, Ibn-i-Arabi, became popular among broad sections in India. Arabi had been vehemntly demounced by the orthodox elements and his followers persecuted because he held that all being is essentially one, and everything is a manifestation of the divine substance. Thus, in his opinion, the different religions were identical. Arabi's doctrine of Unity of Being is known as *Tauhid* (Unity of)-*i-Wajaudi* (Being). This doctrine kept on gaining in popularity in India, and became the main basis of the sufi thought before the time of Akbar. Contact with yogis and Hindu saints went a long way in popularising the concept of pantheism. The Indian sufis started taking more interest in Sanskrit and Hindi, and a few of them, such as Mulla Daud, and Malik Muhammad Jaisi, composed their works in Hindi. The bhakti songs of the Vaishnavite saints, written in Hindi and other regional languages, touched the hearts of the sufis more than Persian poetry did. The use of Hindi songs became so popular that an eminent sufi, Abdul Wahid Bilgrami, wrote a treatise *Haqaiq-i-Hindi* in which he tried to explain such words as "Krishna", "Murli", "Gopis", "Radha", Yamuna", etc. in sufi mystic terms.

Thus, during the fifteenth and the early part of the sixteenth century, the bhakti and the sufi saints had worked out in a remarkable manner a common platform on which people belonging to various sects and creeds could meet and try to understand each other.

iii Literature and Fine Arts

Sanskrit Literature

Sanskrit continued to be a vehicle for higher thought and a medium for literature during the period under review. In fact, the production of works in Sanskrit in different branches was immense and perhaps greater than in the preceding period. Following the great Sankara, works in the field of Advaita philosophy by Ramanuja, Madhava, Vallabha, etc., continued to be written in Sanskrit. The speed with which their ideas were widely disseminated and discussed in different parts of the country showed the important role which Sanskrita continued to play during the period. There was a network of specialised schools and academies in different parts of the country, including areas under Muslim domination. These schools and academies were not interfered with and they continued to flourish. In fact, many of them took advantage of the introduction of paper to reproduce and disseminate the older texts. Thus, some of the oldest available texts of the *Ramayana* and the *Mahabharata* belong to the period from the eleventh or twelfth century onwards.

Besides philosophy, works in the field of *kavya* (poetical narrative), drama, fiction, medicine, astronomy, music, etc., continued to be written. A large number of commentaries and digests on the Hindu law (*Dharmashastras*) were prepared between the twelfth and the sixteenth century. The great *Mitakshara* of Vijnaneshwar, which forms one of the two principal Hindu schools of law, cannot be placed earlier than the twelfth century. Another famous commentator on the *Dharmashastras* was Chandeshwar of Bihar who lived in the fourteenth century. Most of the works were produced in the south, followed by Bengal, Mithila and western India under the patronage of Hindu rulers. The Jains, too, contributed to the growth of Sanskrit. Hemchandra Suri was the most eminent among these. Oddly enough, they largely ignored the presence of the Muslims in the country. Little attempt was made to translate Islamic works or Persian literature into Sanskrit. Possibly the only exception was the translation of the love story of Yusuf and Zulaikha, written by the famous Persian poet, Jami. This might be taken to be as another example of the insularity of outlook of the Hindus which had been mentioned by Albiruni earlier. Refusal to face the existing reality may be one reason why much of the writing of the period is repetitive, and lacks fresh insight or originality.

Arabic and Persian Literature

Although the greatest amount of literature produced by the Muslims was in Arabic which was the language of the Prophet, and was used as the language of literature and philosophy from Spain to Baghdad, the Turks who came to India were deeply influenced by the Persian language which had become the literary and administrative language of Central Asia and Iran from the tenth century onwards. In India, the use of Arabic remained largely confined to a narrow circle of Islamic scholars and philosophers. In course of time, digests of the Islamic law were prepared in Persian also with the help of Indian scholars. The most well-known of these *Fiqh-i-Firuzshahi* which was prepared in the reign of Firuz Tughlaq. But Arabic digests continued to be prepared, the most famous of these being the *Fatawa-i-Alamgiri*, or the Digest of Laws prepared by a group of jurists in the reign of Aurangzeb.

With the arrival of the Turks in India during the tenth century, a new language, Persian, was introduced in the country. There was a resurgence of the Persian language in Iran and Central Asia from the tenth century onwards and some of the greatest poets of the Persian language, such as Firdausi and Sadi, and the great poets of mystic love, Sinai, Iraqi, Jami, Hafiz etc. lived and composed their works between the tenth and fourteenth centuries. From the beginning, the Turks adopted Persian as the language of literature and administration in the country. Thus, Lahore emerged as the first centre for the cultivation of the Persian language. Although the works of only a few of these early writers of Persian in India have survived, we find in the writings of some of them, such as Masud Sad Salman, a sense of attachment and love for Lahore. However, the most notable Persian writer of the period was Amir Khusrau. Born in 1252 at Patiali (near Badaun in western Uttar Pradesh), Amir Khusrau took pride in being an Indian. He says, "I have praised India for two reasons. First, because India is the land of my birth and our country. Love of the country is an important obligation.... Hindustan is like heaven. Its climate is better than that of Khurasan...it is green and full of flowers all the year round. The brahmans here are as learned as Aristotle and there are many scholars in various fields...."

Khusrau's love for India shows that the Turkish ruling class was no longer prepared to behave as a foreign ruling class, and that the ground had been prepared for a cultural rapprochement between them and the Indians.

Khusrau wrote a large number of poetical works, including historical romances. He experimented with all the poetical forms, and created a new style of Persian which came to be called the *sabaq-i-hindi* or the style of India.

Khusrau has praised the Indian languages, including Hindi (which he calls Hindavi). Some of his scattered Hindi verses are found in his writings though the Hindi work, *Khaliq Bari*, often attributed to Khusrau, was in all probability the work of a later poet of the same name. He was also an accomplished musician and took part in religious musical gatherings (*sama*) organised by the famous Sufi saint, Nizamuddin Auliya. Khusrau, it is said, gave up his life the day after he learnt of the death of his *pir*, Nizamuddin Auliya (1325). He was buried in the same compound.

Apart from poetry, a strong school of history writing in Persian developed in India during the period. The most famous historians of this period were Minhaj Siraj, Ziauddin Barani, Afif and Isami.

Through the Persian language, India was able to develop close cultural relations with Central Asia and Iran. In course of time,

Persian became not only the language of administration and diplomacy, but also the language of the upper classes and their dependents, at first in north India and later, with the expansion of the Delhi Sultanat to the south and with the establishment of Muslim kingdoms in different parts of the country, in almost the entire country.

Sanskrit and Persian, in the main, functioned as link languages in the country, in politics, religion and philosophy, and were also means of literary productions. At first, there was little interchange between the two. Zia Nakhshabi (d. 1350) was the first to translate into Persian Sanskrit stories which were related by a parrot to a woman whose husband had gone on a journey. The book *Tuti Nama* (Book of the Parrot), written in the time of Muhammad Tughlaq, proved very popular and was translated from Persian into Turkish, and later into many European languages as well. He also translated the old Indian treatise on sexology, the *Kok Shastra*, into Persian. Later, in the time of Firuz Shah, Shaskrit books on medicine and music were translated into Persian. Sultan Zain-ul-Abidin of Kashmir had the famous historical work *Rajatarangini*, and the *Mahabharata* translated into Persian. Sanskrit works on medicine and music were also translated into Persian at his instance.

Regional Languages

During the period, literary works of high quality were produced in many of the regional languages as well. Many of these languages, such as Hindi, Bengali and Marathi trace their origin back to the eighth century or so. Some others, such as Tamil, were much older. Buddhists and Jains, and the Nath Panthi *siddhas* had used the "corrupt languages" (*apabhramsha*), as also local languages for their works in preference to Sanskrit. Writing in the beginning of the fourteenth century, Amir Khusrau had noted the existence of regional languages and remarked: "There is at this time in every province a language peculiar to itself, and not borrowed from any other—Sindhi, Lahori, Kashmiri, Kubari (Dogri of the Jammu region), Dhur Samundari (Kannada of Karnataka), Tilangi (Telugu), Gujar (Gujarati), Mabari (Tamil), Gauri (North Bengal), Bengali, Awadh, and Delhi and its environs (Hindavi)". He adds, "These languages have from ancient times applied in every way to the common purposes of life."

Some modern regional languages, such as Assamese, Oriya, Malayalam have not been noted. However, Khusrau rightly points to a significant development, viz the emergence of the modern regional languages of India. The rise to maturity of many of these languages and their use as means for literary works may be considered a striking feature of the medieval period. There were many reasons for this. Perhaps, with the loss of prestige by the brahmans, Sanskrit also lost some of its prestige. The use of the common languages by the bhakti saints was, undoubtedly, an important factor in the rise of these languages. In fact, in many parts of the country, it was the saints who fashioned these languages for literary purposes. It seems that in many regional kingdoms of the pre-Turkish period, regional languages, such as Tamil, Kannada, Marathi, etc., were used for administrative purposes, in addition to Sanskrit. This must have been continued under the Turkish rule, for we hear of Hindi-knowing revenue accountants appointed in the Delhi Sultanat. Later, when the Delhi Sultanat broke up, local languages, in addition to Persian, continued to be used for administrative purpose in many of the regional kingdoms. Thus, literature in Telugu developed in south India under the patronage of the Vijayanagara rulers. Marathi was one of the administrative languages in the Bahmini kingdom, and later, at the court of Bijapur. In course of time, when these languages had reached a certain stage of development, some of the Muslim kings gave them patronage for literary purposes also. For example, Nusrat Shah of Bengal had the *Mahabharata* and the *Ramayana* translated into Bengali. Maladhar Basu also translated the *Bhagavata* into Bengali under his patronage. His patronage of Bengali poets has been mentioned earlier.

The use of bhakti poems in Hindi by the Sufi saints in their musical gatherings has been mentioned before. In east U.P. sufi saints, such as Mulla Daud, the author of *Chandayan*, Malik Muhammad Jaisi, etc. wrote in Hindi and put forward sufi concepts in a form which could be easily understood by the common man. They popularised many Persian forms, such as the *masnavi*.

Fine Arts: Music

Trends towards mutual understanding and integration are to be found not only in the fields of religious beliefs and rituals, architecture and literature, but also in the fields of fine arts, particularly music. When the Turks came to India, they inherited the rich Arab tradition of music which had been further developed in Iran and Central Asia. They brought with them a number of new musical instruments, such as the *rabab* and *sarangi*, and new musical

modes and regulations. Indian music and Indian musicians at the
court of the Caliphs at Baghdad had possibly influenced the development of music there. However, systematic contact between the
two began in India under the Sultanat. We have already referred
to Amir Khusrau. Khusrau, who was given the title of *nayak* or
master of both the theory and practice of music, introduced many
Perso-Arabic airs (*ragas*), such as *aiman, gora, sanam*, etc. The *qawwali*
is supposed to originate with him. He is credited with having in-
vented the *sitar*, though we have no evidence of it. The *tabla* which
is also attributed to him seems, however, to have developed during the late seventeenth or early eighteenth century.

The process of integration in the field of music continued under
Firuz. The Indian classical work *Ragadarpan* was translated into
Persian during his reign. Musical gatherings spread from the abodes
of the sufis to the palaces of the nobles. Sultan Husain Sharqi, the
ruler of Jaunpur, was a great patron of music. The sufi saint, Pir
Bodhan, is supposed to have been the second great musician of
the age. Another regional kingdom where music was highly cultivated was the kingdom of Gwaliyar. Raja Man Singh of Gwaliyar
was a great music lover. The work *Man Kautuhal* in which all the
new musical modes introduced by the Muslims were included was
prepared under his aegis. We do not know at what time the musical modes in north India began to differ from those in the south.
But there in little doubt that the differentiation was largely due to
the incorporation of Perso-Arabic modes, airs and scales.

A distinctive style of music, influenced in considerable measure
by Persian music, developed in the kingdom of Kashmir.

After the conquest of Jaunpur, Sikandar Lodi followed its tradition of patronising music on a lavish scale—a tradition which was
further developed by the Afghan rulers. Thus, Adali, a successor
of Sher Shah, was a great master of music. But music came into
its own under the Mughals.

14

THE STATE IN INDIA UNDER
THE SULTANAT

Any state has to be seen in the context of the traditions, ideas and beliefs of the people concerned; social structure, including the character of the ruling class and its relations with other power elites as well as the masses; system of production and relations of production, to mention the main. Such a comprehensive study can hardly be carried out in a brief compass. However, some main points may be delineated.

Debate regarding the nature of the state, its origin, the nature of monarchy, outlook towards the people, relationship with religion and religious orders, the right of rebellion etc. were very old in India, as is clear from the *Arthashastra* of Kautilya which mentions many older schools of political thought which are lost to us. Debate about the nature of the state continued, and figures in the *Mahabharata* and in the writings of Jain thinkers, as well in the *Dharmashastras*. In general, *raj niti* or political conduct, and *dharma-niti* or moral conduct were considered separate, but interdependent entities.

Muslim thinking on the state had a complex evolution. Abu Yusuf Yaqubi (d. 798), al-Farabi (d. 950), al-Mawardi (d. 1031), al-Ghazali (d.1111) etc. gave a definite shape to the Muslim thinking on the subject, specially in the context of the decline of the Abbasid Caliphate and the rise of *de facto* independent states. While the earlier theory of the unity of spiritual authority and secular power in the person of the Imam or Khalifa was retained, the sultans were accorded an independent position, as long as they accepted the theoretical superiority of the Caliph or Khalifa. Thus, the fiction of Islamic unity was retained but, in practice, the sultans were left

free in their political conduct, as long as they did not openly violate the *shara*.

The Turks who came to India were deeply influenced by the Islamic thinking or practices regarding the state, though they could
not completely shake off their tribal/clan traditions. They also
showed themselves to be intensely practical in their political dealings, simultaneously trying to remain within the framework of Islamic law (*shara*).

i. Legal, Political and Social Character of the State

From a legal point of view, the Delhi sultanat can be considered an independent entity with the rise to power in 1206 of
Qutbuddin Aibak, a slave of Muizzuddin Muhammad bin Sam, and
the end of its subordination to Ghazni. However, it was not till
the consolidation of Iltutmish's power that the rulers of Ghazni ceased
to claim suzreignty over the territories comprising the sultanat of
Delhi. In fact, this was a consequence of the conquest of Ghazni
by the Mongol leader, Chingez Khan. It led to the flight of Yalduz,
the successor of Muizuddin Muhammed bin Sam, to Delhi, and his
defeat and imprisonment by Iltutmish.

Although asserting their independence, the rulers at Delhi were
keen to maintain their links with the rest of the Islamic world. One
method of doing this was to get a formal letter of investment (*manshur*)
from the Abbasid Caliph at Baghdad. In 1229, Iltutmish received
such a letter of investiture, along with splendid robes, from the Caliph of Baghdad. Henceforth, the sultans of Delhi inscribed the name
of the Caliph in their coinage, and his name was included in the
khutba at the time of the Friday prayers. The sultans also styled
themselves *Nasir-amirul-mominin*, i.e. the lieutenant of the leader of
the faithful, the Khalifa or Caliph. It has been argued that legally the
sultans of Delhi became subordinate to the Caliphs. However, the
legal aspect was the least important in the eyes of contemporaries.
The legal independence of the sultans of Delhi had not been questioned by any one *before* the receipt of the letter of investment. Nor
was the legal status of the sultan questioned by anyone even when
Mubarak Shah, the successor of Alauddin Khalji, repudiated allegiance to the Caliph, and declared himself Imam or Khalifa. The
question of getting the Caliph's letter of investment was really a
moral question. It also catered to, and helped to maintain the fiction
of the unity of the Islamic world under the leadership of the Caliph.
But this unity had broken down much earlier, partly on account of

the rise of various religious sects, and partly on account of the rise of independent kingdoms under Turkish and other adventurers. The rise of the Mongols fractured this unity still further.

When Muhammad bin Tughlaq was facing a series of internal revolts, he sought and obtained an investiture from a descendent of the Abbasid Caliph who was living at Cairo after the murder in 1259 of the Abbasid Caliph at Baghdad by the Mongol leader, Halaku. This was in 1343. Earlier, he had removed his own name from the coins, and put in its place that of the Caliph. But these steps had little impact on the leaders of the rebellions. Firuz Tughlaq twice obtained investiture and robes of honour from the Caliph, even before he stood forth as a champion of orthodoxy. But the prestige of the Abbasid Caliph had gradually declined. Following the example of Timur, later the Mughal rulers themselves assumed the title of Imam or Khalifa.

Thus, the institution of Khalifat had little relevance in the context of India during the sultanat and the Mughal periods.

With the advent of the Turks, a new type of a state was introduced in north India. During the early phase, maximum freedom was given to the military leaders to carry out conquests in different parts of the country while a strong corp of troops was stationed with, and operated under the direct control of the Sultan. This type of loose or decentralized despotism was replaced by a highly centralised state by Balban. With some interruptions, as for example, under Jalaluddin Khalji, the Delhi sultanat maintained its highly centralized character till the end of the 14th century when, following the downfall of the Tughlaqs and the rise of the Lodis to power, a brief experiment was made at reasserting the principle of decentralised despotism, with Afghan tribal leaders claiming a larger share in power. This led to renewed clashes between the sultan and the nobles leading to the defeat of Ibrahim Lodi at the field of Panipat in 1526.

While a tussle for power between the sultan and the nobles was a constant feature of the sultanat, the precise extent and degree of centralisation varying from ruler to ruler, the basic struggle for power between the nobles and the sultan was settled in favour of the sultan with the accession of Balban to the throne. The Turkish nobles had failed to act as a corp, or to rally around a wazir of their choice, or to set up any institutions to control the power of the sultan.

Despite its outer appearance, the character of the state varied considerably during the 13th and 14th centuries. During the 13th century, the state was very much the institutionalized form of a foreign conquest. The nobles, mostly of Turkish extraction, had little knowledge or links with the country, and exercised control over the countryside from their military cantonments in the towns and the forts sprinkled over the country. It was during this period that the Sufi saints, particularly the Chishtis, played an important role in establishing links between the new ruling class and the populace, as we have already seen.

The 13th century was practically a period of Turkish domination over the state. Most of the nobles, both free and slave, who had accompanied Muizzuddin Muhammad bin Sam to India were Islamized Turks. The Khaljis who were not considered Turks were another important group. But they did not find favour with the successors of Qutbuddin Aibak at Delhi, and preferred to carve out a semi-independent domain of their own in North Bengal.

A second group which held important positions under Iltutmish were the Tajiks. There was a sprinkling of Arabs, Yamanis etc. who were generally appointed in the department of the *sadr*. Unlike the Turks who were rude warriors, the Tajiks whose mother-tongue was Persian, were cultured and refined. Hence, they were generally preferred for administrative posts in the central government. Iltutmish's wazir, Nizamul Mulk Junaidi, was a Tajik. The Turks, both free and slave, resented the Tajiks and their attempt to grab the higher administrative posts. This came to the surface after the death of Iltutmish when most of the Tajiks were massacred by the Turks. The wazir, Nizamul Mulk, escaped, but was not heard of again. This ended the Tajik challenge to the Turks.

The Turkish zealousness of not allowing non-Turks to acquire high office was displayed in their hostility towards the Abyssinian, Malik Yakut, who had been appointed *amir akhur* (superintendent of the Royal stables) by Razia. However, the Turkish nobles did not hesitate to use an Indian Muslim, Imaduddin Raihan, to displace the *chihalgani* slave officers, and to try and establish their own domination over the sultan.

Balban's reign has many contradictions. Balban destroyed the power of the *chihalgani* Turks. Simultaneously, he set his face against the "low born", i.e. the Indian Muslims, even for appointment in the lower rungs of the administration. Thus, he stood forth as the champion of the Turkish domination of the state. Simultaneously he declared himself to be a decendent of the Iranian hero, Afrasiyab, and adhered to pre-Islamic Iranian forms and symbols of suzreignty. Thus, he tried to fuse together Iranian forms and Turkish domination.

Although the institution of slavery played an important role in fusing together different ethnic groups among the Muslims, particularly the Turks who were divided into tribes and regional groupings, the state in India can hardly be called a 'slave state', a term used by early British historians, but now discarded. Many of the nobles started their careers as slaves in the service of a sultan or a leading noble. But they were freed (manumitted) at a stage during their rise to high positions. Thus, Iltutmish presented his letter of manumission to the *ulema* when they called on him after his accession to the throne. According to Islamic theory, only a free person could accend the throne. Thus, it is also wrong to talk of a 'slave dynasty'.

Despite Balban's efforts, the Turkish domination of the State had begun to erode during his life time. Thus, he was compelled to admit a section of the Mongols to the nobility during the last years of his reign. Earlier, following the death of his son, Prince Muhammad, he had to recruit Khaljis under Jalaluddin Khalji to fight the Mongols. Also, during the Bengal campaign, towards the end of his life, he found a section of the Turkish nobles and the army to be inefficient and undependable. He punished the Turkish nobles and soldiers, but he had to fall back upon the support of some of the *rais* of East U.P., and to resort to a *leve'e en masse* to raise local soldiers to suppress the Bengal rebellion.

The Khaljis ended the Turkish domination or policy of Turkish exclusivism. They did not discriminate against the Turks, but threw the doors open to the talents among various sections of the Muslims. Thus, Alauddin's wazir was Nusrat Khan Jalesar, and Zafar Khan his Mir Arz. Both were famous warriors but were non-Turks, possibly Indian Muslims. Another non-Turk who rose to power was Malik Kafur. It seems that there was an influx of a large number of non-Turks including Indian Muslims into the nobility during the latter years of Alauddin Khalji. This alone can explain the rise to power, even though very brief, of the Baradus, an uneducated but fighting group of Rajputs under Khusrau Khan, following the murder of Mubarak Khalji (1320).

It has been suggested that with the rise of the Khaljis, and the end of Turkish monopoly of high offices, an "integrated Indo-Muslim state" emerged in India, i.e., one in which different sections of the Muslims, including Indian Muslims, were admitted to the nobility, and high offices filled on the basis of efficiency and the pre-dilections of individual rulers, rather than on the basis of their ethnic origins. Sufficient research work has not been done to prove or effectively disprove the point. We do, however, know that the ruling classes and the rulers in India strongly believed in the principle of superiority of blood so that only those who could establish their links with 'respected' families, whether in the secular or the religious fields, were entitled to high offices in government. The earliest Muslim political thinker in India, Fakr-i-Mudabbir, who wrote during the reign of Iltutmish, says:

"Posts of diwan, *shagird* and *muharrir* (revenue posts) should be given only to *ahl-i-qalam* (the educated sections) and whose ancestors had served rulers and amirs."

Ziauddin Barani who wrote his political tract, *Fatawa-i-Jahandari*, while in prison during the early years of Firuz Tughlaq, echoes the same views. He says that at the time of creation, some minds were inspired with the art of letters and of writing, others with horsemanship, and yet others in the weaving, stich-craft, carpentry, haircutting and tanning. Thus, men should practice only those crafts and professions "for which men have been inspired (and) are practised by them". He goes on to say, "Even if a man of base or low birth is adorned with a hundred merits, he will not be able to organise and administer the country according to expectations, or be worthy of leadership or political trust."

Barani was, apparently, voicing the prejudices of the ruling sections. But these views had a definite bearing on the character of the state. The state remained the exclusive preserve of the so-called "respectable" classes. The only ruler who tried to breach this policy was Muhammad bin Tughlaq who appointed a number of persons, both Hindus and Muslims, from the so-called low classes on the basis of their efficiency. But there was a strong reaction against this from the established ruling classes. Under Firuz Tughlaq, we find no reference to the appointment of such people, either Hindus or Muslims.

Thus, in a highly fragmented society it is hardly possible to speak of an "integrated" Indo-Muslim state. The position of converted India Muslims from the lower classes hardly changed. The rise of a converted Tailang Brahman, Khan-i-Jahan Maqbul, to the position of wazir under Firuz Tughlaq, or of an Ain-ul-Mulk, a Hindustani, who was governor of Awadh under Muhammad Tughlaq and later was Firuz's *mushrif-i-mamlik* (auditor-general), should not be interpreted to mean that Indian converts from the upper castes had now become a dominant element in the nobility. Muhammad Tughlaq's induction of a large number of foreigners in the nobility, calling them *'aizza'* is an index to the continued preference of foreigners over Indians. It was one of these nobles who later set up the Bahmani kingdom in the Deccan, and another in Gujarat.

The highly mobile central elite, paid by non-hereditory *iqtas*, backed by armed cavalry, un-encumbered by any local vested interests, was the main instrument of Turkish centralization. The state was hierarchical in the sense that there was a definite graded order in society and the state. The nobles, graded into three classes, Khans, Maliks and Amirs, formed the top rung, although great deference was paid to the *ulema* and the *mashaikh* (saints).

ii. Relations with the ulema

The powers and position of the *ulema* in the state, and its relationship with the secular rulers has been a matter of continuous debate in the Islamic world. After the end of the rule of the first four Caliphs at Mecca, there was a division between the spiritual and secular authority, most of the leading clergymen remaining at Mecca, and the centre of political authority being shifted by the Umaiyyad Khalifas to Damascus. With the shifting of the political control to Baghdad by the Abbasids, who claimed descent from the Prophet, an attempt was made to reintegrate spiritual and political authority under their aegis. However, in effect, the political elements often dominated the spiritual. Even this unity, however limited, ended with the break up of the Abbasid Caliphate towards the end of the 9th century, and the rise of independent kingdoms, mostly under Turkish sultans. The Turks who were newly converted to Islam, paid great deference to the clergy, the *ulema*, who were supposed to interpret Islam to the community. But they kept effective political control in their hands. The attitude of contempt towards the clergymen and lower officials (*nawisandan*, or writers) for advising about higher political affairs is explained by the remarks of Alauddin Khalji to Alaul Mulk, the kotwal of Delhi, when he advised Alauddin to persuade the Mongols to depart by using diplomatic and other, i.e. financial, means. Alauddin rejected the advise as "unbecoming", and clinched the argument by saying "you speak thus because you are a *nawisanda* (clerk or scribe) and the son of a *nawisanda*." Elsewhere, Barani says that these sections would not distinguish the head of a horse from its tail! It has been argued that the state set up by the Turks was a theocracy because it was based on the Muslim holy law, the *shara*, which could be interpreted only by the *ulema*. In this connection, it may be pointed out that the word "theocracy" was originally applied to the Jewish commonwealth from the time of Moses to the rise of monarchy, and is understood as "government or State governed by God directly or through a sacerdotal class." It was also implied that for such a sacerdotal class to govern, it should be organised formally, as in the case of Jewish or Christian Churches. It has been said that in the absence of an organised Church, the Muslim *ulema* could not govern, and hence there could be no theocratic state.

The entire discussion is somewhat artificial because a purely theocratic state never existed anywhere for any length of time, as also because the term or concept of a theocratic state as set out above was never discussed in India during medieval times. What was discussed and is relevant is whether a truly Islamic state could be set up in India. And at the back of it was the controversy regarding the extent to which *shara* as interpreted by the orthodox *ulema*, could be implemented in India.

This matter was anxiously debated during the sultanat period, was revived under the Mughals, and continued under British rule. It still arises under various forms.

In general, the sultans in India, while paying deference to the *ulema*, did not feel bound to consult them or accede to their views where matters of state were concerned. Thus, Iltutmish did not consult the theologians before he declared Razia as his successor. Balban introduced pre-Islamic ceremonials in his court, including *sijda* and *pabos* which were considered un-Islamic by the *ulema*. In Alauddin Khalji's time, Qazi Mughis declared that the treasures looted by him from Deogir were *bait-ul-mal*, or part of the public treasury, and that as sultan, he was entitled to take from the treasury only as much as was allowed to a common trooper. Alauddin rejected the advice of the Qazi, and declared:

"Although I have not studied the Book (the Quran), nor am I learned (in religious sciences), I am a Muslim of a Muslim stock. To prevent rebellions in which thousands perish, I issue such orders as I conceive to be for the good of the state, and the benefit of the people. Men are heedless, disresectful, and disobey my commands. I am then compelled to be severe and bring them to obedience. I do not know whether this is according to the *shara*, or against the *shara*; whatever I think for the good of the state or suitable for the emergency, that I decree."

Since Barani wrote more than fifty years after Alauddin Khalji, these may not have been the words of Alauddin, but views attributed to him by Barani. Also, they refer to a particular situation, a situation in which Alauddin had to give harsh punishments to prevent rebellions, and to ensure compliance of his orders. They do not imply that Alauddin Khalji regularly or wilfully disregarded the *shara*. Barani makes the position clear by saying that "when he (Alauddin) attained to kingship, he was quite convinced that government and administration were quite independent of the rules and orders of the *shariat*; and that while the former appertained to kings, the latter had been assigned to *qazis* and *muftis*."

This divergence in the perceived values of the ruler and the *ulema* was not peculiar to Alauddin. Muhammad bin Tughlaq issued many secular decrees (*zawabits*) *to supplement the shariat*. Even an orthodox ruler, Firuz, forbade cutting the hands, feet, noses etc. of criminals even though it had been sanctioned by the *sharia*.

Taking all these factors into account, Barani came to the conclusion that a truely Islamic state based on faith (*din-dari*) was not feasible in India. All that was feasible was an Islamic State based on worldly considerations (*dunya-dari*). In such a state, the head of the state, the sultan, had to be a God fearing Muslim; Saiyyids, religious scholars, shaikhs etc. were to be honoured and given employment; holy wars (*jihad*) and holy campaigns were to be waged against the neighbouring rajas and chiefs; and Muslims not allowed to flout the holy law in their public behaviour so that sins and impurity, wickedness and wrong doing sink low. Barani makes it clear, however, that 'what the sultan did in private, or a citizen in his house was not the concern of the state'.

Thus, the state was not a theocracy. Nor can it be called "ethnocentric" because *shara* as defined by the clergy was hardly the core concern of the sultans. It was formally Islamic in character, but was based not on social equality, but on hierarchy. In practice, there was little distinction between the lives of the ordinary people, Hindu or Muslim. The clergy were to be honoured but the state was run not on their advise, but on political considerations and the interests of the ruling elite. As we shall see, this was not always an easy enterprise, and sometimes, there was a sharp difference of opinion between the orthodox clergy and the sultans, especially regarding the extent of religious freedom to be accorded to the Hindus, and their role in the working of the state.

iii. Position of the Hindus

The state as we have described above, postulated considerable but defined religious freedom to those Hindus who had accepted the overlordship of the Muslim ruler, and agreed to abide by the rules and regulations enforced by him. Such people were called *zimmis* or protected persons. The *zimmis* had the right to worship according to their rites, and to maintain and repair temples "since buildings cannot stand for ever". They were, however, not allowed to build new temples "in opposition to Islam". This clause was vague; it implied that Hindus could build new temples in their houses, or in villages where there were no Muslims. It could also mean that in case of opposition by the Hindus, even old temples could be destroyed. As we have seen, in times of war even temples of long standing were sacked and destroyed. In the early phase, some of them were converted into mosques, or the plundered material from their ruins used for building mosques. But this stopped once the Turks were in a position to erect their own buildings. However, in case of wars with local chiefs or neighbouring rulers, the destruction of their temples became acts of religious merit. Even this came to a stop when Turkish rule had been spread all over the country.

In addition to loyalty and service to the ruler, the Hindus are also required to pay *jizyah*. The origins of *jizyah* are not clear; some trace it to poll-tax on individuals levied in Greece, and pre-Islamic Iran from which it was taken over, others consider it to be a tax in lieu of military service, and still others equate it to land-tax or *kharaj*. This confusion was sought to be resolved by the various schools of *shariat*, which arose towards the end of the 9th century and at the beginning of the 10th century. While some of them, tracing the example of the Prophet towards idol-worshippers in Arabia, argued that idol-worshippers had only the option of Islam or death, a few others gave *jizyah* as the third option. The Hanafi school of *sharia* which was generally followed in India used the formula "Islam or death, or payment of *jizyah*'. We do not know how precisely *jizyah* was assessed or collected during the Sultanat period. In some passages of Barani, the peasants are to pay *kharaj* or *jizyah*, that is, they were considered one and the same and assessed as a lump sum in the villages. Thus, among the cesses collected by Alauddin Khalji, or even Firuz, there is no reference to *jizyah*. How it was collected in the towns we do not know. According to the *shara*, women, children, people who were lunatics, and the indigent were exempt from *jizyah*. This left the artisans and the merchants. Till the time of Firuz Tughlaq, Brahmans too, were exempt.

Thus, during the sultanat period, *jizyah* as a separate tax effected only a small section in the towns. As such, it could hardly be considered a devise for forcing conversion to Islam. For a section of the orthodox *ulema*, however, *jizyah* was a means of harassing and humiliating and insulting the Hindus. Thus, Qazi Mughis went so far as to say that if the collector of the jizyah should want to spit on the face of the Hindu, he should open his mouth. This was on lines of Manu's injunction that if a shudra heard the Vedas, molten lead should be poured in his ears. Both were impractical, but showed a state of the mind.

Some theologians argued that as idolaters, and not having a revealed book like the Quran, the Hindus were ineligible for *jizyah*, and should be given the option of only Islam or death. If Barani is to be believed, such an argument was put forward before Iltutmish by a group of theologians. On behalf of the Sultan, his wazir, Nizamul Mulk Junaidi, replied that such a policy was contrary to tradition, not having been enforced by Mahmud, the hero of Islam, and impractical because the Muslims were too few in numbers, "like salt in a dish (of food)."

Barani perhaps did not know that the Turkish sultans were only following the example of the Arab rulers of Sindh who had granted the Hindus there the option of paying *jizyah*, and employed many of them in civil administration.

It is also necessary to remember that in the Delhi Sultanat, the Hindus formed a predominant section of the population, even in the heart of the empire, Delhi. They continued to dominate the country-side as *khuts, muqaddams, chaudhuri, rana, thakur*, etc., as also trade and finance in the towns, as well as the transport trade (as *banjaras*). As Alauddin told Qazi Mughis, even within 100 kos of the capital, "the *khuts* and *muqaddams* ride upon fine horses, wore fine clothes, shoot with Persian bows, make war upon each other, and go out hunting...give parties and drink wine." In his *Fatawa-i-Jahandari*, Barani referring to them sadly notes:

"....out of consideration for the fact that the infidels and polytheists are payers of tributes and protected persons (*zimmis*), these infidels are honoured, distinguished, favoured and made eminent; the kings bestow drums, banners, ornaments, cloaks of brocade and caprisoned horses upon them, and appoint them to governorships, high posts and offices."

There is, no doubt, an element of exaggeration in this statement because hardly any Hindus were appointed to high offices, except during the reign of Muhammad bin Tughlaq. But there is little doubt about the financial affluence of a section of the Hindus because we are told by Barani that the sahs (bankers), mehtas (administrators) and pandits "build houses like palaces...live in delights and

comfort. They take Musalmans in their service and make them run
before their horses, even in the capital of Islam."

Of course, the affluence affected only a small section of the Hindus. The mass of the people, both Hindus and Muslim, continued
to be poor, and exploited by the ruling classes.

To what extent the Sultanat affected the daily life of an average
Hindu is a matter of debate. According to one view, he was hardly affected because the state did not interfere with his, life as long
as he paid his taxes which, in the villages, continued to be collected by the *khuts* and *muqaddams*, or *rais* and *thakurs*. He got into
trouble only when there was a local war, or famine, or when the
village officials or the local chief delayed or withheld land revenue. In matters of personal and civil laws, the Hindus continued
to be governed by caste panchayats, and by the village zamindar
or chief. The qazis dealt with Muslim law, or only when a Hindu
and a Muslim were involved.

However, in a centralized state, the influence of the state tended to grow, as was shown by the agrarian policies of Alauddin
Khalji and Muhammad bin Tughlaq. In matters of religion, considerable freedom was accorded. Jalaluddin Khalji's observation that
the Hindu passed in procession, beating gongs and symbols, outside his palace, to immerse the images in the Jamuna exemplifies
it. Muhammad bin Tughlaq even participated in Hindu festivals,
such as, Holi, and held discussions with Jogis, and Jain saints. However, in a despotic state such freedom was often regarded as a matter
of grace rather than a matter of right. Thus, local despots could
always act in an arbitrary manner, particularly when a section of
the *ulema* constantly advocated and justified a policy of sternly re-
pressing the Hindus. Thus, they justified Firuz Tughlaq's publicly
burning a brahman on charge of converting a Muslim, or his destroying a number of temples around Delhi on the charge that they
were new, and that in the festivals held around them, Muslims also
used to participate. Perhaps, the only occasion when the *ulema* intervened to prevent a ruler from acting in an arbitrary manner against
the Hindus was when they dissuaded Sikandar Lodi from attack-
ing the pilgrims and destroying and desecrating the old temple and
tank at Kurukshetra on the ground that the temple was an ancient
one, and previous Muslim sultans had allowed the Hindu to bathe
there. It would seem that the traditions of broad religious toleration had become well established by then.

Despite some limitations, it must be conceded that during the
sultanat period, the state allowed more religious freedom than was

allowed to non-Christians, or even to rival sects of Christians in Europe till the 16th century. The state was, of course, formally an Islamic one in the sense explained by Barani. This implied that the Muslims were a privileged group, and that it was a special obligation on the state to look after their moral and material welfare. This was by no means new in India because earlier it were the Rajputs who had formed a privileged group, and their privileges, and the privileges of the brahman were accepted as a matter of course.

iv. Despotism, Benevolence and Development

In their thinking about the state, Muslim political thinkers raised questions about the nature and legitimate objectives of state power, and the basis of the moral authority of the state and the sultan. Political thinkers considered monarchy to be the only safeguard against social anarchy in which property and the honour of women could not be protected. In general, the political thinkers preferred the rule of one individual, the sultan, who had the necessary social and moral qualities, and who, in a sense, enjoyed the mandate of heaven over a oligarchy, or 'noblocracy'. The question of despotism or autocracy bothered many medieval Muslim thinkers. Ziauddin Barani considered despotism to be basically un-Islamic, and considered that religion was the only check against despotism or abuse of personal power by a monarch. However, they did not give the right of rebellion against an unjust ruler, except in some special circumstances, such as open and blatant violation of the *shara*. Barani compromised with despotism because giving of harsh punishments was inescapable in a situation such as India. Specifically, Barani believed that the mean and ignoble, whom he compares to "animals and beasts of prey" were "plentiful and abundant." Their punishment and stern repression by a despotic ruler was not only inescapable but desirable. Thus, Barani finds a social justification for despotism.

The question was: how to maintain the moral authority of the state in this situation? It was in this context that medieval political thinkers emphasized the concept of *adl* or justice. Justice implied making no distinction between rich and poor, relation and stranger, noble and ignoble. Nizamuddin, the author of *Siyasat Nama*, lays great emphasis on the concept of justice. Many thinkers, including Barani, give dispensing of justice even a higher position than discharging religious obligations. For a ruler, an act of justice was greater than seventy years of namaz, according to Barani. However, justice also implies the preservation of the existing social order which was organized on a rigid   hierarchical order in which the mean and the ignoble which included the artisans and peasants were to be kept out of power, and in a position of dependence.

Despite these, justice did provide a certain restraint on the exercise of arbitrary power, especially by the nobles and the lower officials. It should also be seen within the framework of the concept of benevolence, or serving the people. The saints, both Muslim and Hindu, constantly emphasised this point, both for themselves as for the rulers. Within limitations, they also criticized the hierarchical system of society, and upheld the concept of human equality. To that extent, they became a vehicle for postulating popular aspirations, and by their open-ended approach provide them a relief and a means of escape from a rigidly unequal order. However, as we have seen, at the political level, the concept of benevolence was, at best, given only lip service by the rulers. After Jalaluddin Khalji, Firuz Tughlaq was the first Turkish monarch who tried to espouse it, particularly in the context of the Muslims, though non-Muslims could not be completely excluded.

Could such a state, highly centralized and militaristic, with a ruling class which had a narrow social base, promote the economic and cultural development of the country? In the preceding pages we have seen how, despite all these limitations, there was growth of architecture, literature and music in the country in which both Muslims and Hindus contributed. The growth of sufism and the bhakti movements also tended to mitigate mutual hostility, and provide a platform for common interaction. In the economic fields, while only a few monarchs, such as Muhammad and Firuz Tughlaq were actively concerned with the expansion and improvement of cultivation, the centralized system of revenue administration made it possible for the state to intervene more effectively in village life. The centralization of a high proportion of the revenue surplus in the hands of the ruling class gave a fillip to artisanal production of a superior type, and promoted urbanization. The opening up of the frontiers of the country to trade, and wider cultural links with the Islamic world, the improvement of road communications, the provision of a stable currency, the silver tanka, and the active promotion of overseas trade with countries of south-east Asia and China led to the situation that, as modern research reveals, when the Portuguese entered the Indian Ocean towards the end of the 15th century, it was found that trade and prosperity in the region in which India played a key role was at an unprecedentedly high level. But which were the groups and elements which benefited from and participated in this prosperity and which were the ones left out is a question which needs to be tackled separately because, then as now, prosperity and stark poverty continued side by side.

Thus, the Sultanat, far from being a 'dark age' as postulated by some, saw the breaking of the rigid, narrow economic and social mould which had dominated the country between the 8th and 12th centuries, and created conditions for development, even though in a limited form.

Note: How and when in some parts of the country, such as Sind, West Bengal, the Kashmir valley and East Bengal, large sections became Muslim is a question to which no single answer can be given. In many of these areas, large scale conversion, which was a slow and long drawn-out process, has been linked to societies where tribal traditions were strong, with the peoples of the area having their own gods and goddesses, weakly linked to established religions, such as Hinduism or Buddhism. Many of these people shifted to settled agriculture under the aegis of the new Muslim rulers, and, in the process, gradually shifted to Islam. Thus, their conversion were not so much from Hinduism or Buddhism, but from tribal gods and goddesses to Islam. In many of these areas, sufi saints also played a role. In some areas, such as East Bengal, the cultivators became Muslim, while the chiefs or village zamindars who had stronger links with Hinduism, remained Hindu.

In the Kashmir valley where the message of Islam had been carried by a number of eminent Central Asian sufi saints, large scale conversion by force is said to have been carried out by the Mongal leader, Dulacha, during the 14th century. In some other areas, captured prisoners of war also provided a basis for forced conversion, often accompanied by enslavement.

GLOSSARY

Amils—revenue officers

Amir-i-akhur—amir or officer commanding the horse

Amir-i-hajib—officer-in-charge of the royal court

Amirul Mominin—Commander of the Faithful; the
       Caliph

Arz-i-mamalik—minister in charge of the army of the
whole country

Balahar—the lowest grade of the agricultural peasant

Banjara—a corn merchant

Barid—intelligence officer appointed by the state to
       collect information

Charai—a tax on cattle

Chatr—royal umbrella

Dagh—mark of branding

Dallals—brokers

Darogha—a minor officer in charge of a local office

Darul Adl—the market of Delhi or cloth and other
       commodities; literally, place of justice

Darul Mulk—capital

Doab—land between the Jumna and the Ganges

Farman—a royal order

Gazz-i-Sikandari—the yard of Sultan Sikandar Lodi

Gumashta—agent or representative

Hadis—acts or words of the Arabian Prophet

Imam—supreme commander, leader; also the person
       leading the congregational Muslim prayers

Inam—gift; reward

Iqta—a governorship; or grant of revenues of a piece of land

Iqtadar—governor or a person in whose charge an *iqta*
       has been placed

Jagir—a piece of land assigned to a government
       officer by the state

Jama'at'Khana—a house of mystics

Jitals—Copper coins of the Delhi sultanat

Jizya—has two meanings: (a) in the literature of the Delhi
    sultanat, any tax which is not kharaj or land tax;
    (b) in the *shari'at*: a personal and yearly tax on non-Muslims

Kafir—non-Muslim (literally, one who is ungrateful to God)

Karkhanas—royal factories or enterprises for producing or
    collecting commodities required by the state

Khalifa—Caliph, Commander of the Faithful, or
    successor of a sufi

Khalisa—income which went directly went to the king

Khanqahs—a house of mystics but more commoditous than
    the *jama'at khana*

Kharif—a winter crop in India

Khil'at—robe of honour

Khilafat—caliphate; commander of the faithful

Kharaj—land revenue; also tribute paid by a subordinate ruler

Khuts—class of village headmen

Kufr—disbelief

Madad-i-Maash—grant of land or pension to religious or
    deserving persons

Madrasa—an educational institution

Malikut-Tujjar—literally, chief of merchants; a title
    given to one of the highest officers of the state

Mameluks—slave-officers

Mohalla—a section or part of a town; quarter of a city

Muhtasib—an officer appointed to maintain regulations
    in a municipality

Mullahs—persons claiming to be religious leaders of the
    Musalmans

Muqaddam—village headman; literally the first or senior man

Mushrif-i-mamalik—accountant for all provinces

Naib—deputy, assistant, agent, representative

Nawisandas—clerks

Nabuwat—prophethood

Paibos—kissing the feet, a ceremony generally reserved for God

Pir—spiritual guide

Qalandars—a class of Muslim mendicants, generally
    uneducated, who did not believe in private
    property and wandered about from place to
    place and lived by persistent begging

Qasbas—towns

Qazi—a Muslim judge

Rabi'—the winter crop in India, as opposed to the *kharif* or rainy season crop

Rai—a Hindu chief, usually one having his own territory and army

Rai Rayan—the Rai of Rais; the title given by Alauddin Khalji to Rama Deo of Deogir

Ra'iyyat—subjects

Sadah—literally, one hundred; the term *sadah amirs* meant officers controlling territory containing about a hundred villages

Sadr-i Jahan—title of the central officer of the Delhi sultanat, who was in charge of religious and charitable endowments

Sama—an audition party of the mystics

Sarrafs—money-changers, bankers

Sarai—inn

Sarai-Adl—name given to Alauddin Khalji's market in Delhi for the sale of cloth and other specified commodities

Shahr—city, used for the capital, Delhi

Shari'at—Muslim religious law

Shiqdar—an officer-in-charge of an area of land described as a *shiq*

Shuhna—head of the police, mayor, provost

Shuhna-i mandi—officer-in-charge of the grain-market

Sufis—mystics

Tanka—silver coin of the Delhi sultanat

Tauhid—unity of God

Ulema—Muslims of religious learning; plural of *alim*

Umara—Plural of *amir*; amir means ruler or commander

Usar—saline land

Wajh—money, salary

Wajhdar—a salaried officer

Wali—governor

Wali-'ahad—heir-presumptive

Wazir-i mutlaq—wazir with full powers, who could administer without interference by the king

Zawabits—state laws

Zimmis—protected non-Muslims

Index

Abbas Sarwani, 226
Abbasid Caliphate, 14, 111, 129,
    230, 237, 266, 267
Abdul Hasan Ibadi of Iraq, 161
Abdul Wahid Bilgrami, 259
Abdur Razzak, 181, 183
Abu Yusuf Yaqubi, 265
Abul Fazl, 229
Admiral Cheng Ho, 198
Afghanistan, 17
Ahmad Ayaz Rawat-i-Arz, 136
Ainul Mulk Multani, 90, 109
Akbar, 81, 123, 142, 212
Al-Biruni, 33
Alauddin Husain Shah, 22, 177
Alauddin Khalji, 96, 99, 266, 269,
    271, 272, 273, 274
    and Jalaluddin's approaches to
    State, 75
    Market reforms, 78, 81
Amir Hasan Sijzi, 162
Amir Khan, 63
Amir Khusrau, 89, 90, 92, 153, 162,
    163, 165, 168, 261, 262, 264
Amu (rivers), 13
Aqat Khan, 77
Arab Sea, 13, 202
Aram Shah, 39
Architecture, 232
Arthashastra of Kautilya, 265
Ashraf, K.M., 156
Asian Oceanic trade, 194
Assam, 214
Aurangzeb, 125
Awadh, 52
Aziz Khammar, 110

Baba Fariduddin Ganj-i-Shakhar,
    242
Bahlul Lodi, 226
Bahmanid rule (1350-1565), 175
Bahadur Shah, 201, 221
Bahauddin Zakariya, 245
Bahram Shah, 22, 50, 51, 177

Balbam,
    age of (1246-87), 51
    ruler (1266-87), 53
Barka Khan, 67
Bayazid Bayat, 238
Beas river, 66
Bengal relations with Delhi, 43
    campaigns, 116
Bhagawat Gita, 249
    Puran, 250
Bhakti movement, 249
Bihar and Lakhnauti,
    Turkish conquest of, 41
Black Sea, 193, 202
Bosworth, C.E., 21
Bughra Khan, 56, 62, 138, 165
Building industry, 153
Bukhara, 37

Caliph of Baghdad, 45, 111
Caste, 172
Central Asia (10th & 12th)
    Centuries, 13
    Development in, 14
    Centralised monarchy 1236-1290,
    47
Chaghtai Mongols, 66
Chahmans or Chauhan, 21, 23
Chandels, 19, 27
Chaudhuri, Kirti, 206
Chauhan, Prithviraj, 21, 24, 26, 89
Chaulukyas, 19, 23
Chenab, 66
Chihalgani, Balban
    struggle with the, 51
Chingez Khan, 15, 37, 40, 65, 69, 266
Chishtis, 240
Chishti and Suhrawardi
    Silsilahs, 240
Chittor, 23, 70, 88, 90
Christopher Columbus, 193
Court and royal household, 138
Customs, 172

Dalucha Khan, 72

Daman and Diu, 201
Darya Khan, 120
Dawa Khan, 68, 71
Delhi Sultanat,
  disintegration of (causes), 126
  territorial consolidation of, 36
  expansion of, 86
  integrity of, 58
Delhi Sultanat (under),
  Diwan-i-Arz, 136
  Diwan-i-Insha, 138
    Risalat, 138
  Govt. and administration, 129
  Ministeries, 132
  Wazir, 132
Deval Devi, 92
Dilawar Khan Ghuri, 218, 219
Dilwara in Rajasthan, 153
Dor Rajputs, 27
Deva Raya II, 179, 180, 181, 185,
  188
  see also Krishna Deva
Dom Henrique, 192

East Africa, 154
Eastern India, 211
Economic life, 145

Fakhruddin Isami, 133
Fakr-i-Mudaddir, 270
Fariduddin Ganj Shakar, 125
Fatehpur Sikri, 224
Fazl ibn Abul Maali, 233
Firdausi, 21
Firuz, Shah Bahmani, 179, 180, 183,
  184
Firuz Tughlaq, 108, 113, 119, 125,
  145, 154, 160, 171, 211, 225,
  235, 267, 268, 274
  concept of benevolence and
    peoples' welfare, 113
  Military expeditions, 116
Foreign trade, 156

Gamel-al-Din Ibrahim, 195
Ganga Valley, 19, 23, 36
Gauri Shankar Ojha, 89
Ghaznavids, 15
  administration, 29
Ghiyasuddin, 38, 96
  Azam Shah, 212
  Muhammad, 23
  Tughlaq, 91, 94, 115, 117, 119,
    134, 149, 235, 242

Ghurid empire, 37
  rise of, 22
Govindraj, ruler of Delhi, 25
Gujarat, 87, 217
Gupta empire in North India, 144
Gur Khan of Khitai (Central Asia),
  16
Guru Granth Sahib of Nanak, 242,
  255, 256

Habibullah, A.B.M., 29
Hasan Gangu, 111, 177, 179
Hasan Nizami, 26
Hindola Mahal, 222
Hindu Shahi, 29
Hindus, position of, 273
Hindukush mountains, 64
Holi Quran, 164
Hushang Shah, 222

Ibn Battutah, 99, 109, 159, 167, 169,
  173
Ibrahim Lodi, 227, 267
Ilbari Turks, 51
Iltutmish as ruler, estimate of, 45
Imad-ul-Mulk, 158, 168
Imam Ghazali, 245
Imaduddin Raihan, 52, 268
Indian Ocean Trade,
  Portugese impact on, 202
Indo-Gangetic plain, 62
Internal rebellions, 44
Islamic World, 22

Jahaz Mahal, 222
Jai Chand, 24, 27
Jajnagar (Orissa) and
  Nagarkot campaigns, 117
Jalaluddin Khalji, 62, 88, 113, 131,
  133, 163, 167, 267, 269, 276, 278
Jalaluddin Mangabarani, 40, 45, 65
Jama Masjid, 48, 220, 222
Jhelum (river), 18
Jwalamukhi temple, 118

Kabir Khan, 49, 50
Kali Age, 172
Kamal Maihar, 55
Kamla Devi, 88
Kara Khanid, Turks of
  Samarqand, 28
Kashmir, 228
Khajuraho in Bundelkhand, 153
Khalji Maliks, 45

Khan-i-Jahan Maqbul, 119, 120, 122,
    134, 135, 161, 270
Khawaja Hasan, 133
Khizr Khan, 90, 210
Khurasan and Karachil
    expeditions, 102
Khokhars, 36, 65, 127, 226
Khwaja Hisamuddin Junaid, 122
Khwarizm Shah, 37, 40, 64
Kotla Feroz Shah, 124
Krishna Deva Raya, 188, 189, 190
Krishna-Godavari delta, 177
Kulblai Khan, 194
Kurukshetra, 276
Kushan empire, 33

Lakshman Sena, 31
Lambden, K.S., 32
Lodi Garden, 236

Mahabharata, 229, 249, 265
Maharashtra, 91, 94
Mahayana Buddhism, 22
Mahendra Varman, 251
Mahmud Begarha, 219, 226
Mahmud Gawan,
    age of (1463-1482), 185, 186
Mahmud Ghazni, 16, 20, 28
Mahmud Khalji, 222, 223
Malabar, 142, 155
Malik Bakbak, 55
    Chhajju Kishli Khan, 76, 163,
    168
    Ghazi, 140
    Haibat, 55
    Kafur, 78, 88, 92, 93, 94, 133,
    167, 269
    Khusrau, 24, 96, 115
    Muhammad Jaisi, 89, 225, 259,
    263
    Nayak, 71, 78
    Sarwar, 225
    Yakut, 50, 136, 268
Malwa, 90, 221
Mansur bin Hallaj, 238
Masud Sad Salman, 261
Maulana Mahmud Samarquandi,
    220
Mawara-un-Nahar or
    Transoxiana, 13
Max Weber, 254
Mehta, Narsinha, 258
Mettallurgy, 153
Minhaj Siraj, 25, 26, 39, 41, 42, 43,
    49, 50, 52, 158, 261

Mir Hajib, 51, 53, 136
Mongols, 37, 157
Mongol threat to Delhi, 64, 69
Mubarak Khalji, 269
Muhammad bin Bakhtiyar Khalji,
    28, 31, 36, 41, 42, 43, 215
Muhammad bin Tughlaq, 72, 75, 96,
    110-113, 117, 119, 122, 128, 134,
    135, 137, 142, 145, 152, 154,
    156, 157, 160, 161, 162, 166,
    176, 210, 235, 243, 267, 270,
    273, 275, 276
Muhammad Junaidi, 133
Muinuddin Chishti, 244
Muizzuddin Muhammad, 24
Muizzuddin M. Ghuri, 88
Muizzuddin Muhammad bin Sam,
    268
Mulla Daud, 151, 259, 263
Muzaffar Shah, 218, 219

Nasiruddin Chiragh Delhi, 243
Nasiruddin Mahmud, 44, 51, 52, 66,
    127
Nathpanthi movements, 253
Nicolo Conti, 181, 194
Nizamul Mulk Tusi, 132, 158
    Junaidi, 54, 47, 49, 52, 268, 275
Nizamuddin Auliya, 99, 234, 242,
    243, 244, 248, 261
Non-agricultural production, 151
North India,
    economic and social life under
    Delhi Sultanat, 144
Nusrat Khan, 78, 89, 133, 269

Ottomon Turks, 201
Oxus river, 28

Paramaras of Malwa, 19, 21
Peri Rais, 202
Persian Gulf, 14, 195
Persian renaissance, 21
Pilia Khar, 224
Popular Bhakti movement, 252
Prithvi Raj, 45
    raso, 23, 25
Punjab and Sindh, 39

Qazi-Ul-Qazzat, 138
Quibuddin Bakhtiyar Kaki, 233
Quran, 51, 238
Qutb Minar, 46, 125, 232, 233, 234
Qutbuddin Aibak, 26, 37, 38, 43,
    171, 233, 266, 268

Qutubuddin Mubarak Shah, 85
Qutlugh Khan, 52, 69
Quwwat-ul-Islam mosque, 232, 233, 234

Rai Rayan, 92
Raja Ganesh of Dinajpur, 213
Raj Shekhar (Jain Saints), 99
Raja Man Singh of Gwaliyar, 264
Raja Vikramaditiya, 100
Rajputs, 59, 144
    causes of defeat of, 29
Rajput coalition against Mahmud, 20
Rajput Kingdoms, 19
Ram Deo of Deogir, 94
Ramayana, 249
Rana Sanga, 224
Rathors of Marwar, 224
Razia (1236-40), 48
    period of instability, 47
Red Sea, 193, 195, 203
Regional languages, 262
Regional Kingdom in North India, 210
Revenue system, 147
Ruling Class, 164
Rumi Khan, 201
Rural Society, 146

Salt ranges, 65
Samarqand, 37
Sanyogita, 24
Shah Jahan, 123, 236
Shamsuddin Iltutmish, 38, 39
Shara (Islamic law), 266
Sharma, Dashrath, modern historian, 26
Sher Khan, 52, 54, 66, 81
    Shah, 212, 227, 264
Shihabuddin al Umar, Arab writer, 142
Sikander Lodi, 226, 227, 235, 276
Siwalik territory, 26
Slaves, 170
Social life, 158
Southern States, 92, 94
Sufi Hindi poet, 151
    movement, 237
Suhrawardi, 245
Sulaiwan Rais, 201
Sultan Ali Mughayat Shah, 203
Sultan Husain Sharqi, 264

Sultan Saifuddin, 213
Sultan Shamsuddin Ilyas Khan, 211
Suri, Hemchandra, 260
Sutlej (river), 66
Syr (river), 13

Tair Bahadur, 66
Taj Mahal, 236
Tamar Khan, 68
Tarain, battles of, 24
Telangana, 93
Textiles, 151
Thatta campaign, 13, 65-67, 118
Timur, 127
Tomars of Delhi, 21, 23
Trade (Domestic), 154
Tripathi, R.P., 50, 135
Turks, 144

Ulema, relations with, 271
Ulugh Khan 51, 69, 88, 89, 158
Upanishads, 249
Upper Gange Valley,
    Turkish expension, 26

Vaids, 14
Vaishnavite movement, 257
Vasco da Gama, 192, 193, 197, 199, 200
Vigraharaj, 23
Vijayanagar Empire, 175, 188
Vishnu Purana, 250

Wafa Malik, 65
West Asia Countries (10th & 12th), 13
    developments in, 14
West Coast of Africa, 193
Western India, 217
Western Jamuna Canal, 123
Women, 172

Yakub Khan, 17
Yamini rulers of Ghazni, 17
Yadava King Ram Chandra, 91

Zabulistan, 17
Zafar Khan, 69, 70, 120, 218
Zainul Abidin 228, 229
Zamindars, 162
Zia Nakshabi, 162, 262
Ziauddin Barani, 48, 261, 270